TECHTV'S TECHNOLOGY SURVIVAL GUIDE

Lorna Gentry

CONTENTS AT A GLANCE

A Division of Pearson Technology Group, USA
201 W. 103rd Street
Indianapolis, Indiana 46290

TECHTV'S TECHNOLOGY SURVIVAL GUIDE

International Standard Book Number: 0-7897-2601-7

Library of Congress Catalog Card Number: 2001090462

Printed in the United States of America

First Printing: November, 2001

04 03 02 01 4 3 2 1

Trademarks

All terms mentioned in this book that are known to be trademarks or service marks have been appropriately capitalized. Que Corporation cannot attest to the accuracy of this information. Use of a term in this book should not be regarded as affecting the validity of any trademark or service mark.

Warning and Disclaimer

Every effort has been made to make this book as complete and as accurate as possible, but no warranty or fitness is implied. The information provided is on an "as is" basis. The author and the publisher shall have neither liability nor responsibility to any person or entity with respect to any loss or damages arising from the information contained in this book.

ASSOCIATE PUBLISHER
Dean Miller

EXECUTIVE EDITOR
Jill Hayden

ACQUISITIONS EDITOR
Jill Hayden

DEVELOPMENT EDITOR
Kezia Endsley

MANAGING EDITOR
Thomas F. Hayes

PROJECT EDITOR
Tonya Simpson

COPY EDITOR
Molly Schaller

INDEXER
Angie Bess

PROOFREADER
Mary Ann Abramson

TECHNICAL EDITORS
Harrison Neal
Kate Binder
Coletta Witherspoon

TEAM COORDINATOR
Sharry Gregory

INTERIOR DESIGNER
Anne Jones

COVER DESIGNER
Planet 10

COVER PHOTOGRAPHER
Shawn Roche

PAGE LAYOUT
Lizbeth Patterson
Stacey Richwine-DeRome
Gloria Schurick
Mark Walchle

TECHTV EDITORIAL DIRECTOR
Jim Louderback

TECHTV TECHNICAL EDITOR
Phillip Allingham

TECHTV HEAD OF BUSINESS DEVELOPMENT
Dee Dee Atta

TECHTV EXECUTIVE EDITOR
Regina Preciado

CONTENTS

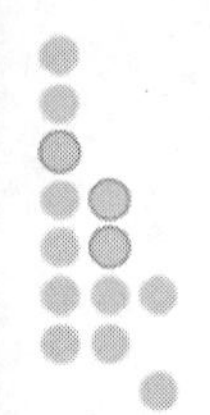

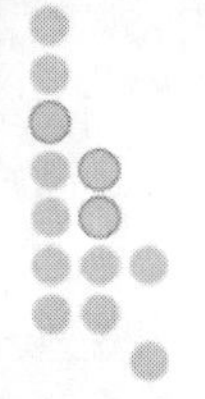

V APPENDIXES

ABOUT THE AUTHOR

Lorna Gentry is a career writer and editor who specializes in explaining technical processes to people who aren't particularly interested in technology. Her writings cover topics ranging from metalworking in ancient Greece to programming with Visual C++. She also has written numerous home, health, and fitness articles, many of which appear on the Learning Network. She is the co-author of *The Complete Idiot's Guide to Home Security*.

ACKNOWLEDGMENTS

I would like to thank Jill Hayden, executive editor for Que Publishing, for her unflagging support and attention to detail throughout the many odd twists and turns of this book's creation. I'd also like to thank Tonya Simpson, Que project editor, for maintaining her good nature and keen editorial eye as she was asked to "morph" the book to each new title, format, and style it assumed. And a special "thank you" to Lyle Neal for assisting with figure shots and those double-pass tech edits.

I also would like to acknowledge TechTV's writers and online contributors, whose opinions, technical processes, and product descriptions make up this book.

TELL US WHAT YOU THINK!

As the reader of this book, *you* are our most important critic and commentator. We value your opinion and want to know what we're doing right, what we could do better, what areas you'd like to see us publish in, and any other words of wisdom you're willing to pass our way.

As an associate publisher for Que, I welcome your comments. You can fax, email, or write me directly to let me know what you did or didn't like about this book—as well as what we can do to make our books stronger.

Please note that I cannot help you with technical problems related to the topic of this book, and that due to the high volume of mail I receive, I might not be able to reply to every message.

When you write, please be sure to include this book's title and author as well as your name and phone or fax number. I will carefully review your comments and share them with the author and editors who worked on the book.

Fax: 317-581-4666

Email: feedback@quepublishing.com

Mail: Dean Miller
Que Corporation
201 West 103rd Street
Indianapolis, IN 46290 USA

TELL US WHAT YOU THINK!

INTRODUCTION

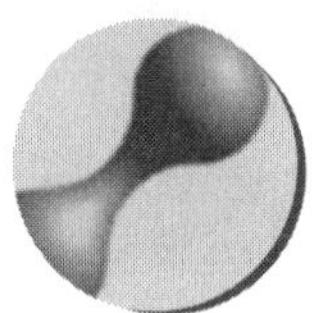

"What can it do for me?"

"Is it hard to set up and use?"

"How much does it cost?"

If those questions sum up your response to the announcement of yet another new computer technology, then you're a TechTV kind of person. When TechTV launched back in 1998 (known then as ZDTV), no one could have predicted how popular the station would become. Now, it reaches millions of viewers every day and just keeps on growing.

TechTV succeeds for a very simple reason: New technologies spring up like mushrooms overnight. Some of them make our lives easier, while others don't deserve our mental energy or the landfill space they'll eventually occupy. Sorting the winners from the losers and explaining how to get the most from changing technologies takes time, energy, and training—plus a healthy love of *la vida geeka*. That's what TechTV is all about, and that's what you'll find in this book.

WHAT THIS BOOK OFFERS

TechTV's Technology Survival Guide compiles the best of TechTV's how-to advice, product reviews, troubleshooting techniques, shortcuts, workarounds, timesavers, and tech-trap alerts. Whether you're an experienced computer junkie or someone who has been dragged kicking and screaming into the computer age, you can benefit from the information and advice in this book.

This guide pulls together the topics, issues, and answers TechTV talks about every day during television programs such as *TechTV Live*, *The Screen Savers*, *Call for Help*, and *Fresh Gear*. After years of answering viewers' questions, reviewing new product releases, and watching the newest must-have device on the tech horizon quickly sink into the sunset of yesterday's news, the TechTV staff has developed a good sense of what matters most to anyone who—for better or worse—is married to technology. That's what you'll find in *TechTV's Technology Survival Guide*.

This book brings you the essential info you need to do the job right, whether you're buying and setting up a new computer system, choosing a broadband connection, building a home network, learning Linux, joining an online gaming community, or shooting and editing your own digital movies. But this guide won't leave you hanging; where you might benefit from more details about a product or process, you can take advantage of the book's many cross-references to the best online resources. And, of course, you can keep up with computer developments every day on TechTV.

HOW TO USE THIS BOOK

Think of this book as a desktop tool. If you'd like to sit down and read the book from cover to cover, have at it! But you can also dip in and grab the info you need when you need it. The book's organization is simple, to make your information-gathering trip as fast and productive as possible. Here it is, in four easy parts.

Part I, "Getting Started"

If you need to brush up on the basics of any computer setup, this part's for you. Learn how to choose a new system and equip it with the components that will work best for *you*. Get some smart tips on how to connect your system and arrange your computer work area for maximum comfort and productivity. Get the information you need to weigh your Internet connection options and decide which (if any) broadband service might work best for you.

Worried about viruses? You'll benefit from TechTV's guide to safe downloading and security basics, plus an in-depth look at using virus protection and firewalls and guarding your privacy online. If you've always wanted to set up the ultimate home network, the information in this part of the book shows you how to do it right. And the tricks you learn in TechTV's insider's guide to using tech support will reduce the time you spend trying to wrangle solutions from overworked, under-paid tech reps.

Part II, "Keeping on Top of the OS Situation"

If you work on more than one computer, chances are good that you don't "live" in just one OS. Many of TechTV's viewers use two or three operating systems in the course of any given day. The information you find in these chapters will help you get the most out of every OS in your life. Get the lowdown on Windows—from making it work the way you do, to troubleshooting glitches, to using the fastest shortcuts and getting in synch with XP.

Then on to the Mac. Make Mac OS X your own, but hang on to the features you loved in Mac OS 9. And, no matter what Mac version you use, this part of the guide shows you ways to wring the most power and speed out of your setup.

Learn what's up with Linux, how to install it as a second OS, and how to keep your Linux system healthy and clean. And, best of all, find out how to make *all* the operating systems you love get along, so you can move your work among different OS setups without losing time or data (or your sanity).

Part III, "Making the Most of Software and Utilities"

Here, TechTV shows you how to choose, use, and *not* abuse the software that can make your daily life simple and sweet. Know the difference between shrink-wrapped software and its downloadable cousin? This part of the guide tells you what you need to know to choose your software delivery method wisely.

You also find out where to get the latest downloadable freeware, shareware, and pay-as-you-go apps, utilities, and system tweaks. With these software gems, you can speed up and protect your system, avoid crashes, and make your computer a more entertaining place to hang out. From maintenance utilities to music, video, and animation, the information in Part III points you to "gotta-have" great software that you won't want to live without.

Part IV, "Computing for All It's Worth"

Because computer technology isn't all about text docs and spreadsheets, this part of the guide offers info and advice that can help you get the most out of *all* the computer devices and technologies in your life. From handhelds to home automation, find out how technology can contribute to your security, comfort, and entertainment.

If you're drowning in a sea of handhelds, you'll appreciate the chapter on how to choose and use PDAs, cell phones, and other mobile buddies. Learn what to look for in hybrid devices and how to keep them all synched up and marching to the same tune.

Are you into gaming? Build the ultimate gaming machine or transform an old PC into a great gaming box with these tips. Learn the ins and outs of online gaming and the how-to of creating your own games—whether you're into programming or not.

When you're tired of shoot 'em ups, dive into the chapter on using your PC as a multimedia studio. From grabbing the greatest MP3s, to listening to PC radio, producing your own music demos, and turning your PC into a DVD home theater, you learn how to use your

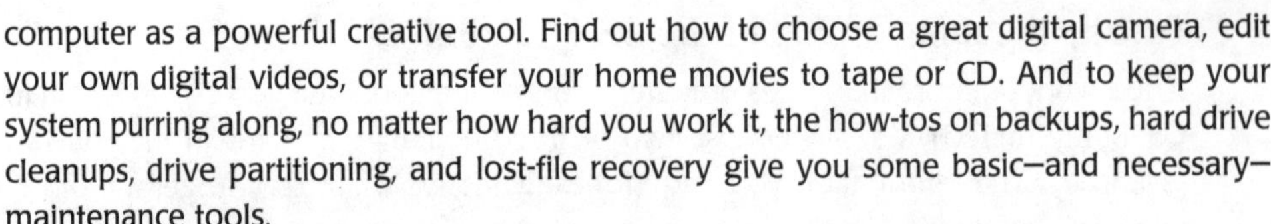

computer as a powerful creative tool. Find out how to choose a great digital camera, edit your own digital videos, or transfer your home movies to tape or CD. And to keep your system purring along, no matter how hard you work it, the how-tos on backups, hard drive cleanups, drive partitioning, and lost-file recovery give you some basic—and necessary—maintenance tools.

Resources

It's hard to talk about computer technology without dishing up a vegetable soup of computer terms and acronyms. You'll find definitions throughout the book, but the "TechTV Glossary" in Appendix A offers a full geek-speak archive. In a tip of the cap to loyal *Call for Help* viewers, the book closes with a collection of short Q&As that offer good factoids and fast-tips reminiscent of the Lightning Round Q&A Wrap-Up that ends each *CFH* broadcast. The Q&A collection is a quick and informative cruise through the common (and not-so-common) questions asked by TechTV's devoted viewers. Maybe you'll see yours!

CONVENTIONS USED IN THE BOOK

Scattered throughout the book, you'll find a number of sidebars and boxes, filled with important or interesting information. Just so you'll know what you're getting into, here's what those elements mean:

TechTV's Favorite Tips, Tricks, and Shortcuts

When you see a Tip box, you'll know you're about to read a way to make your job easier, faster, safer, more productive, more entertaining, or just plain better.

Don't Suffer from Technical Difficulties

It isn't hard to get tangled up in trouble when you're installing new hardware, upgrading software, shopping for a new device, or learning a new operating system. These boxes raise the red flag whenever a gaping tech-trap might be opening up before you. The TechTV staffers test drive so many new products and processes that they've had an opportunity to make just about every mistake possible. Why shouldn't you benefit from all of that experience?

Whassup Out There?

From tech trends and tragedies, to industry developments, to gadgets to watch, these Street Buzz bits will keep you informed and entertained. No, you don't *have* to know this stuff, but it will make you more fun at parties.

PART I

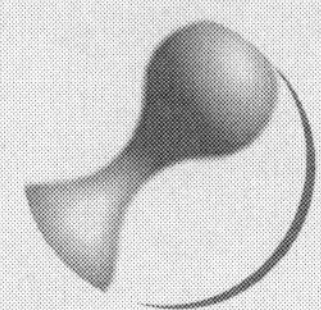

GETTING STARTED

CHAPTER 1

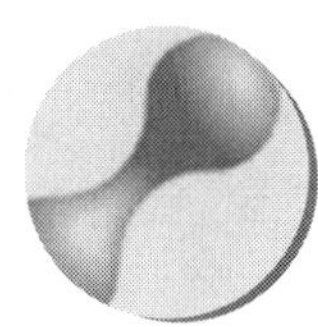

GET SET UP WITH ALL THE RIGHT (COMPUTER) STUFF

- Tick through the desktop PC parts list
- Find the CPU that's right for you
- Compare monitors
- Match printer features to your needs
- Choose a good scanner
- Buy the right CD-RW

Finding a cheap PC isn't difficult today, when complete systems are available for less than $500. But finding the *right* computer can be trickier. Saving money is nice, but you have to live with the bargain you buy. How can you know what system will do the job you need it to do? And how do you figure out exactly what you need?

This chapter is Tech TV's "insider's guide" to desktop PC systems and choosing the one that's right for you. You get a quick tour of basic desktop PC parts, inside tips on choosing major components, and recommendations for sample system setups that do the job—whether you're a gamer, guru, surfer, or SOHO-er. Ready to kick some tires?

A QUICK LOOK UNDER THE HOOD OF A DESKTOP PC

When you buy a computer, what do you get? It's easy to see some of the standard components of the typical desktop PC: the case, a few drives (usually one floppy drive and a CD-ROM or DVD drive), a monitor, some speakers, a mouse, keyboard, and maybe a joystick. But what about the important parts you don't see—the stuff behind the jargon you read in most computer sales ads? Up your consumer savvy by getting familiar with some of the internal workings of the average computer system:

- **The processor:** The processor, also called the *central processing unit* (CPU), reads and executes the commands you issue when you use the computer. Processors are described by speeds, as given in *megahertz* (MHz) or *gigahertz* (GHz).

Don't Assume More MHz Means Faster Computing

In general, the processor's price goes up as its speed increases, but a big jump in price won't give you an equally big jump in actual processing speed. You'll pay hundreds of dollars for a two to three percent increase in processing time. So should you shell out the extra *dinero* for that 1.5GHz processor? If you're a bleeding-edge gamer, or if you do a lot of image editing, maybe the beefier processor is for you. Otherwise, the bump in speed won't justify the dent that faster processor will leave in your wallet.

- **RAM (memory):** RAM (*random access memory*) is the computer's read/write memory, which stores program instructions and data while you're using the system. The RAM size, described in *megabytes* (MB), teams up with the processor speed to determine the speed and capacity of system operation. 64MB is the minimum if you want to surf the Web while you have a couple of applications open. 128MB is better. DRAM (pronounced dee-ram), or *dynamic* RAM, is a type of memory that uses capacitors and regenerates regularly. SDRAM (synchronous dynamic RAM) is a high-speed RAM that synchronizes with the microprocessor's data bus.
- **Hard drive (storage):** Hard drives provide permanent storage, and you need a lot of storage space if you plan to play games, use your computer with a digital camera, or engage in any other system-sucking activity. Cheaper systems ship with 4GB or 8GB drives, but many people prefer to pay more for 16GB or 20GB rather than add drives later.

It's Drive-Alive!

You can pack a lot of drives into a desktop PC. Just about every system comes equipped with a 3.5-inch high-density *floppy drive* and a *CD-ROM drive*. *DVD-ROM* (and CD/DVD-ROM combination) drives are becoming more common, but they're essential only if you plan to watch movies through your computer. If you plan to burn your own CDs for recording music or storing/swapping large quantities of data, you also need a *CD-RW* drive. (You learn more about CD-RW drives in "Get the Right CD-RW Drive," later in this chapter.)

- **Video card/graphics RAM:** The size of your video card determines how quickly your computer can generate images on your screen, which determines the crispness and clarity of the display. A 4MB card is adequate for general PC use. Gamers, artists, graphic designers, and film makers should go higher—16, 32, or even 64MB.
- **Internal modem:** An internal modem manages your PC's Internet connectivity. Modem speeds indicate how fast the modem can transfer information from the source to your system. 56Kbps (kilobytes per second) is the current low-end standard.

Most PCs come with a preloaded operating system such as Windows 2000, Windows Me, or Windows XP. Part II, "Keeping on Top of the OS Situation," gives you an inside look at operating systems.

CHOOSE YOUR WEAPON

Whether you buy a system "off the rack" or order a setup built to your specs, you have a lot of choices in the makeup of your computer system. Prices have come down, and you can get a lot of techno-bang for your buck. You can invest a lot or little on almost every component of your system, so put your computer dollars where they'll do *you* the most good.

A computer shouldn't be an impulse buy no matter how good of a deal you find. Before you buy a system, think about who'll use the machine and how they'll use it. Then, buy the system that best fits that user-and-use profile. That said, the following sections offer the minimum specifications TechTV recommends for some typical PC setups.

Consider Your Connectivity Options

E-mailing, Web surfing, gaming, downloading music, video, or program files, home networking—if you plan on doing any of these things on your PC, you need to buy a machine with the right connectivity options. High-speed connectivity (any Internet connection with download speeds higher than 128Kbps) requires a NIC (*Network Interface Card*). An Ethernet PCI NIC is an important feature on any computer that uses high-speed connections. USB (*Universal Serial Bus*) ports, as shown in Figure 1.1, let you connect peripherals—such as external modems, drives, and so on—simply by plugging in a connection (no PC-breakdown required). Good systems have a few USBs on the back, and might even have a few on the front.

If you'll be using DSL (*Digital Subscriber Line*) Internet access or networking this machine to other PCs in your home, your machine needs a phoneline network card (your local DSL service can tell you what type of connectors it uses). Phoneline connectors are on the back of the PC, and look just like a slightly oversized phonejack. Connectivity is one of the most important features of any PC; think through your connectivity options and be sure the machine you buy offers the connections you need most.

Figure 1.1

A Univeral Seris Bus (USB) port offers a fast and easy way to hook up peripherals such as scanners, printers, external drives, and so on, into your PC. Some models have multiple USBs, located on both the front and back of the PC.

Minimum Specs for the Family Workhorse PC

A family PC might be used for everything from Teletubbies play-along exercises to tracking the family budget. A good family PC is

- Reliable, so you don't have to futz with it all the time.
- Versatile, so both kids and adults can use it for a lot of different things.
- Covered with a good on-site warranty that saves you headaches if something goes wrong with your machine. You might need to pay extra for on-site service, but if you want more than online tech support, the added cost might be worth it to you.

Here are some general guidelines for picking up a good family PC:

- **CPU:** A processor between 500 and 700 MHz should work just fine for this PC. You don't need bullet speeds for most family PC functions.
- **RAM:** If you're running Windows Me, go with 128MB of SDRAM.
- **Hard drive storage:** If your family will load this machine up with lots of applications, MP3s, and graphics files, go with a 20GB hard drive. If you're careful or add a CD burner to keep the MP3s off the hard drive, you can make it on 16GB or even 8GB.

- **Other drives:** You probably don't need more than the standard CD-ROM and 3.5-inch floppy. Get a DVD-ROM only if it also reads CDs *and* you intend to watch movies through the computer.
- **Connectivity options:** Do you want this machine to share Internet access with your other home computers? A 10MB PCI Phoneline NIC lets you do that. If you want to use a high-speed connection for downloading, gaming, or other heavy multimedia tasking, get a 10/100 Ethernet PCI NIC.

You learn more about home networking in Chapter 7, "Bring It All Together in a Home Network." Chapter 3, "Get Internet Access," offers more info on Internet connectivity. And check the TechTV Web site for helpful details about home PC products and options.

Check the Ingredients Carefully

When you shop for any PC, don't assume anything about what the package includes. Be sure you get a modem, check to see which operating system comes in the deal, and find out what "free" software you're paying for, too. Are you getting a 17-inch monitor? And does the warranty offer on-site service? Don't let the sales person rush you through your purchase.

Minimum Specs for a SOHO (Small Office/Home Office) PC

When you run your own business, your PC might be your only working partner. So you need a machine that's

- **Infinitely reliable:** You can't afford to deal with a problem PC.
- **Well-supported:** Get a three-year, on-site warranty if possible, and be sure the manufacturer offers round-the-clock technical support and good diagnostic tools.
- **Fast and beefy:** You need a PC that can handle accounting apps, highly visual presentations, and maybe some Web-site creation software. You also need lots of data storage and high-speed connection capability.

Every business is unique, so research to find the system that best matches your business needs.

General guidelines for the SOHO PC:

- **CPU:** 800+ MHz is a good CPU baseline for a small business PC.
- **RAM:** Don't settle for less than 128MB of SDRAM (Synchronous Dynamic RAM). You need speed and power, and this CPU/RAM configuration should deliver.
- **Hard drive:** You can't go too big. You might get by on 20 gigs, but if you want to postpone upgrading as long as possible, shell out for a 40GB hard drive.
- **Drives:** You might want to add a CD-RW drive, so you can burn CDs for storing data and swapping large files with your clients. If your clients use zip disks often, add a zip drive to the shopping cart.

Bigger Monitors Are Better

When it comes to monitors, size matters. Whether you're working on spreadsheets, surfing the Web, gaming, or earning a living onscreen, a large monitor (19 inches or larger) displays more data per screen *and* it makes the displayed data easier to read. You scroll less and your eyes get a break. If you're buying a computer for a small business, a senior netizen, a gamer, or anyone who works with graphics packages, invest in the biggest screen your wallet and desk can accommodate.

- **Connectivity options:** Many SOHO computers depend on a high-speed Internet connection and a local area network. Your new computer must have an Ethernet adapter that suits the high-speed service options available in your area. A 10/100 PCI NIC and 10MB Phoneline NIC might be good bets for handling these chores (check with your local cable/DSL provider). You learn more about broadband Internet access in Chapter 3, "Get Internet Access."

Minimum Specs for a Gamer's PC

Gaming is serious business, and ultimate gamers want ultimate power. Your wallet's the limit on how high to push the technology in a gaming PC. You need

- **Speed and power:** All you can afford.
- **A fast video card and good monitor:** Your graphics display helps determine your game performance.
- **A fast connection:** Gamers have played at 56Kbps modem speeds, but it ain't a pretty sight. If your area has broadband access and you're serious about gaming, get wired.

Although the ultimate gaming PC doesn't stay "ultimate" for any length of time, these rock-bottom recommendations will help you spec out your gaming PC:

- **CPU:** Don't even try to game with less than a 500+ MHz Pentium III chip, and (though the stakes get higher every day) most gamer's opt for a 1GHz chip.
- **RAM:** Start with at least 256MB. You can never have too much RAM.
- **Hard drive:** Again, go big. A 20GB hard drive gives you the gaming room you need.
- **Drives:** A floppy and a high-speed (52x) CD-ROM are all you need for high-burn gaming, although many gamers opt for a DVD-ROM drive, too.
- **Video/Sound:** A gaming machine needs blazing good sound and video. Be sure yours has a 64MB video card and a high-quality sound card. An *AGP* (Accelerated Graphics Port) graphics system is designed to give you faster, better-looking 3-D graphics. If the system doesn't have built-in AGP, it should have an AGP slot so you can add the feature.
- **Connectivity options:** Again, you need a fast connection, so get a machine with an Ethernet PCI card to support the speed you need. The 10/100 PCI NIC is a must for good gaming.

It's on TechTV

To take an up-close look at the specs for an ultimate gamer's machine (UGM) and a cheaper (sub-$1000) gamer's nirvana, visit the TechTV Gamers' archives (`www.techtv.com/help/games`).

SHOPPING FOR A MONITOR

The monitor is one of the most important components of any system. When you buy a new machine, you typically can opt to upgrade to a larger monitor for just a few hundred dollars more—and that small jump in price can deliver big gains in productivity. Whether you're crunching spreadsheets, editing images, or getting your game on, a better display means higher productivity.

What matters most in monitors?

- **Size:** Bigger is better. Smaller monitors have less screen space and run at a lower resolution, and that translates into more eyestrain, more scrolling, and less productivity. A *PC Computing* magazine Usability Test found user productivity rose by an average of 17 percent when users switched from a 17-inch to a 19-inch monitor.
- **Refresh rate:** The higher the monitor's *refresh rate* (the rate at which the image on the screen refreshes or updates with new data), the easier on your eyes. Your monitor should refresh at a rate no lower than 75 to 80 MHz. Lower refresh rates cause flicker and eyestrain.
- **Maximum resolution:** Screen resolution determines the size and clarity of the image displayed on your screen. The lower the number of pixels—say, 640×480 versus 1,024×768—the less information you can fit on your screen. Screen resolution usually is linked to refresh rate. Your new monitor should support a refresh rate of 75 to 80 MHz when set to your desired screen resolution.

Remember the Connection Between Your Graphics Card and Your Monitor's Refresh Rate?

Your PC's graphics card plays a key role in your monitor's capability to deliver a high refresh rate and resolution. The refresh rate your card can deliver is tied to the screen resolution. As the resolution increases, your card's deliverable refresh rate drops. If your graphics card can't refresh at a rate of 75–80 Hz at the screen resolution you've chosen, you need to upgrade the graphics card (or lower your monitor's resolution).

GET IT ON PAPER—HOW MUCH PRINTER DO YOU NEED?

When it comes to choosing a printer, your first decision is inkjet or laser, followed closely by black-and-white or color. Both decisions hinge on how you intend to use the printer, and how much you want to invest in it.

Laser Pros and Cons

Laser printers offer excellent quality, delivering crisp, clear documents at about 600 dots per inch (dpi) (DPI determines the clarity of reproductions). They're fast, too. Many laser printers consistently churn out 16 pages per minute. Laser printers reproduce images by burning toner onto the paper, and most toner cartridges last a *long* time. That means you have fewer timeouts for replacement and a low per-page cost of about 1.5 to 2 cents. Finally, laser printers are quiet. You can set one right next to your phone and chatter away as it whispers its way through a print job.

So, what's bad about laser printers? Laser printers carry a hefty price tag. You'll pay at least $300 for a black-and-white laser, and more than $1,000 for a good color laser printer. The laser's color photo reproduction isn't as good as that of a high-quality color inkjet, although the laser excels at color graphics and presentation slides.

Inkjet Pros and Cons

As the name implies, inkjet printers reproduce images by laying ink on the page. The best thing to say about inkjets is that they're cheap. Prices vary, but you can get a relatively good three-color inkjet printer for well under $100. A high-end color inkjet printer will cost about the same as a low-end, monochrome laser printer. And inkjet printers produce excellent color photo reproductions that are better than a laser's color photo reproductions.

What's not-so-hot about inkjet printers? Three-color inkjets won't produce true black. The cheapest models require that you swap out the black-and-white and color cartridges. Ink cartridges don't last long, contributing to a higher total cost of ownership. You'll pay as much as 8 cents a page for inkjet prints.

Your Best Printer

How will you use your printer? If you primarily print business documents, color printing might not be as important as the laser's fast, high-quality results and low total cost of ownership. If you're buying a printer for kid-art projects or printing color photos (and you're willing to pay for the ink cartridges and photo paper), get an inkjet. Other questions to answer in your research:

What About Those All-in-One Printer/Fax/Copier/Toaster Models?

The technology continues to improve in the world of all-in-one equipment, such as combination printer/fax/copier machines, but at this point they seem to work best for very specialized situations. These combo packages save space, and that might be a plus for a small home office. But come over to the dark side for a minute: Combo machines produce fewer pages per minute in all functions and print quality isn't as high as with most single-use printers. And if the thing blows up, you're down three functions until you get it fixed—four functions, if you opted for the toaster add-on.

- **Is it quiet?** You don't want to share a workspace with a noisy printer.
- **Does it hold a decent amount of paper?** If you do high-volume print jobs, you don't want to have to feed the thing every three minutes.
- **Does it have a good reliability rating?** Check *PC Magazine* or another reliable source to see whether the printer earned good reviews.

Don't Forget the Cost of the Cartridge

When calculating any printer's cost, don't forget to check the price and capacity of the replacement cartridges. When companies sell inkjet printers at unbelievably low prices, they might intend to make the difference by beefing up the charge for replacement cartridges. A car can't run on one wheel, and a printer can't live forever on one cartridge. Look down the road when planning total printing costs.

GET A GOOD SCANNER

Since digital cameras came on the scene, scanners don't seem quite so "buzzy," but they're still useful tools to have in your home office. Scanners are great for creating electronic copies of old photos, text documents (no retyping necessary!), posters, and other fragments of your life's memorabilia. At as little as $80 a pop, why not put one of these useful imaging devices on your desktop?

How Scanners Work

Scanners come in flatbed and sheetfed models, and they operate much like photocopiers. Put an object or image on the scanner bed, push a button, and the scanner reads the image and creates an electronic reproduction of it. You can store this copy on a hard drive or CD, e-mail it to your friends, post it on a Web site, or print and frame it.

Don't Fill Your Hard Drive with Scanned Images

Scanned image files hog disk space, so don't scan your entire family album into your home PC's hard drive and expect to use your computer for anything else. If you're going to store a lot of photos as JPEG, TIFF, or BMP files, add a CD-RW drive or other removable storage option to keep your machine unclogged with shots of your dog wearing sunglasses at the beach.

What to Look for in a Scanner

A good mid-range scanner produces about 1200×2400 dpi resolution—a perfectly acceptable quality for most business or personal uses. You'll also see scanners rated according to their *bit-depth* or *color-depth* (that's the number of color levels the scanner's lens can sense). 36-bit should be fine for most purposes. Though low-end scanners cost less than $100, you can get a good mid-range scanner for about $200, and a great one for about $500. Those are today's prices; expect them to come down in the future (and you can always check TechTV's product reviews for the latest developments in scanners and other equipment).

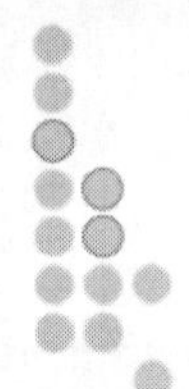

Like most desktop hardware, scanner profiles are slimming down, and you can find flatbed scanners that are less than an inch thick. Portable scanners weigh less than five pounds, and some can scan three-dimensional objects as well as flat documents.

When you shop for a scanner, look for one with at least 1200×2400 dpi resolution. And get one that has a USB connector, so you don't have to do anything mechanically challenging to hook the thing up. Your scanner should come bundled with software. Be sure the bundle includes an image-editing OCR (optical character recognition) program that will let you scan and convert printed documents into electronic files.

Get More Than You Need

If you're buying a scanner for storing and sharing family photos, get one with the highest resolution and bit depth you can afford. The printer you own right now might only be able to reproduce 30-bit color or 1200×2400 resolution images, but 10 or 20 years from now, your kids' printers will do better. When they pull out those CDs of stored photos you made for them way back when, your kids will appreciate all the resolution you handed down to them.

GET THE RIGHT CD-RW DRIVE

You probably need a CD-RW (rewritable compact disc) drive, and that's why they're becoming more and more common on home and small business PCs. They're the most efficient PC storage medium available today. CD storage is cheap. You pay less than $2 for every 650MB of info you archive on a CD. With a CD-RW, you can burn your own CDs to back up data, store and share files, and create both conventional and MP3 audio CDs. What more could you ask from one drive? (You learn more about MP3 and other audio technologies in Chapter 17, "Having It All: The Jukebox/Music Studio/Radio/Movie Theater PC.")

How CD-RW Technology Differs from CD-R

CD-R drives use a laser beam to heat a dye layer on a compact disk, which "burns" a record of data permanently into the disk surface. Burning a CD is an inexpensive and efficient way to store and swap large quantities of data.

CD-RW drives use phase-change technology to both record *and* erase data on CDs. That means you can write and then rewrite data on the same disk, again and again. You can use a CD-RW to create a CD of your favorite music, and then update that same disk next week when your favorites change.

Get Your Technologies Straight

It's important to remember that CD-RW disks require a "multiread" drive to access the data. As a result, CD-RW cannot be played in most CD audio players and they cannot be read in some older CD-ROM drives. Always be sure to use compatible technologies when you plan to swap data or storage media between systems.

It's on TechTV

Equip your computer with a video capture card, and you can digitize your analog video for storage on your hard drive or transfer to a CD via CD-RW. You also can digitize video if you have a digital video camera and a FireWire port. Saving video to CD is a two-step process. After you have the digitized video on your hard drive, you can burn it onto a CD using capture software. Learn all about it on TechTV's Help & How To Web site (`www.techtv.com/help/`).

What to Look for in a CD-RW

Although CD-RW technology changes daily, you face a few simple decisions when choosing a good CD-RW drive in your new computer (Figure 1.2 shows the external MicroSolutions backpack CD-RW drive). First, do you want an internal or external drive? An external drive is more portable and easier to install, but it requires an available USB or SCSI port. Your computer's configuration and capabilities limit how many devices it can support, and that determines what kind of CD-RW you should opt for when you buy your computer. Check your machine's specs to match the drive you buy to the machine you own.

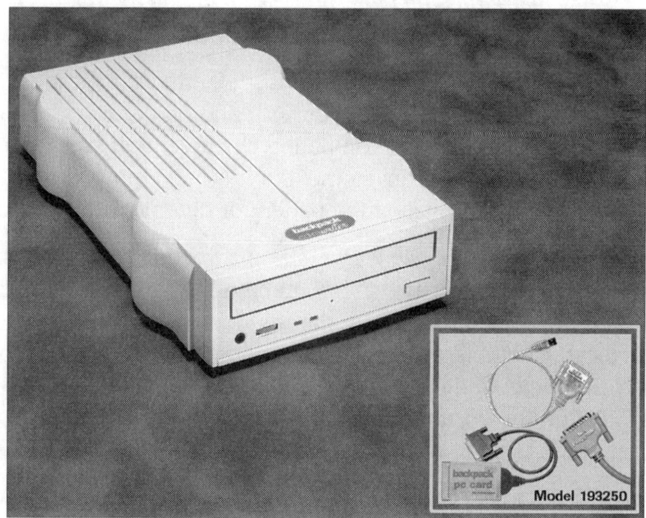

Figure 1.2

A CD-RW drive is an important feature in any PC; use it to back up critical files, create music CDs, and more. *Photo courtesy of MicroSolutions.*

Manufacturers rate CD-RW drives by their speeds: reading or playback (CD-ROM), recording or writing (CD-R), and rewriting (CD-RW). CD-ROM speeds start around 24x, with 32x the low-end standard. Look for CD-RW rewriting rates of 4x and CD-R recording rates of 8x or 12x.

A typical listing for a mid-range CD-RW drive would rate it as "12x write, 4x rewrite, 24x playback." A mid-range CD-RW should create a full 650MB CD in less than six minutes. These drives cost about $300 and the prices keep dropping even as the technology improves.

LIGHTNING ROUND Q&A WRAP-UP

My first computer came with all kinds of software on a master disk. I just bought a new computer, and it has only an operating system installed. Can I copy the old programs and files from my old computer onto my new system?

First, check your original machine's software agreement. Some software licenses only allow you to run the product on one computer. Sometimes the license permits the use of the software on more than one machine, as long as it's used only in one place at a time. If you're allowed to use the software on only one machine, uninstall the programs from your first computer. Then install the programs into your new computer from your original CD.

If you don't have the original CD, use a combination of Laplink (`www.laplink.com`) and Norton CleanSweep (`www.symantec.com`) to move the applications from the old computer to the new one. CleanSweep tells you which files you need for each application, and Laplink enables you to move them over to the new computer.

I am going to college in the fall at the Nebraska College of Business in Omaha. Mainly I will be working with word processing and networking. I am wondering if I should take a desktop computer, or will a laptop do, and why?

Both types have pros and cons. Desktops are easier to upgrade, give you more power per dollar, and they're more durable and harder to steal. Laptops work great for taking notes in class, computing wherever you happen to be, and hauling back and forth on trips home. But they cost more, are easy to damage in transit, and require a really good battery or nearby power source.

Provided that your school will let you bring a laptop to class, we suggest you get a cheap computer (such as the $500-or-less Emachine) and a cheap handheld device like the HP Jornada or the Windows Clio. The combined prices of these two can be less than a fancy laptop and will offer the best of both worlds. Take the handheld—add a portable, laptop-sized keyboard for about $100—when you're on the go, and then bring it back to the dorm and copy your work to your desktop to store or print.

What are the differences between EIDE and SCSI hard drives?

SCSI and EIDE are both hard-drive interfaces, but each suits a different type of computing. The SCSI drive is fast but expensive, and requires a SCSI controller card. EIDE drives require no controller card and cost less but aren't as fast as SCSI drives. They also don't handle multiple devices as well.

If you're running a server or you like to open several applications at once, opt for the SCSI. If you have a small desktop setup that doesn't get a heavy multitasking workout, stick with the cheaper, easier-to-install EIDE.

CHAPTER 2

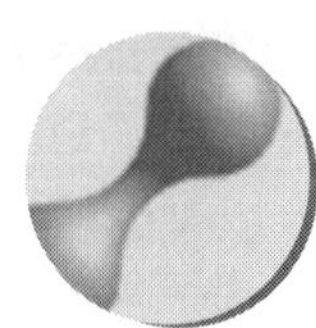

SET UP YOUR HOME COMPUTER

- Unpack the system
- Get connected
- Build in basic ergonomics

When you get ready to unpack that new computer, don't forget the old story of the tortoise and the hare. Sure, you're in a hurry to start using that new machine, but "slow and steady" definitely is the best (and, in most cases, the quickest) way to go.

In this chapter, you walk through the setup process and learn a few special tips for organizing and storing your product warranties, instructions, and printed documentation. And your new computer setup should be a healthy place to work, so this chapter shows you TechTV's best tips for incorporating basic ergonomics into your PC workstation.

BEFORE YOU DIVE IN

Don't start hacking into packages yet! Move the boxes to the room where you're going to set up your workstation, and then gather a few tools to help keep the unpacking process organized:

- A sharp letter opener, box cutter, or mat knife (such as an Exacto knife)
- A pen or marker
- An expanding folder, a binder, or a large, resealable plastic bag or envelope for storing your documents
- A power strip or surge protector

Put the computer near adequate electrical outlets and a phone jack in a dry, well-ventilated room. Clear away all drinks. You're working with a lot of large, unwieldy pieces here, and you don't want to knock a soda over your system before you even have a chance to use it, do you?

Don't Go It Alone

A can-do spirit is a wonderful thing, but find someone to help you unpack your computer. Components come packed tightly in their boxes, and you probably can't just lift them out. Removing a large tower or monitor from its box is much easier when one person holds the box while another lifts or pulls the component free.

GET IT ALL OUT IN THE OPEN

If any documentation is taped to the outside of the crate, remove it and set it safely aside. Then use that sharp box opener and gently—*very gently*—slit the top of the packing crate. You don't want to destroy the packing crate or any of the materials inside.

Follow these steps to unpack the components of your new system:

1. Take your time removing components from their boxes. Be neat, and label all Styrofoam and/or cardboard packing materials with the name of the component they surrounded. Keep *all* packing materials in the original cartons. As you unpack each box, set the labeled materials aside, and then return them to the empty crate.
2. Now, get that packing list, and use a pen to check off each item as you unpack it. That way, you know you have everything the list says you should.
3. Keep all documentation, CDs, disks, registration materials, and so on in that expandable folder or resealable envelope. Keep registration and rebate information handy—you'll return to it as soon as you get your system set up.
4. Read through the instruction booklets, and look for information about connecting your equipment. Most systems come with large, foldout guides that take you through the connection process step by step. Keep this information handy for reference as you set up the system.

Don't Toss That Packaging

Don't throw anything away! You might need to return some or all of the PC, and manufacturers can get nasty about wanting all the packing materials (if you ship it back, you *have* to include all the original packing). If you have space, hang on to this packing indefinitely—it comes in handy if you move. If you can't keep it forever, at least hold on to it for a few months.

In addition to the packing materials, here's a list of all the things you should save as long as you have the computer:

- Receipts for the system unit, monitor, cables, peripherals, and delivery costs
- Warranties, mailback registration, and rebates
- All disks that came with the system

CONNECT YOUR SYSTEM

With the components unpacked and your instruction book nearby, you're ready to hook it all up. Your system probably has a keyboard, mouse, monitor, speakers, printer, and maybe a Web camera. All of those peripherals plug into the back of your system unit.

Connect the Components

You shouldn't have any trouble with this part of the process, because most manufacturers label (with words or icons) or color-code connectors and receptacles to help you match them up. Many peripherals have unique connectors, so you don't have to worry about accidentally plugging the keyboard into the speaker receptacle. Many connectors have a flat side, arrow, or other alignment marker to show exactly how to orient the plug to the receptacle (see Figure 2.1). Don't forget to check the installation instructions if you get confused—they just might help!

Connect all the peripherals, *except* the netcam (if you have one). The camera hooks into a USB port, and you need to install the netcam software first, before you plug the camera into the USB port. Other than the USB-connected netcam and other USB peripherals, connect all your peripherals before you plug the computer into a power source.

To Register or Not to Register...

If you suspect that manufacturers use owner registration cards to gather demographic information and create junk mailing lists, you're absolutely right. In fact, registering hardware helps you only if the manufacturer recalls your equipment.

Register your software, though, because that's the only way to ensure you get the tech support you need. When you register, fill in the basic contact info and equipment identification, and skip any requests for personal information.

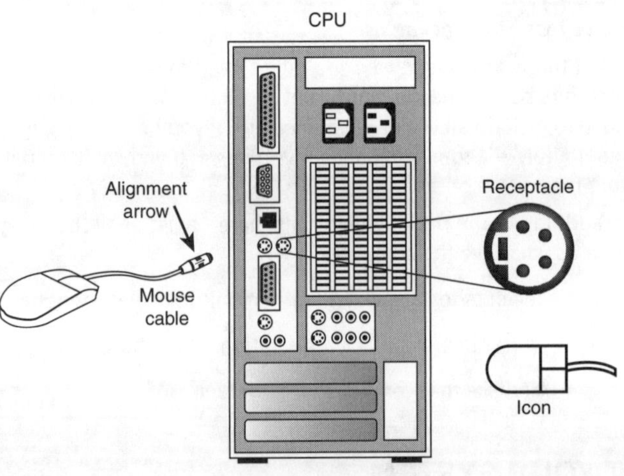

Figure 2.1

Don't let all the cables and connectors throw you. They're all labeled to show you what goes where. If the plug aligns specifically in the connector, you'll see an alignment arrow or other indicator.

No Muscles Required

Don't force anything! If you can't easily slide a component plug into its receptacle, something's wrong. Check the alignment, be sure you're putting the right plug in the right place, and—if all else fails—check the directions for help. If you bend or break a connector, you're in for a long, annoying delay in your setup process. Remember, if you have to force a plug into a receptacle, it doesn't go there.

Power Up

After you check the manufacturer's instructions to verify that your peripherals are properly connected, you're ready to tackle the power connections. Your computer probably requires a lot of power connections–the monitor, modem, and printer each have their own electrical plugs. That's why you have that power strip or surge protector nearby and ready to go.

Plug your equipment into the power strip, plug the power strip or surge protector into an electrical outlet, and then turn on your machine. Those friendly humming noises you hear tell you that your computer is ready to be your pal.

Don't Get Too Comfy with That Surge Protector

Don't let a surge protector give you a false sense of security. It won't protect your equipment from big power surges like you get in an electrical storm or when repowering after a brownout. The only way to protect your system from damage during a strong electrical storm or in the aftermath of a power outage is to unplug your equipment from the power source (and don't forget to unplug any phone line connected to your system, too). For about $150, you can buy an uninterruptible power supply (UPS) that is, by definition, a battery backup system; that's a wise investment. A UPS can condition the power going into your machine and keep it going for a short time after a power outage. Use that grace period to save your work, shut down, and unplug your system from the outlet.

Work It!

After you hook everything up, abuse that computer! Put it through its paces while it's still under warranty. Leave it running even when you're not using it (for at least a few weeks), connect all the peripherals you can, and use the computer as much as possible. If the machine keeps ticking along, you're probably in for a long, happy relationship. If things are going to go wrong with your system, better now than after you've become attached to each other (and the warranty has expired).

Remember That Rebate

Remember to send in your rebate coupons! Companies can only afford to run rebate programs because most people don't follow through on them. Your rebate coupon could expire faster than lettuce in a crisper drawer, so fill it out and send it in NOW.

HEALTHY COMPUTING WITH BASIC ERGONOMICS

All the coolest PC tips and toys won't make for a good computing experience if you don't set up a healthy workspace. You'll be happier, healthier, and more productive if you follow basic ergonomic principles.

Ergonomics is the study of work and the way people stand, sit, and move while they do it. When you're deciding how to set up your computer workspace, answer these questions:

- How will you use your computer? Will you need plenty of desktop space around it for propping up books, magazines, or other printed material? Will you use dual monitors?
- Will you work at the computer most of the time when you're in this workspace, or will computing be a secondary function? If you'll use the computer only once in a while, set it to the side of your desk so you won't have to work around it.

The medical world is still debating the connection between repetitive stress injuries and computing, but to be on the safe side, set up your system for maximum comfort and minimum strain. The two most important factors in your area's ergonomic design are the positions of your chair and your computer.

Put Your Chair in Position

You can find computer chairs costing thousands of dollars—and you can find others for less than $100. In the end, you know what kind of chair best suits you (and your wallet), but here are some general tips for positioning *any* computer chair:

- Your chair should hold your hips slightly higher than your knees.
- You should be able to rest your feet flat on the floor or on a footrest.
- Your back should arch slightly. Most chairs curve in to provide lumbar support, but if yours doesn't, use a small pillow to support the curve of your back.
- Your hips, ears, and shoulders should be vertically aligned.

- Adjust your seat height to keep your elbows at a 90–110 degree angle when you're typing, your wrists flat, and your fingers curved down toward the keyboard.

Don't Compromise Your Position

Don't adjust your body to fit your workspace—make your workspace fit your body. You'll suffer (and so will your work) if you try to cram or twist your body into an unnatural position during long hours at the computer. Pay attention to how your body feels while you work, and if you detect any strain, track it down to its source. Adjust your seat height or angle, and use pillows, footrests, wrist supports, and any other props necessary to support your body while you sit at the computer. Better a little trouble now than lots of trouble later.

It's on TechTV

Learn more about the ergonomics of small offices and student study areas at www.TechTV.com.

Position Your Computer

That $1700 computer chair won't help a thing if you don't get the other piece of the ergonomic puzzle in place—your computer position. Follow these general guidelines to get it right:

- Your monitor should rest squarely in front of you when you're typing, and no closer than 18 or 24 inches from your eyes.
- The top of your monitor should be at eye level when you sit in your chair.
- Position your keyboard so that you can reach it with your arms bent, elbows close to your side, and wrists flat.
- Keep your mouse as close to your body as possible. If you have to reach for it, you'll end up straining your wrist, arm, and elbow.

Don't give up on finding just the right setup for your computer workspace (see Figure 2.2). It's worth investing some time, trouble, and experimentation in the beginning to come up with a good setup that will give you comfortable computing for years down the road.

Do All Those Ergonomic Gadgets Really Work?

Special input devices, footrests, wrist-supporting mousepads, document rests—the world's full of devices that promise to give you the ergonomically correct computing experience you crave. Only you can decide what works for you, but here are a few of the ergonomic gadgets you could try:

- Trackballs, pens, and other input devices are designed to help alleviate the repetitive stress injuries some say result from too much mousing. With any input device, keep it as close as possible to your body. If your keyboard has the numerical pad and other extended keys on the right, a right-side mousepad will be way the heck to the right of where your hands normally rest. If mouse you must, try mousing on the left, so your mousepad can snuggle up closer to your hands. It takes a few days for right-handers to get the hang of this, but don't give up!

- Rocking footrests cost less than $50, and many people claim they do help alleviate bad posture at the computer. Rock or not, use a footrest if your feet won't rest flat on the floor at the proper seat height adjustment.
- Those backless, forward-leaning computer chairs work well for some folks, but lots of users say they put too much pressure on the knees. Try it before you buy it.
- Curved and split keyboards have enthusiastic users, but a lot of those "ergonomic input" dudes end up in the accessory bone pile. Again, test drive any new keyboard. Most ergonomic experts agree that the shape of the keyboard matters a lot less than its positioning.

Before you buy any ergonomic device, ask the retailer about the return policy in case the item doesn't work out.

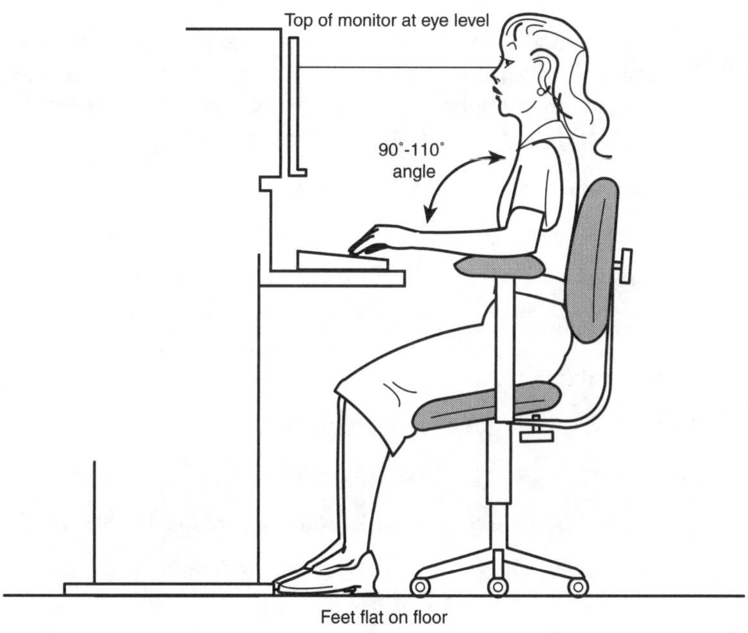

Figure 2.2

You don't need a $12,000 computer desk to work comfortably. If your keyboard, monitor, and chair are positioned correctly, your time at the computer should be happy *and* healthy.

LIGHTNING ROUND Q&A WRAP-UP

During a recent storm, there was a lightning strike near my house. Even though I have a surge protector, my modem died. How can I avoid this problem in the future—is there anything more efficient than a surge protector?

The only way to truly protect your computer from lightning or a sudden power outage is to unplug your PC from the power outlet and unplug the phone from the modem. You can take other steps to better your chances of keeping your computer safe. First, be sure that your phone line goes through your surge protector, and use a surge protector that supports modems. Most surge protectors guard against slow, low-power changes but won't stand up to major surges like the ones resulting from lightning strikes.

When you buy a surge protector, check its clamping speed (the speed at which the surge protector responds to a power surge) and the amount of voltage it can handle. Faster clamping speed is better, as is higher voltage capability.

One of my friends told me that I need to create a boot disk for my new computer. What's a boot disk, and why do I need one?

Computers crash, and when they do, they lose data. A boot disk, or start-up disk, is a disk you can use to start your computer—even if it's crashed and your hard drive isn't working right. Like a smoke detector, you hope you never need to use your boot disk, but you gotta have it, just in case.

To create a boot disk in Windows 98 or ME:

1. Insert a formatted floppy disk into your floppy drive.
2. Click Start.
3. Select Settings.
4. Select the Control Panel.
5. Double-click Add/Remove programs.
6. Click the Startup Disk tab on the far right.
7. Choose Create a Startup Disk. Windows creates the startup disk for you.

To use the boot disk, put the disk in your floppy drive as you start your computer.

CHAPTER 3

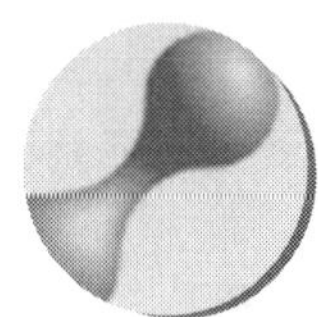

GET INTERNET ACCESS

- Weigh your access options
- Consider a cable modem connection
- Decide whether DSL is for you
- Size up satellite Internet
- Choose fixed wireless
- Use a dial-up networking connection (for better or worse)

Internet connection options have grown—but they might shrink again soon. You still can choose to use a dial-up networking connection through a 56Kbps modem, or you can opt for one of the screamers—cable modem, DSL, or satellite connection. However you do it, you need to know the best way to make and manage your Internet connection.

You can use this chapter as your "superguide" to Internet connectivity. In it, you learn the ups and downs of the major connection options and basic modem management techniques.

EYEING YOUR INTERNET CONNECTION OPTIONS

Many people buy a computer solely for Internet access. Web surfing and e-mailing are a big part of most people's computer experience. With the growing demand for broadband content—animation, audio, and video with a need for speed greater than a traditional 56K transfer rate—the demand for faster connection methods grows, too.

So how does everyone get on the Internet? Here are the most common ways people access the Net today:

- Dial-up networking (DUN) is still the most common method of Internet access used in the United States. DUN is built into Windows and MacOS. It uses standard phone lines, software, and an internal or external modem to dial in to an ISP and make the PC/Internet connection.
- Cable modems are external devices that connect to an Ethernet network card called a NIC (network interface card) in your PC. Cable TV companies provide cable modem access, which is available in most (but not all) areas.
- DSL (Digital Subscriber Line) services are high-speed Internet connections that usually are provided by the local phone company. Like cable, DSL requires a NIC and a DSL modem or router installed for your system.
- Satellite Internet service is available, but it's not as common as other connection methods. Only a few providers exist so far, with a Microsoft joint venture called Teledesic scheduled to open in 2005. Satellite Internet requires a satellite dish and mount, satellite modem, receiver, transmitter cards, and a few hundred bucks worth of software. In most cases, that's it—no additional phone line or dial-up connection is required.

Each of these Internet connection options has its own list of pros and cons, as you see in the information that follows. As technologies evolve and become more widespread, expect the Internet connection landscape to change dramatically. Right now, you have some interesting choices for getting online.

CHOOSING A CABLE MODEM CONNECTION

In 2000, more than 63 million U.S. homes subscribed to cable TV service, which means all those homes are wired for cable modem Internet access. Although cable modem access isn't available everywhere, more and more cable companies are adding it to their service lists. It's a popular option, but is it right for you?

Pros and Cons

As with any connection option, the important factors to consider about cable modem Internet access are cost, speed, and reliability. So how does cable modem stack up? Here are cable modem's pros:

- The monthly cost of cable modem is about the same as that of a phone line and ISP—currently, right around $40 per month. If you don't find a free installation deal, you'll also pay an installation fee (about $100).

- Cable modem connections are fast. Most provide speeds as high as 1.5 Mbps. That's 10,000 Kbps, as opposed to the 56 Kbps you get from a DUN/phone line connection.
- Cable modem connections are "always on," meaning you don't have to dial in (and tie up a phone line) every time you want to go online.

But cable modem has its cons:

- When you connect through cable, you're really on a LAN (local area network) with everyone else in your neighborhood. The more users that jump online at the same time, the slower your connection will be.
- LANs allow file sharing, and so does your cable modem connection. If your file-sharing capabilities are activated, anyone on your cable line might have access to your files. This doesn't happen regularly, but security is a big concern for cable modem users. (You can disable file-sharing capabilities in the Network Control Panel settings of your PC, or in the File Sharing section of the Sharing Setup Control Panel of your Mac.)

Given the predictions for growing numbers of cable modem users, these "sharing" problems aren't likely to go away. Look for them to get worse before they get better.

Can You Do Cable Modem?

To find out whether cable modem access is available in your area, ask your cable company. If they don't offer it now, they soon will.

Most home computers can support a cable modem connection. The current standards call for a PC with at least a 66Mhz 486 processor or a Mac with at least a 68040 processor and 16MB of memory. The faster your machine, the better your performance will be; most pros recommend 32MB of RAM and a 166MHz Pentium or 250MHz PowerMac.

The good news about signing up for cable modem service is that the provider does most of the installation work for you. In most cases, the cable company sends a technician to your house to install the cable modem and to make sure that your computer can handle the connection.

Don't Let Fear Of NIC Keep You From Exploring Cable Modems

If your computer doesn't have a network card, the cable company will help you arrange to have one installed. They might have you take your computer to a service shop for NIC installation. If you're willing to do the installation yourself, the cable company might provide installation instructions. If you're uneasy about the install, though, don't mess with it; leave it to the pros, even if you have to pay a bit more for startup costs.

WEIGHING IN ON DSL

DSL (Digital Subscriber Line) is a technology working hard to catch up to its potential. DSL is popular because of its speed and always-on connections (more about that later). But in a TechTV broadband user survey, the complaints most frequently cited by DSL users were "failure to receive advertised connection speeds and frequent inability to connect to their service." DSL could be great, but it's still getting there.

DSL connects your computer to the Internet by sending high-speed data through copper phone wires. DSL isn't offered everywhere, but phone companies are working hard to add DSL service to their offerings.

Even if your local phone company offers DSL service, you might not get hooked up right away. The number of ports in each of the phone company's central offices determines the number of DSL users the system can support. If no port is available in your area, you won't be able to get DSL service until the company adds more ports, or a current user unsubscribes.

Upload, Download—What's the Dif?

When you start researching broadband connection options, you'll see speeds rated for *uploading* and *downloading*. Those terms refer to the direction of the data transfer through the connection. Data passing from your computer to the Internet is being uploaded; information feeding into your machine from the Internet is being downloaded. The speeds for the two types of transfers are always different, because uploading is slower than downloading. Because most Web activities—from surfing to e-mail—require both actions, both upload and download speeds matter.

DSL Pros and Cons

DSL is becoming one of the most popular Internet connection methods. Some experts predict that by 2002, more than half of all Internet users will receive broadband transmissions, and DSL and cable modem are the two current technology leaders in broadband delivery. Here are some of the good things about DSL:

- DSL is fast; from most services, you should look for speeds up to 384Kbps for downloads and 128Kbps for uploading.
- Most DSL connections are "always on" (though some, like Earthlink, use PPPoE or point-to-point protocol over Ethernet, where you're assigned an IP address and have to connect, just as in DUN).
- DSL works through dedicated lines—no line-sharing or security worries, like those you have with cable modem.
- Even though DSL works through phone lines, it doesn't tie up yours. You can be online and talk on the phone at the same time, without adding a second line.

Now, take a look at the DSL "dark side":

- Offerings and services vary, but DSL can be expensive. In addition to the hardware costs, your phone company might charge you a monthly DSL fee (the amount varies, but it's usually between $40 and $50) and a separate ISP charge of $10 or more. Again, the pricing and "packaging" of DSL varies from area to area, so be sure you determine exactly what *your* DSL deal provides.
- The farther you live from the phone system's "hub," the less speedy your connection will be.
- If your system goes down, you might have to wait a long time for service. Many phone companies launched DSL services without knowing how much maintenance and repair the services would require. As a result, they got off to a rocky start, with lots of down time and slow service response. Look for this issue to resolve itself as the systems—and providers—get "broken in."

"Free" DSL Might Not Be

You might see ads for free DSL, but take a close look at the details of the contract (and they *will* ask you to sign one). Some services offer free DSL because they pump continuous advertisements onto their subscribers' screens. You'll pay an additional fee if you don't want to be bombarded with ads. Other companies want you to sign up for an extended period—say five years—and charge a hefty fee if you break the contract. Or they might require you to take on additional phone services the company offers in your area. As always, read the fine print before you sign anything. And if it looks too good to be true...well, you know the rest.

Can You Use a DSL Connection?

Most modern home computers can handle DSL with little modification. You need a DSL modem (about $200, but often included free by the provider when you sign a contract) and an Ethernet card (anywhere from $10 to $50) if you don't already have one. In some cases, you still need an ISP. The phone company charges about $10 a month for theirs. Most companies will install your DSL equipment and service for a fee.

Maybe You Don't Want to Install Your Own DSL

Lots of DSL providers encourage new subscribers to install their DSL system, providing a reduced start-up cost and a "self-install" kit that includes instructions, a DSL modem, and a number of microfilters you need to install to keep the DSL signal from interfering with your phones. Those microfilters are important parts of your DSL setup; they also prevent your telephones from interfering with your DSL service.

The problem is that self-install doesn't always work. Problems ranging from poor house wiring to lighting dimmers can slow down or even stop your DSL performance. And you can run into problems getting the special software that DSL demands to run on your computer. If you give in to the self-install "lure," be prepared to spend some time arranging for a service technician visit if you run into problems.

More importantly, you also need to live within three miles or so of a telephone switching station if you want your DSL connection to be at all speedy and reliable. For a basic monthly DSL fee, you should get downloads at about 384 Kbps and uploads at about 128 Kbps. Those speeds work great for most users, but not everyone gets the same speeds.

DSL providers farm the service out to you through a central hub. Users located close to the hub receive great speeds; move on down the line, and the quality of your service degrades. Pack a large number of users on the hub, and you lose even more quality. In other words, you get no guarantee that you'll get the DSL speeds you pay for.

INTERNET IN THE SKY: SATELLITE INTERNET ACCESS

Satellite Internet service is still in the early stages of developing a user base—and its technology. Satellites can "broadcast" the Internet directly to homes using the same kind of small-dish antennas used for TVs. Satellite access has some real benefits going for it:

- It can be available to you no matter where you live.
- You don't have to share lines (or service access) with other users.
- Under the right conditions, satellite Internet access provides very fast downloads.
- Second-generation satellite Internet doesn't require a modem. Although its predecessor required a modem for uploading information (from you to the Internet), services such as StarBand and DirecPC offer systems that both send and receive data via satellite.

But look at these down-to-the-ground drawbacks:

- You don't have a lot of provider options. Only a few companies offer satellite Internet access (Hughes Network system's DirecPC (`www.direcpc.com`) and Starband (`www.starband.com`) are the current biggies).
- Peak-period Net access can be much slower than the 400 Kbps download/128 Kbps upload "optimum" speeds.
- The signal is subject to interference from weather, other buildings—even trees. Anything that stands (or moves) between your satellite dish and the satellite can interrupt your connection.
- The startup costs can be way-high. You need a dish and mount, a satellite modem, and software. All of this can run you hundreds of dollars.

Something's Gotta Give

Right now, it looks like DSL and cable modem are *the* contenders for high-speed Internet connection, but DSL customer complaints were loud and strong during the first half of 2001. The DSL landscape is still riddled with service and connection quality landmines, but smart providers will clean up their messes soon. Keep an eye on TechTV to follow developments on the DSL-delivery front.

No technology gets to remain a cyberkid for long. Expect improvements in satellite Internet access as the number of players in this field grows.

It's on Tech TV

Get the latest on developments in broadband delivery technology and check out the results of the TechTV broadband survey by visiting the TechTV Web site at `www.techtv.com`.

FIXED WIRELESS ISPS HIT THE STREETS

Wireless Internet service providers (WISPs), from small, local operations to nationwide giants, are beginning to attract customers to one of the latest forms of broadband Internet connectivity. WISPs use high-powered transmitters and transceivers that send data over radio waves along the 2.4GHz spectrum. All data is delivered wirelessly from an access point to a transceiver located on your roof and then routed to a stationary computer in your home.

Pros and Cons of Fixed Wireless Internet Connection

Fixed wireless is still in its infancy, but it offers some real advantages. But before you decide to retire your cable or DSL modem, you need to consider the option from both sides.

Here are the pros of going with a WISP:

- The cost is reasonable. Rates vary, of course, but in most cases monthly rates are equal to or less than those of a DSL or cable modem connection. Colorado River Internet, as an example of a small local WISP, charges $20 a month; Sprint charges $49 a month for similar service.
- The download speeds are good. Advertised speeds vary among WISPs, but most are comparable to that of a DSL provider. In most cases, upload and download speeds fall between 500 and 1,000 Kbps.

Now for the cons:

- The hardware isn't easily transferable. If you decide to move, your hardware might not be compatible with the service provider you have in your new location. No dominant fixed wireless standard is in place.
- You get shared access. As with other connection services, as the total number of users accessing the network increases, expect throughput speeds to diminish.
- You might get line-of-sight interference. This might or might not be a problem for you, depending on your locale and proximity to the first available access point. If you live in a flat location, then chances are good that you'll have little interference. But in a hilly city such as San Francisco, you'll need a bigger antenna with increased signal amplification to send and receive data without any problems.

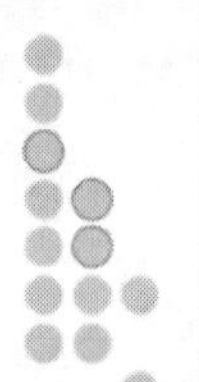

What You Need for a Fixed Wireless Connection

A typical fixed wireless installation requires an antenna or transceiver, cabling, and either a modem or a special wireless PC card. Because there's no hardware standard among WISPs yet, hardware setups will vary among providers.

For the service to work right for you, your setup must have a clear line-of-sight between transmitter and transceiver. The more man-made structures, trees, and hills between the transmitter and transceiver, the more interruptions and slowdowns your service will suffer. Most providers station access points every few miles.

You can learn more about fixed wireless at `www.isp-planet.com/fixed_wireless/` and at `www.epinions.com`.

OLD FAITHFUL: DIAL-UP NETWORK CONNECTIONS

Dial-up networking (DUN) is still the most common form of Internet access used in America, although experts think that will change over the next few years. For now, DUN is just about the only Internet connection method that's available in every area, and that's what keeps it ticking along in the first place. Like the internal combustion engine, it's a technology that just never seems to go away—no matter how many disadvantages it offers.

Surf the Slow Lane

Dial-up networking uses a modem, a telephone line, and software to connect your computer to the Internet through an ISP. Here are the reasons so many people use DUN and an ISP to access the Internet:

- You don't need special phone lines or high-tech gear to use DUN access.
- It's relatively inexpensive; about $20 for an ISP, plus your usual phone line charge.

Here's why people are leaving DUN to move to cable modem or DSL service:

- DUN is slo-o-o-o-w. Even if you have a 56Kbps modem, you will *never* get speeds that high.
- You must dial in and establish a connection every time you want to get on the Net. Depending on the size of your ISP and the number of subscribers, you could get busy signals or bumped off-line during peak usage periods.
- You simply can't get broadband content through a 56Kbps modem in any really usable format.
- If you don't install a separate line for your DUN connection, your phone line is out of commission while you're online.

What's Ahead for DUN?

Many people stick with DUN because it's easy to do, uses their computers' existing equipment, and they aren't that concerned with high-speed access. As broadband content builds, and functions such as telephony, online film broadcasts, and so on become more common, the tried and true DUN/ISP Internet connection will go the way of the Model T.

Note that V.92, the new standard for high-speed modems, is an improved version of the V.90 standard that high-speed modems have been using for a couple of years. However, it must, of course, be supported by your ISP, and many ISPs don't yet support it.

Bigger Might Not Mean Better

When choosing an ISP, don't assume that bigger automatically means better. Huge national ISPs offer 24×7 service departments, but you often get quicker and better response from the good old mom-and-pop ISP in your area. When you're one of a few hundred—versus a few million—accounts, you carry a lot more weight as a customer. Every service is unique, so explore your local ISP to see if it can provide the services and support you need. When evaluating any ISP, look for a local-call access number for your area, national access, reasonable service response time averages, and any auxiliary services you need (e-mail accounts, Web page hosting, and so on).

LIGHTNING ROUND Q&A WRAP-UP

I use a dial-up connection, so I know that I'm not going to get blazing connection speeds. But what can I do to get the fastest speeds this setup is capable of?

Just because you still use a dial-up to connect to the Internet doesn't mean that it has to take forever to get online. Use this tip to speed up connection time to your ISP.

For Windows 98:

1. Open My Computer.
2. Double-click Dial Up Networking.
3. Right-click on My Connection (or whatever you named the shortcut when you first entered your connection settings).
4. Select Properties.
5. Click the Server Types tab.
6. Uncheck the Logon to Network box.
7. Under Allowed Network Protocols, check only the TCP/IP box.

For Windows Me:

1. Right-click your dial-up connection.
2. Select Properties.
3. Click the Networking tab.
4. Under Allowed Network Protocols, check only the TCP/IP box.
5. Click the Security Tab.
6. Uncheck Logon to Network.

Immediately after your password is accepted you should be online.

I keep getting disconnected while I'm online. What's up with that? How do I put a stop to unwanted disconnects?

Sometimes ISPs boot users offline during peak usage periods if they see that the user's computer has been idle for a given period of time (the ISP decides when your time is up). You can fend off some unwanted disconnects by tweaking your computer settings. Here's how:

1. In the Start menu, open Settings.
2. Click Control Panel.
3. Click Internet Options.
4. Select the Connection tab.

5. Click Setting.
6. Click Advanced.
7. Uncheck the box next to "Disconnected if idle for (blank) minutes."

Unfortunately, this doesn't help you if your ISP is doing the disconnecting. If you've taken the preceding steps and still suffer way too many unwanted disconnects, ask your ISP for an explanation.

CHAPTER 4

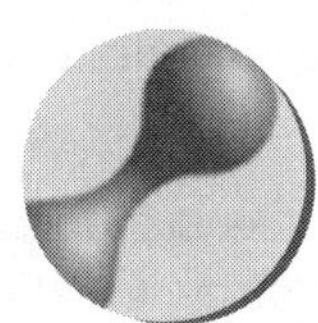

THE GOOD LIFE ONLINE

- Browse beyond the basics
- Download programs
- Shop online
- Chat and instant messaging

Going online is all about getting instant access to information, people, ideas, and products—the Net has no limits. With so much happening, it's easy to miss new developments or overlook shortcuts and workarounds that make your online time as productive (and non-frustrating) as possible.

In this chapter, TechTV shares some of its favorite tips, products, and technologies for online happiness. Learn no-fail ways to speed up your browser, use the quick guide to online shopping to buy with confidence, and get the inside scoop on Internet chat and telephony.

BROWSING BASICS (AND BEYOND)

A browser is a program that pulls online documents through your Internet service provider and displays them on your screen. Enter an address in your browser's address bar, press Return or click Go, and you move immediately (well, you hope so, anyway) to your chosen destination.

In addition to taking you to specific addresses, browsers let you move forward and backward through document pages and search the Internet for just the information you need.

Choose a Default Browser

Most computers today come with a browser or two all loaded up and ready to go. The two big contenders in the browser wars are Microsoft Internet Explorer (IE) and Netscape Navigator. Both are good browsers, but they do have an annoying tendency to want to be your "steady" browser.

But IE and Netscape aren't your only browser choices—check the Street Buzz for some interesting alternatives. If you do stick with one of the "big two," here's how to set one or the other as your default.

Setting a default browser in a MacOS machine is simple. Users can make any browser their default by choosing it from the Default Web Browser pop-up menu in the Internet control panel's Web tab (Mac OS 9) or in the Web tab of the Internet pane of the System Preferences (Mac OS X).

To make Internet Explorer your default browser in Windows:

1. Open IE.
2. Open the Tools menu and choose Internet Options.
3. Click the Programs tab and select the "Internet Explorer should check to see whether it is the default browser" box (down at the bottom of the tab).
4. Click OK, and then close the Internet Options box.
5. Close IE, and then relaunch it.
6. When the "Do you want to make IE your default browser?" message box opens, click Yes. Uncheck the "Always perform this check" box, and then close the box, as shown in Figure 4.1.

It's not quite as easy to make Netscape your browser of choice, but it can be done. Take a deep breath, and then follow these steps:

1. Open the Netscape folder on your hard drive.
2. Open the Users subfolder and double-click on your name.
3. Find the file named prefs.js. That's your preferences file, and you're going to edit it (even though it will tell you not to).
4. Open Notepad.

5. Drag prefs.js into it, to open and read the file.
6. Read down through the file—from the top line that says "Netscape User Preferences" and the "Do Not Edit!" line that follows it. Keep going until you find a line that reads

   user_pref("browser.wfe.ignore_def_check", true);
7. Delete the word **true** and in its place type the word **false**, as shown in Figure 4.2.
8. Save your changes and close Notepad.
9. The next time you launch Navigator, you get the "Do you want to make Netscape your default browser?" box; click the check box, and then choose Yes.

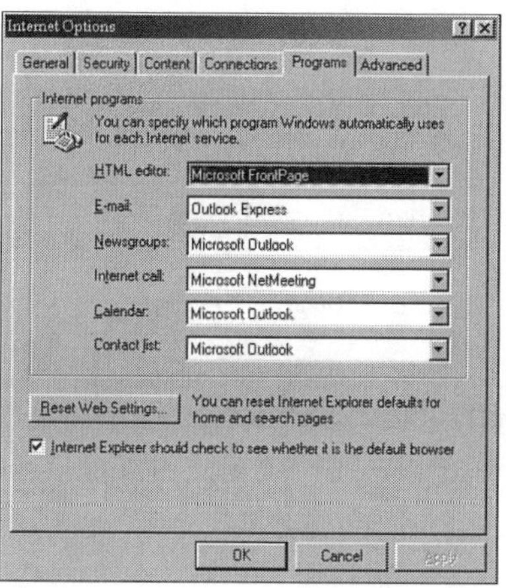

Figure 4.1

To make Internet Explorer your default browser, be sure to check the "Internet Explorer should check to see whether it is the default browser box."

Be sure to change "true" to "false"

prefs.js - Notepad

File Edit Search Help

```
user_pref("browser.url_history.clear", 1);
user_pref("browser.wfe.ignore_def_check", true);
user_pref("browser.wfe.show_value", 3);
user_pref("browser.window_rect", "80,86,710,529");
user_pref("custtoolbar.Messenger.Location_Toolbar.showing", false);
user_pref("custtoolbar.personal_toolbar_folder", "Personal Toolbar
Folder");
user_pref("editor.author", "Lyle Neal");
user_pref("ldap_2.servers.infospace.csid", "UTF-8");
user_pref("ldap_2.servers.infospace.filename", "infospace.na2");
user_pref("ldap_2.servers.infospace.replication.lastChangeNumber", 0);
user_pref("ldap_2.servers.netcenter.csid", "UTF-8");
user_pref("ldap_2.servers.netcenter.filename", "netcenter.na2");
user_pref("ldap_2.servers.netcenter.replication.lastChangeNumber", 0);
user_pref("ldap_2.servers.pab.csid", "iso-8859-1");
user_pref("ldap_2.servers.pab.filename", "pab.na2");
user_pref("ldap_2.servers.pab.replication.lastChangeNumber", 0);
user_pref("ldap_2.servers.verisign.csid", "UTF-8");
user_pref("ldap_2.servers.verisign.filename", "verisign.na2");
user_pref("ldap_2.servers.verisign.replication.lastChangeNumber", 0);
user_pref("ldap_2.version", 2);
user_pref("mail.addr_book.version", ".na2");
user_pref("mail.compose_window_rect", "75,75,629,475");
```

Figure 4.2

To make Netscape your default browser, be sure to change "true" to "false" in the command line shown here, and then save your changes.

Speed Up Your Browser

You can speed up any browser, even IE and Netscape. Anyone can benefit from these speed tips, but if you're working with a 56K modem, you'll find them especially valuable.

Who likes to wait for a browser's default home page to load? All that advertising and over-designed, recycled info on the latest star marriage meltdown or stock market survival tip weighs down the page and steals your time. Set a blank or uncluttered home page, to lose the wait, and reduce your browser start-up time.

Make Your Home Page Your Own

If you want more zip to your new, fast-loading home page, use FrontPage Express or some other WYSIWYG (What You See Is What You Get) HTML editor to dress it up. Give your new home page a cool color, add links (such as your favorite search engine, or local movie listings), and otherwise make it your own, and then save the file in your My Documents folder. Now you have your own slim and fast home page that appears on your screen much faster than the prefab versions.

To set your browser to use a blank page (or a page you've created) in Internet Explorer, do this:

1. In Windows, open IE, and choose Tools, Internet Options.

   In MacOS, choose Edit, Preferences, and click Browser Display.
2. In the section labeled Home Page, Windows users choose Blank or click the Browse button to select the page you've created (see Figure 4.3).

   Mac users, click Use None in the section labeled Home Page, or click Use Default and enter a URL for the page you want to use.

Alternative Browsing

Maybe you don't want *either* of the memory-gobbling "big two" browsers. As Netscape and IE continue to battle it out, newer, more agile, and maybe even better contenders have joined the smack-down:

- Opera (find it at `www.opera.com`) is a small but mighty browser that offers real benefits to its users. You can get a free version, or register and pay a small fee ($39 street/$20 or less for educators) for a no-ads version. Opera is incredibly fast and it doesn't suck up storage space, either. Visit its Web site for details.
- Neoplanet, available free at `www.neoplanet.com`, offers online communities and more than 500 different "skins" or customized looks.

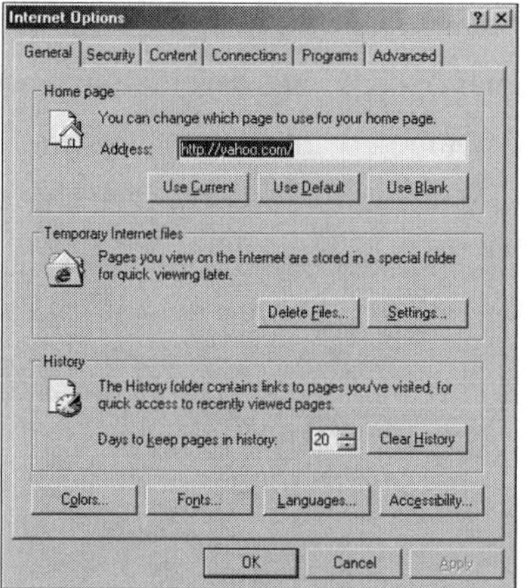

Figure 4.3

You can set Internet Explorer to a blank home page or any page you like by entering the correct address under Home Page.

In Netscape, Windows and Mac users follow the same steps:

1. Choose Edit, Preferences, and select Navigator.
2. Choose the page that you want your browser to launch with, as shown in Figure 4.4.

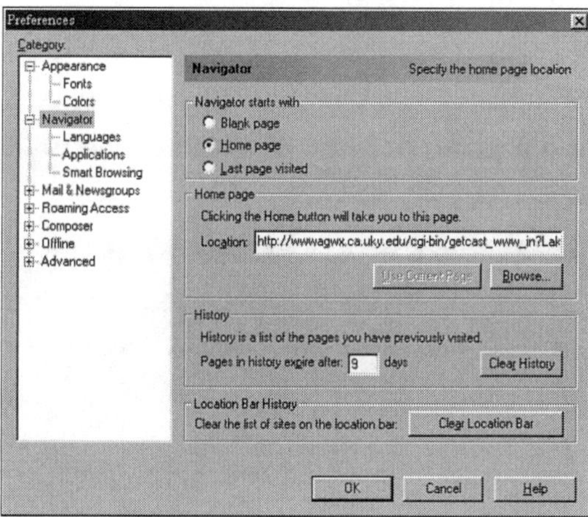

Figure 4.4

Select a blank page or enter the address of a Web site to change the home page in Netscape.

Save more time by setting your Web cache big enough to hold plenty of pages. When you revisit a Web page, it loads much faster from the cache than from the server.

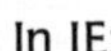

In IE:

1. Choose Tools, Internet Options, and click the General tab.
2. Click Settings in the Temporary Internet Settings area.
3. Move the slider under Amount of Disk Space to Use. Set your cache size at about 10% of the available space.
4. In the Check for New Versions of a Page area, select the Automatically button or choose Every Visit to the Page so your cache won't deliver stale pages (see Figure 4.5).

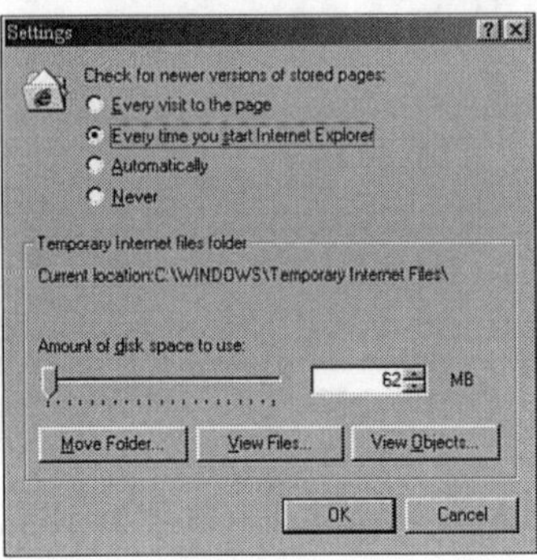

Figure 4.5

Speed up the loading time of Internet Explorer by moving the slider to allow more room in the cache.

In Netscape:

1. Choose Edit, Preferences, and click Advanced. Then select the Cache panel.
2. Use the editable fields in the Cache Preferences panel to set the size and location of your cache, as shown in Figure 4.6.

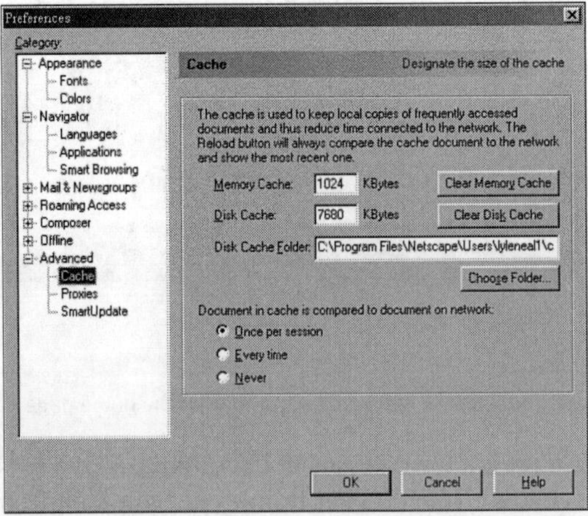

Figure 4.6

Adjust the size of your Netscape cache to allow more pages to load quickly from memory.

Know When to Say "When" on Cache Size

Don't set your cache size larger than 10 percent of your available hard disk space. You'll slow down your system and lose whatever speed benefits you gain by using cached files. If your system gets too bogged down, clear your cache. In IE, choose Tools, Internet Options. In the General tab, click Delete Files in the Temporary Internet Files area. In Netscape, go to Edit, Preferences, and click Advanced. Open the Cache preferences panel, and click the Clear Memory Cache Now and Clear Disk Cache Now buttons.

If you work in MacOS, to clear your IE cache choose Edit, Preferences, Advanced and click the Empty Now button in the Cache error. In Mac Navigator, choose Edit, Preferences, Advanced, Cache and click Clear Disk Cache Now.

If you work in Windows, here are other ways to cut down on keystrokes and mousing (and time) while you surf the Web:

- **Skip the "www":** In IE, access any Web site by typing its domain name, and then pressing Ctrl+Enter. For example, to visit TechTV's Web site, type **techtv** in the address box, and then press Ctrl+Enter. Voila!
- **Page down:** Press the space bar to page down on a Web page.
- **Move forward and back:** Press Alt+left arrow to move to the previous Web page. Alt+right arrow takes you forward through Web pages you've viewed. (The Backspace key also takes you back through previously viewed pages.)
- **Close it:** Close your browser quickly by pressing Ctrl+W.

DOWNLOAD FILES

The Net's a treasure chest full of valuables: games, software, utilities, music, video...you name it. Most of these gems lie just a few clicks away, if you know how to download. The first rule of good downloading is

1. Follow safe downloading rules!

Safe Downloading Rules:

- Only download files from reliable sites—you don't want to download a virus-infected file.
- Install a virus-scan program (such as McAfee VirusScan or Norton AntiVirus) on your computer.
- If you download frequently, scan your hard drive at least once a week for viruses.
- Remember where you save your downloaded files. They won't do you any good if you can't locate them.

Try Another Time Zone for Speedy Downloads

You might speed up a sluggish download by using a server located in a time zone where it's the middle of the night. For example, say you want to download a copy of the newest version of IE from a Microsoft site. At 10 a.m., Microsoft's Redmond site might

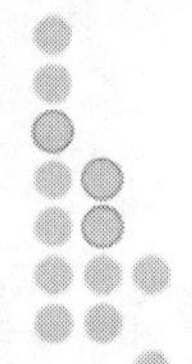

be really busy, so downloading could take forever. But if you choose to download from Microsoft's site in Japan, where the local time would be about 2 in the morning, the download could zip through in no time. If you use a 56K DUN connection, a bad ISP line could also cause slow downloads. Call your phone company and ask them to check your line for excessive noise (you might need to be persistent). If that doesn't help, check alternative dial-in numbers for your ISP; one might offer a faster connection.

Find and Download Goods from the Net

From games, to desktop applications, utilities, and other software and programs, you can find great downloadables all over the Internet. These download sites have proven themselves reliable:

- `www.ZDNet.com/downloads/`
- `www.tucows.com`
- `www.download.com`
- `www.superfiles.com`

If you download from one of these sites, you'll get all the info about the file you're interested in up front (see Figure 4.7)

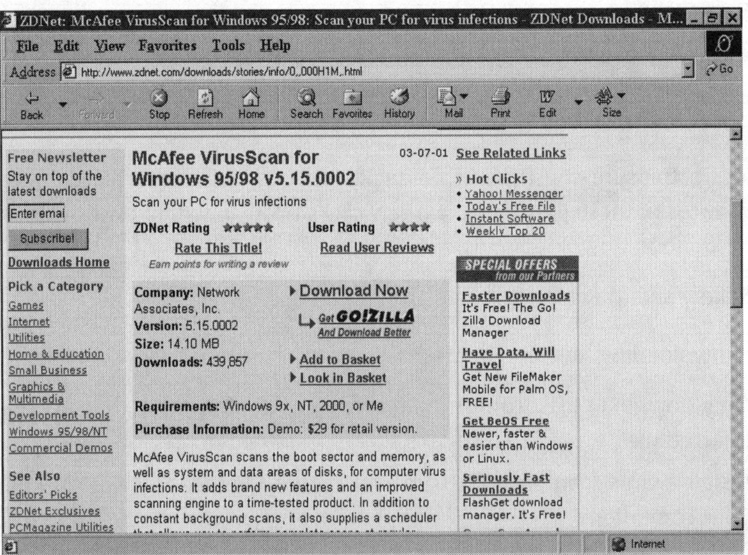

Figure 4.7

The ZDNet download site lists the size, version number, and cost of downloads, along with user ratings and other useful info.

Anti-Virus Protection Is a Must!

A word of warning is worth repeating here: Don't set off on a downloading spree until you've protected your system with anti-virus software. Downloads are the Typhoid Marys of the computer world, and you don't want to be infected by a rogue bug. Download only from reputable sites and use a virus-scan program (such as McAfee VirusScan or Norton AntiVirus) on your computer.

Downloading is relatively simple:

1. Create a download folder on your hard drive (store it on your Desktop if you like). This is where you'll stash the files you download.
2. Use your browser to find a file you want to download, and then click the Download Now button (or whatever hotlink to the download is given). A message box asks you where and how to save the file (see Figure 4.8); click the Save to Disk option.

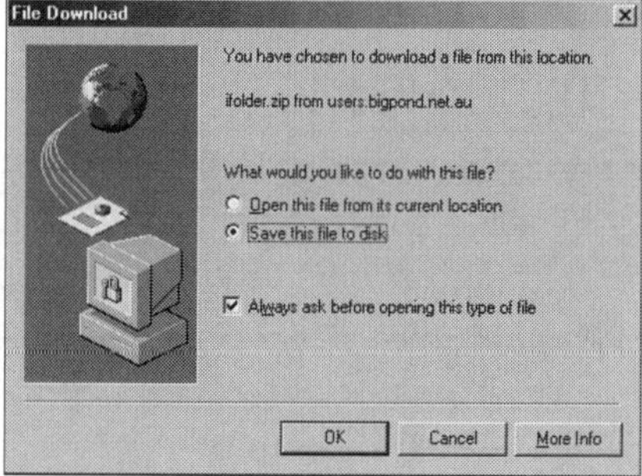

Figure 4.8

You always get to decide where to save your downloaded files.

3. Type in the location and name you want to give the program, then click Save and proceed with the download. A progress indicator will tell you when the download is finished.

Most downloadable files are compressed into a smaller file size to speed up transfer. Your computer might have come preloaded with WinZip or Stuffit Expander (common decompression utilities for Windows and MacOS, respectively). If not, check out the following section, "Must-Have Downloads," to find out where you can download a shareware version of either.

If you double-click a compressed downloaded file, it automatically opens in the compression utility. In the contents list of the decompressed file, open the readme.txt file for instructions on installing the program you've downloaded.

If your download isn't compressed, look for the .exe file. That's the program's *executable* file, and if you double-click it, the program will either begin running or you'll receive another instruction box to walk you through installation. MacOS users won't find an .exe file, so they just have to try to spot the program file based on its name or icon.

Must-Have Downloads

These programs help you run and protect your system, listen to music, watch video, and use other downloadables you'll snag from the Net.

- **Protect against viruses:** Get McAfee Virus Scan (free demo, $30 to keep) or Norton AntiVirus (free demo, $40 to keep) at `www.zdnet.com/downloads`.
- **Unzip archived files:** Get shareware versions of WinZip and StuffIt Expander from the ZDNet downloads site (`www.ZDNet.com/downloads/`).
- **Listen to MP3s:** Winamp (`www.winamp.com`) is the standard Windows MP3 player; Mac users like SoundJam. (`www.soundjam.com`).
- **Watch video:** You have some options here, and all are free. RealPlayer, at `www.real.com/player`, Windows Media Player at `www.microsoft.com`, or Apple's QuickTime at `www.apple.com`. Might as well get all three because none of them can play video encoded for the others.

PRACTICE SAFE ONLINE SHOPPING

Everybody shops online these days, and why not? It's fast, convenient, and doesn't require that you put on weather-shielding outerwear or start your (car's) engine. Whether you're browsing, searching, or catching up on the latest developments at TechTV.com, you encounter a rash of shopping-cart laden links wherever you turn online. And with sites like eBay (`www.ebay.com`) and Priceline (`www.priceline.com`) appealing to everyone's inner bargain hunter, online shopping won't die any time soon.

Online shopping is safe, if you follow a few basic rules.

- **Be sure the site is legitimate:** The site should display a phone number and street address. If you have any question about the site's legitimacy, call the number. If the store doesn't post a number, shop elsewhere. Check the Better Business Bureau Online (`BBBOnLine.com`) to see if the site's registered with the Bureau. If it is, it passed the entrance requirements and can most likely be trusted.
- **Protect your privacy:** Before you enter any information about yourself, look for the locked padlock symbol on the browser, and be sure that the address bar shows **https** (evidence of a secure socket layer) in the URL. That guarantees that you're in a secure server. Read the site's privacy policy. If the site doesn't have one, say "buh-buy." Finally, look for the TrustE symbol. TrustE (`www.truste.com`) sets standards for online privacy (see Figure 4.9).
- **Don't give them too much information:** Most online merchants ask you to fill out a form when you make a purchase. Complete only the necessary fields (they're usually marked as mandatory) such as your name and billing address. Don't give information about your age, income, or other non-essentials, and *never* give your Social Security number. Provide a fake phone number if the site insists you list one.

- **Pay with a credit card:** You can cancel the payment if something goes wrong, and in a worst-case scenario, you should be liable for no more than $50 of unauthorized charges. *Don't* use a debit card. You don't want to give anyone access to your checking account.

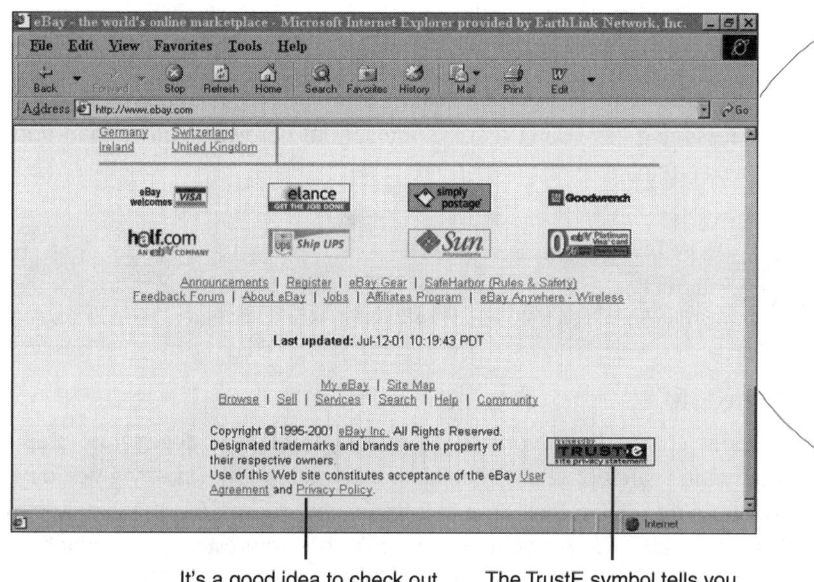

It's a good idea to check out the privacy policy of any online merchant; if the site doesn't list one, watch out.

The TrustE symbol tells you that the site adheres to online privacy standards.

Figure 4.9

The TrustE symbol and a good privacy policy, such as those shown here on the eBay online auction site home page, are good indications that you're dealing with a reputable online merchant.

Find Out Where They Stand

You can see how a site compares to others of its kind by visiting `Bizrate.com`, an online business ranking service. Find out how your online merchant compares to the competition in areas such as ease of ordering, customer service, and on-time delivery. If you're interested in other customers' opinions about an online service or product vendor, visit `Complaints.com`. That site lists online shopper complaints, categorized by type of business.

TALK IT UP ONLINE

Although you might not have reached the space-age standards of videophoning predicted by the Jetsons, you can use your PC as a day-to-day instant communication device. *Internet telephony*, a combination of hardware and software that allows long-distance voice and video sharing through a PC, continues to grow in popularity. If you doubt that, just watch all those NetCam calls broadcast on TechTV (you learn more about Netcams in Chapter 18).

Two of the most popular forms of instant communication– Internet Relay Chat (IRC) and Instant Messaging (IM)—don't require any special hardware (other than your modem) or much special training.

It's on TechTV

You can find detailed information on both IRC and IM by checking out the TechTV Web site's Help and How To information at `techtv.com`.

Chat with IRC

If the words "chat room" automatically make you think of degenerate predators trawling the Internet in search of young, gullible prey, you're right. On any given day, the worst of the worst are occupying their time in Internet chat rooms. But that's only part of the chat-room story. A lot of good people, with valuable, interesting, unavailable-anywhere-else information also hang out in chat rooms. In fact, most of the TechTV program hosts pop in the network's moderated chat rooms every day to talk with viewers. With 30,000 people using Internet chat at any give time, you can't judge all of them by the actions of a few.

It's on TechTV

Meet TechTV hosts, producers, Web gurus, and fans at `www.techtv.com/interact/chat/`. It's safe, moderated by TechTV-approved hosts, and you might even get answers to your burning tech questions like "Why won't my PC recognize my printer?" and "Is that Leo's real hair?"

IRC isn't the only chat platform, but it's the most popular. To use it, you need client software that provides an interface for you and connection information for your modem. Windows users can download a copy of mIRC, a popular client, as shareware from the ZDNet download site. A similar product for MacOS, Ircle, is a shareware download available from `www.ircle.com`.

When you install and launch mIRC, you get a message box asking for your name, e-mail address, and nickname. *Don't ever use your real name and e-mail address here or in any chat room communications.* Enter fake information and move on.

Choose Your Nickname Wisely

When choosing a nickname for mIRC, Ircle, or any chat program, be sure the name you choose sounds totally asexual. Everyone sees your nickname as your identification while you're chatting, and you don't want to attract any sickos. A nickname like Throbulizer, therefore, isn't as advisable as, say, Oaktree.

Don't Let Kids Chat Alone

Don't ever, ever, ever let your children participate in chat rooms without your direct and constant supervision. Chat rooms aren't safe places for youngsters—some of them aren't safe for adults, either. Chat rooms can be vile and disgusting places, so don't let your kids wander around in them.

You can only chat with others on the same server. mIRC presents you with a list of servers from which to choose; if you're signing up to chat with friends and family, be sure everyone knows which server to connect to.

After you connect to a server, choose a channel. Channels are chat rooms devoted to specific topics such as Labrador retrievers, single parenting, or Star Wars. (If you don't see the channel listings, open the mIRC channel folder or click the List Channels button.) To join a specific channel, type /**Join#Channelname** (enter your chosen channel after #) in the text box at the bottom of the mIRC window. You can create your own channel by entering a name of your choice after the #. For example, /**Join#smithfamilyreunion**.

You'll find full instructions for using mIRC online, along with an extensive help section. Don't be afraid to play around with mIRC; you'll be chatting like a pro in no time.

Use Instant Messaging

Instant messaging (IM) conversations are sort of like e-mail, but–as in IRC–the exchanges take place in real time (see Figure 4.10). Instant messaging first became popular as a medium for conducting online conferences and seminars. Now, people use it as a daily method of communicating privately over the Internet (and skipping those long-distance bills).

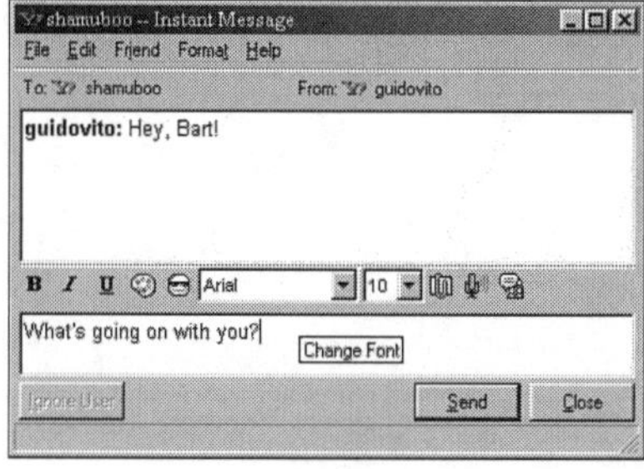

Figure 4.10

Instant messagers, such as Yahoos!'s Instant Messenger, enable you to carry on private conversations in real time.

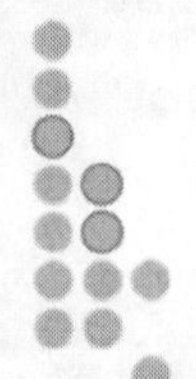

You need an IM client. America Online probably is the most popular, but it certainly isn't the only client available. Lots of folks at TechTV use Yahoo!'s IM (downloadable at `messenger.yahoo.com`). Yahoo!'s IM is easy to use, and its features and commands are similar to many other IM clients.

After you download the IM client, create a list of friends that you want to talk to with IM. In Yahoo!'s IM, choose Messenger, Add a Friend/Group, and then fill in the information the dialog box asks for. When you're ready to go, select Messenger, Start a Conference, and then add people from your lists to the group.

If you have headphones and microphones, the folks in your group can chat out loud to each other. Choose Messenger, Start a Voice Chat, and you're ready to go.

Most IM clients have slight delays in the sound transfer, but IM is a lot cheaper than paying for a long-distance call. Depending on the IM client that you choose, you can send file attachments while chatting, keep up with stock quotes, or follow the action of your favorite sports teams. Your program will contain full info on its features.

LIGHTNING ROUND Q&A WRAP-UP

What's the difference between shareware, freeware, and all those other file types I see available for download?

Most downloadable files fall into a few major categories. You can use **freeware** and **public domain** at no charge, indefinitely, though the author might ask you to return demographic information. You can "test drive" **shareware** and **demonstration** (demo) software for a given period of time—say 30 days—before you're asked to pay. Demos and shareware are often only partial programs. If you want the full version, you'll have to pay a fee.

How can I be sure the program I'm downloading doesn't have a virus?

First of all, remember that you're more likely to get a virus from a friend's floppy disk than from a reputable download site. If you download from reputable sites only, such as America Online, CompuServe, and ZDNet, you're safe. These sites check all their downloadable files for viruses before posting them.

On the other hand, if you frequent places like "Jerry's Hacker Page," scan the files with an antivirus program before you open them. Some programs, like McAfee Antivirus and Norton Anti-Virus, can scan software as you download it.

CHAPTER 5

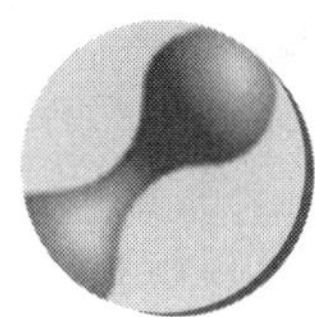

LOCK DOWN BASIC SECURITY

- Know your security risks
- Protect your privacy online
- Fight off viruses
- Build your firewall
- Use e-mail encryption

Over the years, computer security risks—and prevention measures—have changed dramatically. Used to be you only worried about your own data—backing up properly, not deleting important program files, and so on. Now, you have to worry about protecting your data from outside forces you can't predict or control.

But the good news is that you *can* protect your data, your privacy, and your sanity, and still lead a happy, active online life. This chapter brings you TechTV's must-do security safeguards, tips for finding and using must-have security tools, and an inside look at some of the must-know developments in cyber-crime prevention.

KNOW WHAT'S BUGGING YOU

The first step in safe computing is to know your enemy. TechTV viewers report a wide range of computer security problems. Here are some of the most common:

- **Viruses:** These programs (or mini-programs) sneak into your system through e-mail attachments or downloads and can destroy your hard drive's data.
- **Online privacy invasion:** Web pages can copy information from your hard drive, but most often they just plant cookies to track your Internet use history. The more newsgroups and mailing lists you belong to and the more browsing you do, the more vulnerable you become to having your information stored, shared, and sold to interested parties for online commerce, mailing lists—or whatever.
- **Hack attacks:** Because you share your cable modem connection with other users in your area, cable modems open up the possibility for hacker access. Hackers have been working hard to grab and decrypt wireless network transmissions.
- **User oversight:** Still one of the easiest ways to lose your precious data is to forget to take care of it in the first place. If you don't use the right kind of backup and surge protection, you put your computer data (and equipment) at risk. If your system crashes, your hard drive fails, you use a friend's infected floppy, or you get hit by lightning or a virus, you can lose it all if you haven't been practicing safe computing.

Follow the Four Rules of Internet Safety

No matter what other security measures you use, *always* follow our four basic rules for Internet safety:

1. Use good passwords. The best passwords are gibberish words of *at least* six to eight characters, made up of a combination of numbers and both upper- and lowercase letters. Be creative and use a full sentence with capitalization and punctuation, the initials of your first love mixed with the date you met him or her, or anything else you can remember without writing down. Don't use a spouse, parent, child, or pet's name, or birthdate, or any other personal data that could be guessed by someone with access to those details of your life.
2. Don't start services you don't need. Turn off file sharing, and don't run an FTP or Web server if you don't need to. These activities open your ports—and thus your system—to intrusion.
3. Keep personal info personal. Don't put your name or address in your computer, and don't associate your personal name with your computer in any way.
4. When you're on the Internet, hide your IP address. Programs such as Freedom from Zero Knowledge Systems (`www.zeroknowledge.com`) hide your IP from everyone).

PROTECT YOUR PERSONAL INFORMATION ONLINE

You are the first line of defense in protecting your personal information. When you browse the Net, join a mailing list or newsgroup, shop online, or host your own Web page, you leave a trail of information that gives advertisers, businesses, and who-knows-who a profile of your life. You might not need to live invisibly, but if you want to stay out of the scopes of spammers and voracious online marketers, take precautions in the way you behave online.

Keep It to Yourself

Any time you provide your name, address, and phone number to someone on the Internet, you put your listing in the Net's telephone book, so to speak. Assume that whomever you share that info with plans to sell it to someone else. So, don't give your personal information to any site unless you are certain that it's secure and trustworthy, and then don't give out any information that isn't absolutely necessary. (Read "Practice Safe Online Shopping," in Chapter 4, "The Good Life Online," for rules about passing out info to online merchants.)

Want to find out whether you've been sold out? Go to a Yellow Pages site—like the Netscape People Finder—and search on your name. You might be unpleasantly surprised to see how quickly you show up. Most directory sites give you the option of removing your listing—take advantage of it.

Lock It Up

Lock down your online security by looking for the security "padlock" whenever you're entering sensitive information on a Web site. The padlock symbol appears on either the right or left side of your browser's status bar. The padlock is closed when you're in a secure, encrypted location and opens when you move on to unsecured servers. Double-click the lock to determine that you're at the correct site and haven't been relocated to another, unsecured location.

Gated Security for Your IP

Your Internet Protocol (IP) address is your computer's "street address." When you're online, your IP address makes it possible for the rest of the online world to respond to your queries and prompts. Unfortunately, spammers and other unsavory types can use your IP address to track you down and load you up with their e-junk. If your Internet connection method has a static IP address, you need to guard against such intrusions. If you have a static IP address (check with your IP provider), look into software products such as DHCPMan, which release your IP address after you boot up. To learn more about this and other IP protection software, visit `www.zdnet.com`.

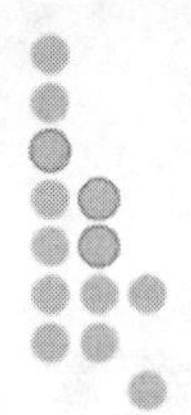

Be Careful of the Company You Keep

Newsgroups and mailing lists are public meeting rooms. When you join a mailing list or post a message to a newsgroup, you basically make your whereabouts—and opinions—public knowledge. Although mailing lists circulate among subscribers, anyone can access and read newsgroups.

The information posted to a newsgroup stays there indefinitely, so look upon it as your permanent record—one that can wreak much more havoc than the one your high school principal always threatened you about. Be careful about the kind of messages you post to newsgroups if you want to avoid the attention of someone scouring the Net for folks with opinions on a pet topic.

Be an Anonymous Poster

Don't use a signature line in your public postings, particularly if it includes other contact information. Your perfectly innocent opinions can be misconstrued by any wacko with a religious or political axe to grind. You don't want to be targeted on some idiot's mailing list (e-mail and or snail) because, for example, you support school lunch programs or want better sidewalks in suburban neighborhoods. Don't give anyone easy access to your address, phone number, and other personal information, but be particularly cautious about releasing it online.

Browse a Trail

When you browse the Internet, every site you visit notes your presence and keeps a record of your stay. The site might send a cookie (a message file that contains identifying data about you and/or your computer) to your machine that could tell other sites about your visit, too. Companies use cookie files to collect marketing data; that's good for the company's marketing efforts, but it might not be good for you.

Close the Cookie Jar

You can disable cookies on your system so that your machine doesn't allow companies to store their marketing devices on your machine. Your browser probably offers you the options of disabling cookies entirely, having the machine prompt you before it allows a cookie to enter your machine, or storing only those cookies that disappear at the end of the session. To set cookie options in Internet Explorer, choose Tools, Internet Options, and click the Security tab. Click the Custom Level button in the Security Settings area. When the Settings list appears, scroll down to the Cookies listings and click the button next to your choice. (Mac users choose Edit, Preferences, Cookies.) In Netscape, Mac and Windows users choose Edit, Preferences, Advanced to adjust cookie settings.

To keep your browsing safe and as untrackable as possible, regularly clear your cache and temporary Internet history files and—again—don't give out personal information to the Web sites you visit (read more about managing your cache in Chapter 4).

Host Your Own Web Record—I Mean Web Page

Web pages can be a great way to promote your career and expand your creativity, but never forget that you open a window into your world when you put a personal page on the Web.

Most people want their sites to draw attention—that's why you publish them in the first place. But prepare to deal with the spam, e-mails, and potentially negative attention your site might draw. Take care about just what you "give up" on your Web page.

If you use the site as a job-search center, you might want to keep your personal and political views off the site. That kind of information rarely helps your job search, and it can be a real nut magnet. If you use the site as a political forum, do you really need to exchange addresses or other contact info with the readers? Use your common sense and expect your page to fall in the firing line of Web trawlers at one point or another.

Button Down Your Mac

You can be completely safe online if you make your Mac an island. But what fun is that in the Internet age? While you're out surfing, err on the side of safety. To button down your Mac against unwanted access, do this:

- In Control Panels, go to File Sharing and be sure it is off. If you run Mac OS 9, be especially careful to leave the Enable Over TCP/IP box unchecked.
- In Control Panels, go to Web Sharing and be sure it is off.
- iDisk is very handy, but be careful what you put in those folders. Although only the public folder is easy to get to, any of the data you store there could be vulnerable.

Slam Spam

No matter how much you hate spam, you might as well face it: Spam is a fact of cyberlife. But you don't have to take spam lying down. Here are some of TechTV's favorite cybercrime tips for fighting spam:

- **Maintain a spam e-mail account.** Web-based e-mail accounts are free and easy to set up, so why not get one that's strictly for spam? Don't use your spam e-mail

Say "No Thanks" to Spyware

Some marketers include spyware in free software and downloads to bombard you with ads and report on your activity whenever you surf the Internet. If you want to make sure your computer rebuffs any such ad-vances, use an ad-busting software product such as OptOut. OptOut is a free download for Windows 9x systems. It lets you know you have spyware on your system, and then gives you the option of removing it. Learn more and download it at `zdnet.com`.

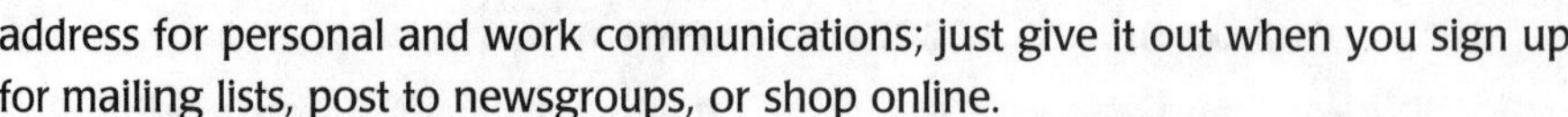

address for personal and work communications; just give it out when you sign up for mailing lists, post to newsgroups, or shop online.

- **Don't give out your real e-mail address.** When filling out online registration forms, use your spam e-mail address or leave the e-mail address space blank. If the site requires an e-mail address, enter a fake address. "Munging" is the practice of altering just a few letters in your e-mail address, to keep your inbox free of messages sent to that address.
- **Never open or reply to spam.** Although federal legislation is in the works to require companies to provide—and honor—opt out mechanisms in all unsolicited e-mail ads, none of the legislation currently is enacted. So you don't want to reply to a spammer, even to say "leave me alone." Your reply tells the spammer your e-mail address is active and is likely to trigger even more spam. In fact, when you get a message that looks like spam, delete it without even opening it. Some spam messages are programmed to contain Web bugs that notify the message's sender when a sent message has been opened. Opening such messages is just another way to convince a spammer that your address is active.
- **Screen for spam.** Program your e-mail client to filter out certain messages, such as those that don't have your correct e-mail address. You also can screen out messages with subject lines in all caps, those with a lot of dollar signs, exclamation points, or words like "unsubscribe," "X-priority," "adv," "bulk e-mail," "authenticated sender," or "make money fast." And take note of the domains from which you receive a lot of mass e-mail, and then block messages from those domains.
- **Get a spam filter.** Many ISPs come with a spam filter that you can add to your existing e-mail client. Earthlink offers one called Spaminator, and Hotmail provides one called InBox Protector. You also can purchase Novasoft's SpamKiller for $30 (`www.spamkiller.com`), or download one for free from Spam Bouncer (`www.spambouncer.org`).
- **Get unlisted.** Contact Internet directories such as WhoWhere and 411 and ask them to remove your name, e-mail address, and personal information from their databases.
- **Periodically change your e-mail address.** Although this can be annoying, changing your e-mail address on a regular basis, say every six months, will help keep spam from getting out of control. By the time spammers have figured out your new address, it will be changed again. This is a plan of last resort, only for those who just cannot seem to avoid spam.

WARD OFF VIRUSES

Every month or so, a new virus alert pops up in the national news. Viruses are manmade problems—programs designed specifically to worm their way around the world, via e-mail and downloads, and to wreak havoc by destroying or hopelessly gumming up computer systems. Because viruses are computer programs, they can do just about anything a program can do. They'll delete files, rework documents, and copy and send information. You probably can't even guess all the evil deeds a virus can do.

Basic Virus Protection

Viruses tend to spread through e-mail attachments in the form of executable files (.exe files) and Visual Basic script (.vbs) files. They also spread through the macro templates attached to Word or Excel documents. To avoid contracting a painful virus, follow these two rules:

- DON'T OPEN E-MAIL ATTACHMENTS from unknown sources and don't download software from sites that you aren't 100 percent certain you can trust.
- Use good antivirus software from a reputable company such as Norton AntiVirus or McAfee VirusScan and update it frequently.

Downloading an antivirus program doesn't protect you for life. Update your software periodically from your anti-virus software's home page to get protection from the newest virus going 'round. Symantec's antivirus research site at `www.sarc.com` lists the latest threats and fixes.

"What Big Attachments You Have!"

Don't assume that the innocent-looking file attachment you received from your sweet old grandmother really contains her brownie recipe. Some computer viruses search your e-mail for addresses of folks who frequently send you attachments. The virus then attaches itself to an e-mail from one of those senders. That's why you need to carefully examine *every* attachment for a .vbs or .exe extension before you open it—no matter who it comes from. If grandma's brownie recipe is in a file labeled brwnie.doc.vbs or yummythings.exe, don't open it until you scan it or verify that it's legit.

The Language of Love (bugs)

Viruses come in many flavors, but you frequently hear about two types, *worms* and *Trojan horses*. A worm is a virus that spreads from computer to computer through e-mail, leaving a path of destruction (and very angry people) in its wake. A Trojan horse is a virus designed to destroy just one computer. Trojan horse viruses can act as remote-control agents, allowing the virus writer to control an infected computer over the Internet.

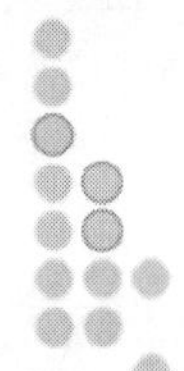

When Viruses Attack

If your computer does contract a virus, you still might manage to salvage some of your data (depending on the nature of the virus). If you download the latest fix for your virus, following the "fix" directions should clean the virus from your system. If the virus has infected your master boot files, you can boot from a DOS disk, and then copy data files from your system and load them onto another (protected) system, cleaning the files with antivirus software as you go. (You learn how to make a boot disk in "Building Your Own PC-Problem Life Raft," in Chapter 6, "TechTV's Computer User's Survival Guide").

Don't Fall for a Hoax

Pay attention to reports of new viruses, but be aware that many of those reports are hoaxes. For some odd reason, people get a kick out of starting rumors about viruses that simply don't exist. To find out whether the virus warning you receive is "word" or hoax, visit www.CIAC.org, the U.S. Department of Energy's Computer Incident Advisory Capability Web site. CIAC keeps a good up-to-date list of computer hoaxes of all types, including fake virus warnings.

FIREWALL YOUR ALWAYS-ON CONNECTION

A firewall is hardware, software, or some combination of both that protects your system from unauthorized access. Big businesses have used firewalls for years to monitor and protect information entering and leaving their corporate networks. Today, many private computers have always-on connections through DSL and cable modems that make them vulnerable to hackers. As a result, personal firewalls are a good idea for many home and small-business computer setups.

A study by SecurityPortal (www.securityportal.com), a company devoted to developing and testing online security products, showed that computers have a 50 percent chance of being scanned by a hacker within 24 hours of hooking up to the Internet with an unprotected connection. If the hackers' automated tools find anything "useful" on your computer, the hackers might come back to take advantage of it.

Personal firewalls protect your system from access by an unauthorized site or computer, but they do it in a variety of ways. Some standalone firewalls filter arriving packets by type, source, and destination address. Other, more comprehensive personal firewalls also block viruses, spam, and inappropriate content. You can find firewalls available as free downloads, such as eSafe Desktop from esafe.com or Tiny Personal Firewall from tinysoftware.com. Many Mac users rely on IPNetSentry from Sustainable Softworks.com (www.sustworks.com). Read the excellent firewall reviews and descriptions at www.securityportal.com and at www.zdnet.com.

KEEP YOUR E-MAIL PRIVATE

Antivirus software and personal firewalls offer good front-line security measures, but you can do even more to keep your information where it belongs. Use e-mail encryption to stop unauthorized folks from reading your private e-mail for their own personal pleasure or profit. If you send private information through e-mail, e-mail encryption can help you keep that information from prying eyes.

How E-Mail Encryption Works

E-mail encryption translates data into a secret code, so that only someone who has the key can decipher the data. Public-key encryption is probably the most popular e-mail security technology around today. Public-key technology follows the old "two-key" approach; you send someone a message encrypted with their publicly available key, and they decipher it with their private key. Together, the public and private keys are known as a Digital ID.

How to Use E-Mail Encryption

If you send private information via e-mail and want to use e-mail encryption, get a Digital ID by visiting `www.verisign.com`. Verisign's Web page gives you full instructions for downloading and using your Digital ID. Some major e-mail clients, such as Microsoft Outlook, use native encryption options. Here's how to use encryption in Outlook:

1. Open Outlook, and from the Tools menu, choose Options.
2. Click on the Security tab, and then click the Digital IDs button. If you don't have a digital ID, choose Get Digital ID to go directly to the Microsoft Web site.
3. Microsoft has a deal with Verisign for a free trial digital ID; fill out the information that Verisign requests and they'll send you a follow-up e-mail that tells you how to install your digital ID.
4. After you've installed your digital ID, return to Outlook's Security screen and choose Digital IDs to view your personal information.
5. Check the Encrypt Contents and Attachments for All Outgoing Messages option to encrypt your messages.
6. To include a digital signature with your message, check Digitally Sign All Outgoing Messages.
7. To activate revocation checking, warnings, and other extra-tight security measures, click the Advanced Security Settings button.

Wireless Hack Attacks

Wireless technology is still relatively new, but hackers are already busy finding and exploiting vulnerabilities in wireless (Wi-Fi) networks. Hackers have found ways to use modified Wi-Fi equipment to intercept and decrypt wireless data transmissions. Wireless networking isn't going away, so you can believe that labs around the world are working on new security technologies to keep wireless data safe. Keep an eye out for new developments; and take care when sending messages via Wi-Fi from your corner coffee shop!

Remember, when you use public-key encryption, the recipient must have your public key and his or her own private key. You can set these options with each message you send.

Don't Become a Victim of E-mail Wiretapping

In early 2001, the Privacy Foundation, an Internet privacy watchdog group, uncovered evidence of hackers using a bug to monitor messages attached to forwarded e-mails. The hackers simply send a bugged e-mail message, and then sit back and read the "wiretapped" messages as they move from sender to sender. Hackers use e-mail wiretaps to get inside information on business negotiations and to capture e-mail addresses as the forwarded e-mail travels from reader to reader. If you use Outlook, get the Outlook e-mail security patch at `www.microsoft.com` to help protect against these wiretaps. Visit `www.privacyfoundation.org/advisories/advemailwiretap.html` for more information on e-mail wiretapping and how to prevent it.

LIGHTNING ROUND Q&A WRAP-UP

What is port scanning, and do I need to be worried about it?

Port scanning is just one of the ways hackers can use an unprotected IP address to get inside your computer system and extract information. It's very likely that automated tools scan millions of Internet-connected systems every day. Here's how it works: Before a hacker tries to enter a system, he or she scans the available ports, looking for one with an active listening service, such as file sharing. If hackers detect an active service, they can directly connect to that service and gain access to the system. Most firewalls block port scans to prevent this kind of unauthorized entry.

How do I keep my kids from seeing specific kinds of online content?

You can use software packages as your own Internet censor. CyberPatrol (`www.cyberpatrol.com`) and NetNanny (`www.netnanny.com`) are two of the most popular. Products like these are a good first step, but they can't guarantee that your young ones won't get access to places—or people—you'd rather they avoid. The best way to protect your kids is to place the computer they use in a high-traffic area of the house. Check on them frequently while they're online, and go into the cache and history files to see where your kids' surfing adventures have taken them. In the end, your eyes are the best weapon against nasty Internet invasions of your children's world.

Should I be worried about sending my credit card information online?

When you send your credit card into the back room of a restaurant with a 19-year-old waitress, do you worry about what's happening to it back there? Credit card numbers can be used illegally in any number of online or offline ways. The best way to protect your numbers online is to check the site's privacy policy and look for the padlock symbol in your browser's status bar when you send *any* kind of sensitive personal information. And check your credit card bills with a fine-toothed comb. Hackers have learned that small charges have a better chance of slipping through undetected. Be sure that you can account for any charge, no matter how small, that appears on your monthly statement.

CHAPTER 6

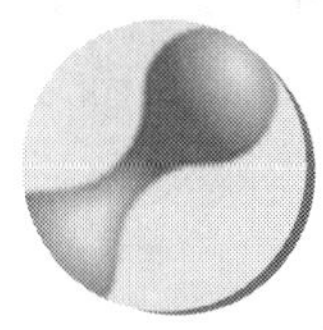

TECHTV'S COMPUTER USER'S SURVIVAL GUIDE

- Set your preferences
- Find and use online help and tech support
- Translate geek-speak terminology

If you want your computer life to remain productive and stress-free, prepare to survive the challenges of the user's road ahead. You can't avoid every sinkhole, but with foresight you can miss the deepest ones—and have a rope handy when you do fall in.

This chapter opens with sound advice for any computer user. A brief review of some basic preference settings can help beginners get the best performance from their computer setup. No matter how savvy you are, you need access to good online help, and this chapter shares some of TechTV's favorite online help sites and tips for how and when to call for help.

SET YOUR PREFERENCES

Every operating system, application, or hardware peripheral comes with instructions for setting its preferences. This chapter doesn't replace any of those guides, but it adds some valuable additions to the information the manufacturers' guides contain. TechTV staff and crew have spent a lot of time behind the keyboard, and they've learned a trick or two for tweaking preference settings for maximum performance. You can use these settings to make your device or program or system dance to *your* tune; you spend more time getting what you want from your system, and less time trying to coax it to perform.

Handy Windows Preferences

You might not realize it, but you have some say-so over how you communicate with your computer. Most of that communication takes place through a keyboard or a pointing device (such as a mouse or trackball). Windows offers several options for customizing both types of "great communicators," so you can make them work the way you want them to.

It Pays to Play

Why would you want to mess with the mouse settings? Well, if you spend a lot of time at your keyboard, you might want to switch "mouse hands" occasionally, to avoid any potential for repetitive stress injury. Believe it or not, you can become "ambi-moustrous" pretty easily, and it's a good idea to learn how before you blow a tendon or develop "mouse shoulder" in one overworked mousing arm.

To adjust the button, pointer, and motion properties of your mouse or other pointing device in Windows, follow these steps:

1. Open Start, Settings, Control Panel, and double-click the Mouse icon.
2. Use the Buttons tab to configure a left-handed or right-handed mouse. Changing mouse hands occasionally is a good way to avoid inflamed tendons and other mouse-related aches and pains. To change the double-click speed of your pointing device, click the Options button to open the double-click speed settings. Play around with the slider and the test area until you find the speed that's right for you (see Figure 6.1).
3. Want to use big, fat pointers, animated pointers, or 3D versions of your pointer favorites? Use the Pointers tab to choose your pointer's style. In Windows 2000, you can choose from more than 20 cursor "schemes" listed on the Pointers tab. Windows Standard or Large pointers give the fastest performance, and Extra Large schemes are great if you have trouble seeing the pointer onscreen. Animated pointers tend to get in the way, and some schemes change pointers into things that don't really resemble pointers, so you can lose those schemes after an initial test drive.
4. Use the Motion tab to change the pointer's speed and acceleration rate. If you choose to accelerate your pointer, you'll get better performance in dialog boxes by choosing the Move Pointer to the Default Button in Dialog Boxes option. You want pointer control, not speed, in those little boxes; choosing this option gives it to you.

5. If you work with multiple pointing devices, choose your weapon in the Hardware tab.
6. Whatever changes you make, click Apply to put them in action.

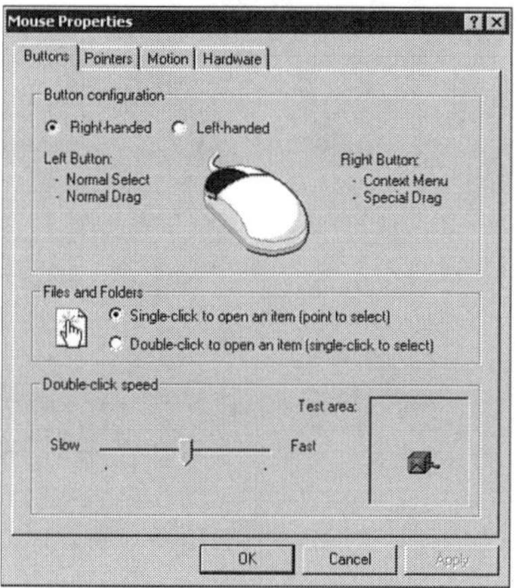

Figure 6.1

Use the Mouse Properties Button tab to customize the way your mouse operates.

Don't be A Stranger to Your Computer

Many people never take time to get to know exactly what makes their computers tick. You don't have to dismantle your computer to find out what's going on inside it—though you can learn a lot about a machine that way. To get a "no-tools-required" view of your computer's inner workings, go to your desktop, right-click the My Computer icon, and then choose Properties. Cruise through the Properties screen's General, Hardware Profiles, and Performance tabs to find out who manufactured your system, where you can get support, what kinds of drives, connections, and disk settings your system uses, best troubleshooting techniques, and more. Don't be afraid to click around, open directories, and choose Advanced buttons for more info. This kind of cruising is the only way to truly get to know the system you're working with.

To change keyboard settings—language preferences, cursor blink rate, repeat delay, or keystroke sensitivity—follow these steps:

1. Open the Control Panel again and double-click the Keyboard object.
2. Use the settings on the Speed page to adjust repeat delay, repeat character, and cursor blink rates (see Figure 6.2). Take time to make sure you have these settings right. If the keyboard doesn't work with you, you'll work more slowly and make more errors.
3. When you've fine-tuned the speed settings, click the Language tab if you want to add a second language to your keyboard.
4. When you've set everything to your liking, click OK, and then close the box.

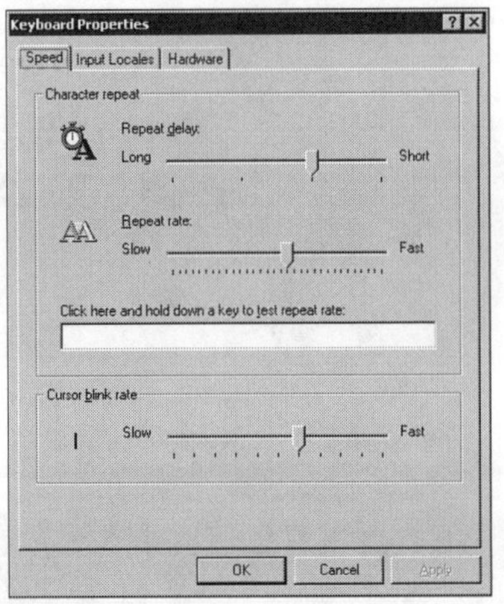

Figure 6.2

When your key-repeat speed and delay settings are right, you have fewer typing errors.

Speed-Launch Windows Apps

You can program your system to quick-launch Windows apps at the press of a few keys (don't worry, this isn't complicated). Launch apps using the function keys (the F keys at the top of your keyboard) or a combination of Ctrl+Alt+"Shortcut Key," or both. To program either method, do this:

1. Right-click the icon of the program you want to quick-launch.
2. Choose Properties from the menu and open the Shortcut tab.
3. Place your cursor in the Shortcut key field, and then press the function key or letter combination you want to use in your shortcut.
4. Click Apply.

To open the program, press Ctrl+Alt+the letter or function key you assigned to the shortcut.

SET SIMPLE MAC PREFERENCES

Macs are easy to customize, and it's always worth your time to let your system know what you expect of it. These Mac settings are favorites at TechTV; try them to see if they work well for you.

Most Mac applications let you save your printer settings with this handy trick:

1. From within an application (such as Microsoft Word), first be sure no documents are open, and then go to the File menu and select Page Setup.
2. Adjust your page settings the way you like. For example, maybe you prefer to orient your pages as landscape rather than portrait mode, or to print at a lower dpi to extend your print cartridge's life.

3. In Microsoft Word, click the Default button. In most other applications, simply click OK to save these settings as the default for all new documents (see Figure 6.3).

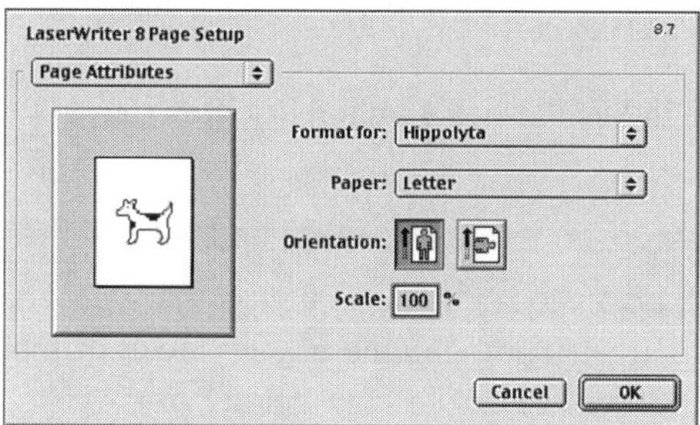

Figure 6.3

If you make Page Setup settings with no document open, they're applied to every new document you create.

If you have only one printer connected to your network, you can remove the Printer Selector module from your Control Strip. To remove unused controls from your Control Strip, do this:

1. Open your System Folder.
2. Open the Control Strip Modules folder (see Figure 6.4).
3. Drag any items you don't want to the Trash or drag them into another folder.

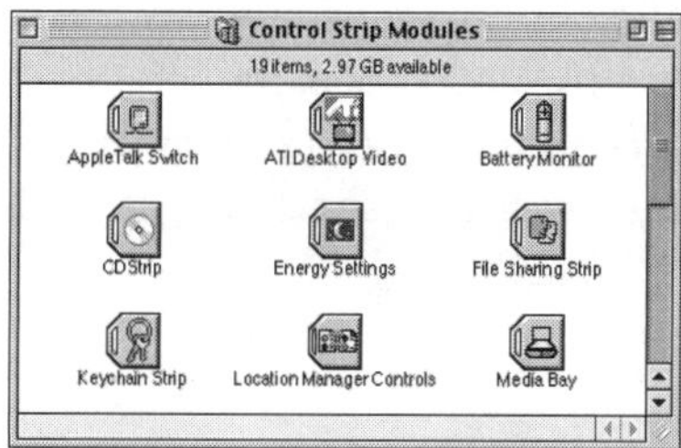

Figure 6.4

You can remove a module from the Control Strip by dragging it out of the Control Strip Modules folder.

To change the order of the modules:

1. Open the Control Strip.
2. Press the Option key and drag the modules into a new sequence.

Want a new desktop? You can choose from an amazing variety of new icons at Icon Factory (`www.iconfactory.com`), where the icons are available as free downloads. When you find an icon you like, follow these steps to change the icon of your file or folder:

1. In the Finder, select the icon you want to use and choose Get Info from the File menu.
2. Click once on the picture in the window and type Command+C to copy it.
3. Highlight the file or folder to which you want to assign the new icon.

4. From the File menu, choose Get Info.
5. Click once on the current icon image in the window and press Command+V to paste the new icon over it.

Like most programs, the Finder has a number of preferences you can use to customize its performance.

1. From your desktop, go to the Edit menu and select Preferences.
2. Click the check boxes to set the information that appears in Finder windows. For example, you can change the name of your labels or make a "simplified" version of the Finder in the three tabs of this dialog box.

GET THE MOST FROM TECH SUPPORT

Good tech support is any computer system's most important feature. Unfortunately, many users don't find out how good—or bad—their tech support options are until it's too late to change them. Don't wait until your machine is smoking on your desk or staring at you with the blue screen of death to test the manufacturer's commitment to tech support. Check out your tech support system *before* you need it.

Before you buy a PC, call the manufacturer's tech support line. If nothing else, ask about its hours and any special support packages available for purchase. Read the company's support policies and talk to reps in both tech support and customer service. Judge how promptly they respond to your questions and how helpful the technicians are in their responses. If a company's tech support department is lousy, don't buy the product unless you're confident that you'll never need tech support, anyway. Tech support is part of what you pay for when you buy the system, so be sure you're buying prompt, helpful service—not a passport to future headaches.

Conserving Electricity Is Smart

Anyone who's experienced the joys of rolling blackouts knows that the need for energy conservation is more than a soft and fuzzy memory from the seventies. To save power and prevent unnecessary wear and tear on your Mac's hard drive, put it to sleep now and then:

1. Choose Apple menu, Control Panels, Energy Saver.
2. Click the Sleep Setup tab.
3. Drag the slider to set the amount of time your computer can be inactive before the hard drive goes into sleep mode.
4. Click Apply.

Check Out the Street Buzz on Your System

If you have Internet access on another computer, go online to search for customer ratings and newsgroup discussions about the vendors of computer systems you're interested in buying. You can learn a lot about a company's product and tech support system by reading the remarks of its current customers.

Build Your Own PC-Problem Life Raft

You have a problem with your PC, and it's time to put the vendor's tech support network to the test. But before you toss yourself into the murky depths of tech support, follow these tips:

1. Read your owner's manual. If you haven't already gone through this (undoubtedly boring) important source of information about your system, do it now. You might stumble across the source of and solution to your system's woes. Even if you don't, your reading will help you pinpoint issues and describe the problem to the tech support representative.
2. Check the obvious. Be sure that none of your connections are loose, all power supplies are turned on and working, all of your devices' "on" buttons are pressed, and that your cat hasn't nibbled through any of the connecting cables.
3. If you have online access, start with the company's Web site for relevant help or information. Many companies post large FAQ lists, white papers, and databases of recommended fixes and troubleshooting tips for a wide variety of common problems. The answer to your questions might be waiting for you.

And don't forget to have your boot disk handy, just in case your hard drive gives you fits. Even if your computer has crashed and the hard drive goes down, you can get your computer up and running with a boot disk. If you haven't already made a boot disk, do it now. To create a boot disk in Windows:

1. Insert a formatted floppy disk into your floppy drive.

Scrub Up and Get Ready to Offer PC First Aid

The much-complained-about meltdown of customer service hasn't spared the computer industry. Savvy computer owners arm themselves with PC first-aid kits to keep systems from flat-lining in the absence of a professional. The hardware and software you purchased with your system might come with its own troubleshooting and diagnostic applications (check your system and software user manuals and Help menus). If so, use them as your first line of defense when a problem arises. Third-party utilities are another good answer: Symantec's Norton Utilities and McAfee's Nuts and Bolts are just two examples.

2. Click Start.
3. Select Settings.
4. Select the Control Panel.
5. Double-click Add/Remove programs.
6. Click the Startup Disk tab on the far right.
7. Choose Create a Startup Disk. Windows creates the startup disk for you.

To use the boot disk, put the disk in your floppy drive as you start your computer.

Before You Pick Up the Phone...

Take a deep breath, contemplate all the *good* things in your life, and then get ready to make the call or send the e-mail. To make the experience as productive and painless as possible:

1. Position yourself and your phone in front of your computer and boot your system.
2. Have your ID information handy. The technician's likely to ask you for all of it: customer number, serial number, warranty number, service agreements, and so on. Know the version number and name of your processor and operating system, too.
3. Write down a list of everything that happened. The reps will want to know exactly what you were doing and the exact wording (if possible) of error messages you received. Again, if you tell the technician "the program won't run" or "the commands don't work right" or something equally vague, you're in for a long, nerve-wracking tech support nightmare.

Enjoy Non-Peak Perks

Put the odds in your favor, and call tech support at what might be its slower times. In other words, you know they get a lot of calls on weekends and on Monday mornings. If you can wait, try to call mid-morning or mid-afternoon on a Tuesday or Thursday. If the company offers 24×7 support, call late at night to get the fastest service. You'll have to wait whenever you call, so do yourself a favor and—if you can—time the call so that you can keep your wait to a minimum.

When You Realize Your Tech Relationship Is Going Nowhere

Wake up! There's a human voice on the other end of the line. Brush away the cobwebs that have formed between you and your PC screen, pull out your notes (see preceding section), and deliver your tale of woe to the beleaguered technician at the other end of the line. But what happens when the response doesn't solve your problem? Or, worse yet, what if you never even *get* a response?

Before you abandon all hope of getting tech support help from your system's manufacturer, be sure you've explored all support avenues. If you have the luxury of time—and Net access—send an e-mail. If you tried e-mail the first time, call the company's tech support hotline. If it becomes clear that your system's manufacturer isn't going to provide the tech support you need, make a note of the company's poor performance (you won't want to reward it with future purchases) and get ready to move on. You do have other options for solving your technical troubles:

1. Clear your head; you won't be able to tackle the problem or track down help if you're in a frustrated panic. Walk away for a few minutes, get a drink of water, take deep breaths, then return to the broken beast on your desk.
2. Make like Sherlock Holmes and use your powers of deductive reasoning. When did the problem start? Have you added or deleted any programs or files recently? What was the latest change you made to your data or system right before the problem started? If the problem cropped up after you added a new program or hardware device, uninstall the newcomer, then reboot; check the program manufacturer's Web site for clues.
3. Scan for viruses; the problem could be as simple as a buggy e-mail attachment.
4. Try to get third-party advice. Many companies offer online tech support (see the following section for examples and contact info).
5. Find advice on a Usenet newsgroup. You aren't getting *bona fide* tech support from these sources, but you might very well run across an informative discussion of the problem you're experiencing—along with some helpful "fix-it" advice.
6. Turn to TechTV! The TechTV experts are there to answer your questions whenever they can. Start by searching for Help and How To information on the `techtv.com` site; you might find that one of TechTV's shows or online articles has already tackled your problem. If not, you can submit questions via e-mail to `callforhelp@techtv.com` or `screensavers@techtv.com`; or call TechTV at 888-989-7879. The TechTV message boards (accessible from the TechTV site) are good sources of troubleshooting info, too.

Don't Give Up!

If you're looking for phone, versus e-mail, support, don't be discouraged by hard-to-locate contact numbers. Many companies tuck their tech support/customer service phone numbers away in the darkest corners of their Web sites. But if you poke around long enough (try the Contact Us link on their Web site, if all else fails), you usually can ferret out the phone number of a real human contact. Well...most of them are humans, anyway.

Searcher's Guide to Tracking Down Tech Support

To find tech support at *any* company connected with computer technology, visit `www.zdnet.com/companyfinder`, or go to `www.comspec.com/mfglist/`. At either site, use the alphabetized index to companies to find and link to company Web sites and (usually) tech support.

The Ultimate Industry Connection, www.acehardware.net/complist.html, offers alphabetized indexes to hardware and software companies, plus a helpful list of links to operating system info and support, FTP support archives, newsgroups and mailing lists, and the home pages of top computer magazines.

It's Not Your Fault!

You've heard us at TechTV say it time and time again. It's not your fault that you weren't born with an intimate knowledge of everything cyber. If you want to join the company of other proud NGTUCs (non-geeks that use computers), visit Scott's CyberPrimer (www.mphcomputing.com/newsletter/cybertips.asp). There, you'll find answers to basic computer questions that you might be too embarrassed to ask your local geek friend. From "How am I supposed to know what program to open this file with?" to "When should I use the three-fingered salute (Ctrl+Alt+Del)?" the CyberPrimer gives you the straight facts, without any eye-rolling, snickering, or long-winded stories about other stupid questions it's heard that morning. Got a question? Go for it!

LIGHTNING ROUND Q&A WRAP-UP

What should I do if I get an online tech support rep who is really, REALLY bad?

Some tech support reps are worse than bad; dealing with one of these characters can bring out the monster in anyone. But you won't gain anything by blowing up at a bad tech support rep. Unless you're the bonehead's lucky first caller, he or she has already heard a long list of threats and abuse from irate customers, so save your breath. If you can't get anywhere with the rep you're with, you can say good-bye and call again, in the hope of reaching a more...enlightened technician. Or, you can ask to speak to the tech's supervisor. In either case, prepare for another long wait and another response to the "what seems to be the problem" question you just spent 20 minutes answering. And remember the advice listed earlier in this chapter: Be specific about the problem and be sure you've read through the manual and checked the Web site for answers (if possible) before you call.

What am I supposed to do when I get that "Choose what program to open this file with" message box when I try to open files with unfamiliar extensions? Most of the time, I don't KNOW what program the file should be opened with. If I guess wrong (as I always do), the thing won't let me choose another option. Any answers?

If you try to open a file that Windows doesn't recognize as having been written by a specific program, Windows asks you to tell it what program to open the file with. Chances are good that if Windows doesn't know, you won't either. Before you try *any* program, go to the checkbox underneath the applications list and uncheck that box that says "Always use this program to open this file." Otherwise, if you "guess" wrong, you're hosed, because Windows will *always* try to open the file with the wrong program. To recover your file's freedom of association, hold down the Shift key while you right-click the file. The "choose a program" box appears, along with the opportunity to uncheck that nasty box. But to find the right extension, I recommend you visit `www.extsearch.com`. Use the site options to enter the file extension and get a description of the file type. Then, choose your weapon from the "open with" message box back in Windows, and you're good to go.

CHAPTER 7

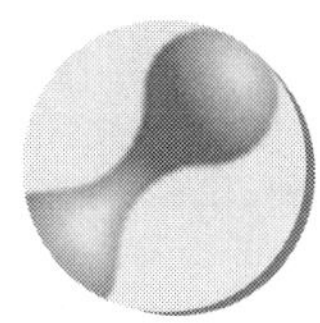

BRING IT ALL TOGETHER IN A HOME NETWORK

- Know your networking options
- Choose the right combo of wired and wireless networking alternatives
- Share printers and Internet access
- Add a laptop to your network
- Bring your home entertainment center into the mix

You probably have more than one computer in your home. Constantly improving technologies and falling computer prices have convinced many people that it's cheaper to buy a new machine than to upgrade an old one. With everyone in the family clamoring to use a PC—for homework, e-mail, research, gaming, and so on—most families *need* more than one computer. If you live in a multi-computer household, you might find that home networking is the best, cheapest, and easiest way to manage all that equipment under one roof.

This chapter will convince you that home networking is a geek-free option. Here, TechTV shows you how practical (and easy) home networking can be. After you look at the technology options, you learn how to combine the options into simple systems that make your family's computers play nice with shared data, programs, devices, and Internet access.

A QUICK REVIEW OF HOME NETWORKING OPTIONS

It all starts innocently enough. You add DSL to your home office computer, and suddenly everyone in the family just has to have high-speed connectivity. You can get all of them broadband access, or you can forget about ever using your computer again—it's your choice.

Beyond proving that you love everyone in your family equally, home networking has many advantages: You can move data from one machine to another, and everyone can share an Internet connection, printers, drivers, and other precious resources.

If you're still recovering from making the DSL-cable-satellite-dial-up networking decision, you might cringe at the idea of weighing more technology options. Buck up! Home networking technology choices are relatively simple and they aren't "all or nothing." To choose the setup that works best for you, you need to know your choices. Right now, four major players make up the home networking technology market:

- Conventional Ethernet
- Phone line (HomePNA)
- Power line (HomePlug)
- Wireless (Wi-Fi and HomeRF—for now)

Don't Blink!

Home networking technology is hot right now, and it's changing rapidly. HomePlug came into its own in late 2001, while HomeRF seemed to be fading into the twilight (this technology isn't dead yet, though, as you learn in "Networking Without Wires" later in this chapter). And by the time you finish reading this paragraph, 20 new home networking technologies might have emerged. So what's the message? When you're ready to set up your home network, be sure you know about *all* the latest and greatest ways to do it. Keep up on home networking developments by watching TechTV. Online, you can follow home networking news at TechTV's site (`www.techtv.com`), the *PC Magazine* online info center at `www.zdnet.com/pcmag`, or through other reliable tech news providers.

Stick with the Classics—Networking via Ethernet

Ethernet is the classic choice for home networking. To set up an Ethernet network, you connect two or more computers with special cables, either directly to each other or through a router or hub. Each machine on the network requires an external Ethernet adapter or an Ethernet card. Right now, a traditional Ethernet setup is the fastest (100Mbps and rising), least expensive, and most reliable home-networking setup you can configure.

But Ethernet networking brings its share of challenges. Many folks hesitate to run Category 5 wiring (the wiring used to cable this type of home network) in walls, ceilings, and floors—or to leave piles of cable visible to toddlers, pets, and guests. Others don't relish the idea of opening up a computer and tinkering with its innards (good news for Mac users; your system came with built-in Ethernet, so you can just plug in the cable and go). On the other hand, many people start with a wired system and add other technologies as needed.

Major players, such as 3Com, NDC, and NetGear offer, two-PC Ethernet network starter kits for less than $100. A starter kit for a two-PC network includes two network cards, cabling, and a hub that enables you to connect more PCs later on as your networked family grows. Most kits come with good, clear instructions that make the process do-able by anyone with enough chutzpah to stare a PC in the guts.

Build for the Network To Come

If you're preparing to build a home, build your networking plans into the blueprints. Talk to your builder about installing "home-run wiring" from a central point in the basement. Category 5 wiring also can be used as phone wire, and you should be able to get it for pennies a foot. You also might want to have your contractor install conduit piping to channel your networking wires around the house (but the contractor has to know what he or she is doing; the placement of conduit and wires in relation to other wiring, security systems, telephone, lines, and so on is critical). That'll make it easier to run wires later, as your system expands. And finally, do your research. Your contractor might not know how to build in "smart home" expansion capabilities.

It's on TechTV

TechTV online (`www.techtv.com`) can help you plan for and build capabilities for the ultimate home-networking system. Click on The Screen Savers and then on Show and Tell. Search under "Tips for Networking Your Home."

Tap Those Phone Lines

Phone-line networking is one of the most popular home-networking solutions. The original HPNA (Home Phoneline Networking Alliance) standard used PCI add-in cards and your home's existing phone lines and jacks. But that system was slow, allowing only about 1Mbps transfer rates. The HPNA 2.0 specifications boosted speeds to about 10Mbps, making the system more competitive with other networking methods. One real benefit of HPNA is that it uses equipment manufactured to one set of standards, so you don't have to worry about your system's equipment being incompatible with another vendor's stuff. Learn more at `www.homena.org`.

You can set up a three-computer HPNA network for as little as $100 (plus USB adapters if you don't already have them). It's easy to install, because your phone lines are already in place. However, HPNA is still slow—at 10Mbps, it's faster than transferring from a floppy disk, but much slower than a 100Mbps Ethernet line. HPNA requires a phone jack near every piece of your networked system. Current HPNA systems don't mesh well with PCs that are already set up for a network (like your commuter notebook). Look for these issues to be resolved in the months ahead.

Like Ethernet, you set up an HPNA system using a USB adapter or by installing a HomePNA network card in each PC (many Gateway and Compaq models come with the cards already installed). With the adapter attached to your machine, plug it into a phone jack, and you're connected. Most HPNA kits come bundled with software that walks you through the network setup. If you need a simple, inexpensive home network that's *very* easy to install, this is your best bet.

Phone Line Networking Won't Interfere with Telemarketing Calls

Don't worry about losing a phone line to your new HPNA network. The adapter has a pass-through for your phone. Even if you're busy trying to clean all the spam out of your day's e-mail, telemarketers can still get through to you on your phone line. Now, isn't that a relief?

Networking Without Wires

Wireless networking is the big buzz in home networking channels right now. Wireless networking lets you roam all over your house with your notebook computer and connect to the Net or other computers and peripherals on your home network without running a single wire.

The most popular wireless networking standard—802.11b, also known as Wi-Fi—transfers your data through radio signals at speeds up to 11Mbps. Every computer on your system shares a single Net connection, and several manufacturers support the standard, including Apple Computer, 3Com, Cisco systems, and Lucent Technologies.

Although wireless isn't the cheapest way to go, prices for the system are dropping all the time. You should be able to network three computers for as little as $100 to $200 per device. The 802.11b cards deliver ranges from 100 to 300 feet and offer 40-bit or 128-bit encryption to keep your data safe. Wi-Fi requires access points if you want to connect more than two computers to the Net. These cost less than $300, and that price is sure to drop, too.

Network Through Your Power Lines

The HomePlug Power Alliance (`www.homeplug.com`) hopes to create a home networking system that is the ultimate "plug-in." HomePlug uses your home's electrical outlets and existing electrical wiring to network your computers. This isn't a new idea—intercoms and wireless light controllers have used AC lines for some time—but the technology underwent rapid redevelopment in late 2001.

The pioneer in AC networking, Intelogis, stopped making its Passport two-PC networking kit in early 2001. Today, the company, under its new name of Inari, no longer is a member of the HomePlug Alliance. Although 3Com, Intel, Cisco, and other computer tech giants are founding HomePlug Alliance members, the market isn't flooded with kits that take advantage of this technology. 3Com (`www.3com.com`) currently offers a 10Mbps phone-line kit based on the HomePNA standard. Look for other companies' offerings to bring serious competition to the field of home networking options.

The most famous version of 802.11b is Apple's AirPort system. The AirPort design works well, and with special software, such as FreeBase (`baseport.sourceforge.net`), you can configure the AirPort base station to work with PCs.

Keep an Eye on Bluetooth

A year or so ago, the tech world was buzzing about Bluetooth—a wireless technology that uses multidirectional radio waves to transmit data through walls and other non-metal surfaces at speeds of 720Kbps. Bluetooth operates within a range of 30–300 feet, but its transmission speeds take a hit with any kind of interference from other devices. As Bluetooth technology moves beyond PCs and into other handheld gadgets, expect to see this technology make inroads into the wireless home-networking market. TechTV's Web site offers more detailed information about this technology, as does the `bluetooth.com` site.

BRING IT ALL TOGETHER IN YOUR HOME NETWORK

You have several home-networking technologies from which to choose—so how do you decide which one is right for you? Here are some tips for weighing your options:

- Research until you understand exactly what you want to include in your network and how you want it to work.
- Sketch out a plan for your network. What will go where and what kind of connectors (plugs and phone jacks) will you need in those locations?
- Think about how your system is likely to grow in the future. Will the setup you design today handle more components tomorrow?

Wireless Wars

Although Wi-Fi seems destined to become the home-networking method of choice for many consumers, HomeRF, one of the earliest wireless networking techniques, remains a contender. Wi-Fi carries clout in the market, because it's a standard used by many businesses, airports, and hotels. But HomeRF technology keeps improving, and manufacturers promise newer, faster speeds, and greater Wi-Fi compatibility with each new version. HomeRF came out of the gate with the lowest prices, but in early 2001, Wi-Fi prices began to drop, too. Bottom line: Any consumer interested in setting up a home networking system is a sure winner in this neck-and-neck race to own the wireless market.

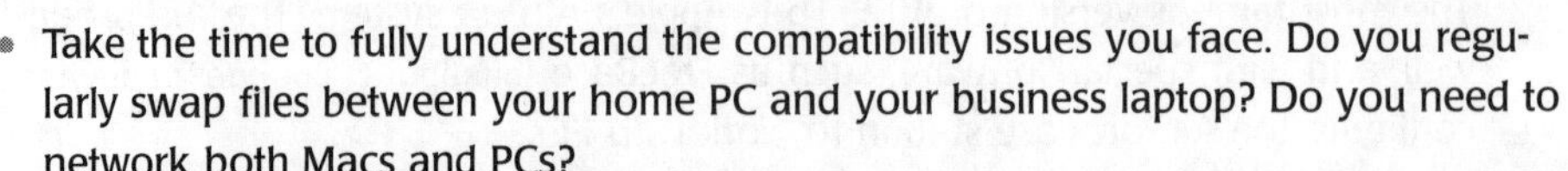

- Take the time to fully understand the compatibility issues you face. Do you regularly swap files between your home PC and your business laptop? Do you need to network both Macs and PCs?

When you know where you want to go with your home network, you're ready to start building it. If you decide that all or part of your home networking system will be hard-wired Ethernet, your first big job is running all of your Category 5 wiring. Remember, if you don't know how to work with Cat 5 wiring, get an expert's help and advice. Without the proper tools and training, you can run into real problems trying to cable, connect, and terminate Cat 5.

With your wiring in place, your next task is to install at least one NIC (network interface card) in each machine that you want to include in the network. If you intend to use one machine as a router for Internet access to the whole network, add two NIC cards to that machine. For a two-machine Ethernet hookup, you'll also need an Ethernet crossover cable (for more computers, use a switch or a hub).

HPNA, HomePlug, and wireless systems don't require any special wiring, but you will need the appropriate cards and access points. Follow the kit instructions, and you'll have no problems setting up those systems.

Test Your Connection

Test your Internet connection before you connect the first two computers in your system. If your connection isn't working right, you could spend hours trying to track down a nonexistent problem in your network. Rerun the Windows Internet Connection Wizard (or Mac Internet Setup Assistant) or use another method for diagnosing the connection problem. Then you're ready to get back to work on home network.

Most networking kits come bundled with the necessary networking software. Windows 98SE and later versions come with built-in networking software that's relatively simple to use. Windows Me and XP support mixed-technology networks to make the setup process even simpler and more flexible. The Windows Home Networking Wizard walks you through the configuration process. If you need to go back and add more "pieces" to your puzzle later, you just run the wizard again to update the system. All Mac systems come with necessary networking software built-in.

Share Drives and Peripherals

When you configure your home network, you turn on the appropriate protocol within the networking control panel; then, you turn on file sharing and share your hard drives. Keep in mind that when file sharing is on, you're on the Internet. Hackers and other malicious folk could break into your system, so you should consider implementing a firewall or other security system (see Chapter 5, "Lock Down Basic Security," for complete details about securing your system).

You're a Server, Now

Your network might have a *client/server* setup. If you use one computer as a server, it can manage disk drive, file, and Internet access for all other computers (the clients) in your network. If you use one computer as the server for a shared-Internet-access setup, leave the server computer on all the time. Make sure that you password-protect the server computer in your setup, and that you have a firewall in place so you're comfortable leaving the server chugging along in your absence (for more information, see "Firewall Your Always-On Connection," in Chapter 5).

Share Internet Access

Whether you connect to the Net over a phone line, cable modem, or DSL modem, your home network can give multiple users Internet access over that single connection. To share a Net connection, you add an Internet gateway, also known as a router or proxy server, to your network. You can create the gateway using software installed on one of your computers or a freestanding "box." Or, you can use a hardware gateway that connects directly to your network.

Hardware gateways cost more than software solutions, but they have the advantages of replacing the "always on" server computer connection, so you don't need to leave your connected machine running all the time. Software gateways are available for just about every system. Windows 98SE and later versions come with built-in networking software, so you don't have to buy and install any other programs for Net sharing. Just turn on the appropriate protocol in the networking control panel, and you're set. Windows automatically assigns IP addresses out to other machines on the network and acts as a local DNS.

That Gateway Keeps You Safe

Both software and hardware gateways give you firewall protection that blocks access from unsolicited Net traffic and provides security for your local network. That's a good thing—especially if you have an always-on broadband Net connection such as cable or DSL modem.

If you share Internet access through the Apple AirPort system, your connection experience should be simple and slick. The AirPort base station works on the Wi-Fi standard, and it comes with an Ethernet port to attach to a cable or DSL modem and a built-in 56Kbps modem. You can use the AirPort software with no base station, which means that you'll leave one system running all the time to maintain your Internet connection, or you can use a base station to connect to the Internet. If you want to use the AirPort base station with PCs, you have to run special software to configure it, or get a wireless access point such as the Linksys WAP11 or Dlink's WirelessLAN Access Point.

Network Your Laptop

If you have an existing Ethernet home network, it's easy to add your laptop to the mix. Right now, your best bet for wireless connection is the Wi-Fi (802.11) networking technology.

Begin by deciding whether you want to leave a machine running constantly to host the connection through a wireless NIC, or whether you'd prefer to go with a dedicated wireless hub, such as Apple's AirPort Base Station. If you don't work with Macs, skip the AirPort, because you need a Mac to configure it. Even the least expensive PC-friendly hubs cost nearly twice as much as the wireless card.

The downside to using a wireless NIC is that your performance suffers slightly on the machine that hosts the card, and you have to tolerate the fan noise from the constantly running machine. Otherwise, it's a cheap and easy solution.

If you set up a peer-to-peer network (one card in a machine that connects to the Ethernet network, and a second card in the notebook), your setup process is easy. You just drop the cards in, load the software that came bundled with them, and make sure your gateway is in place between the server and the rest of your network. If you use a wireless hub, you also need to configure it.

That's it; your laptop is wirelessly connected into your network, and you're free to roam about the premises.

Build That Bridge

If you want to extend an existing Ethernet network, you probably can "bridge" other technologies into that system. Maybe you install a home networking adapter and software in a PC that already runs traditional networking software. As another example, you can connect your laptop to your wired computer LAN by using a wireless Ethernet PC card (more about that later in this chapter). Windows XP knocks out the need for expensive new bridge materials by letting you manage multiple networks from a single "server" PC. You just have to install a separate NIC in the server for every technology you want to connect to your home network. As home networking technology develops, the possibilities for cross-tech systems keep right on growing. So be creative, and choose a networking combo that meets your needs.

LIGHTNING ROUND Q&A WRAP-UP

I work in a Mac environment using an AppleShare file server. Can a Windows NT machine share files with Macs using AppleShare?

You can use a software program called, believe it or not, Dave. Dave 2.5.2 lets Macs and PCs work together using standard TCP/IP protocol. Both parties have access to full peer-to-peer operations, including shared directories and the capability to print to shared PostScript printers on the network. You also can use Dave to network Macs to other Macs.

To overcome hassles reported in the configuration and installation of earlier releases, Thursby touts its latest version of Dave as coming complete with an easy-to-use setup assistant. Perfect or not, Dave does what it's supposed to do—it offers network connections between Macs and PCs. You can find out more about Dave by visiting Thursby Software Systems (`www.thursby.com`).

I have a cable modem connected to my system and a network with three PCs on it. When I want to connect my system to the three other PCs, I have to crawl under the desk, unplug the cable modem from my Ethernet adapter, and then plug in the cable connected to the other systems. There's gotta be a better way!

You could add another Ethernet card to the system to solve this problem, but instead, try using Linksys's Cable/DSL Ethernet Router. You can plug the cable modem into one side and the three systems into the other. With this setup, you'll add security and, best of all, never have to crawl under the desk again (unless you drop some candy and it rolls under there).

I have two notebook computers and only one cable modem connection into the house. I understand that Windows XP supports hybrid wireless/wired setups, but I work in 98 and I'm not ready to upgrade. Any suggestions for linking both notebooks to the same connection?

If you're working in Windows 98 SE, you're in luck, because it can handle Internet sharing. To set up a wired solution to this problem, you'll need

- One crossover cable
- One hub (such as a D-link)
- Your two computers; you'll use one as a proxy server and the other as a client
- Proxy software
- An official Internet address and a non-public address

When you have all your "ingredients" together, your setup is simple:

1. Connect one end of the crossover cable to the cable modem, and then connect the other end to your hub.
2. Plug both computers into the hub.

3. Install the proxy software on the computer you've chosen to be the proxy server (read the software documentation for the setup details).
4. Use the IP address supplied by your cable modem company for the server computer.
5. Give your other computer the non-public address (such as 10.0.0.1). This computer will use the other one to communicate with the Internet.

PART II

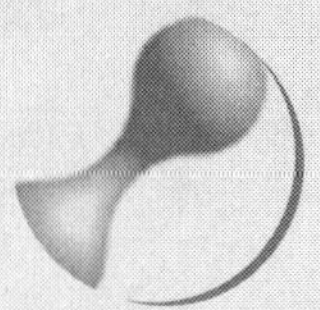

KEEPING ON TOP OF THE OS SITUATION

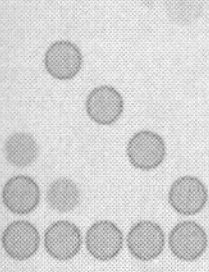

CHAPTER 8

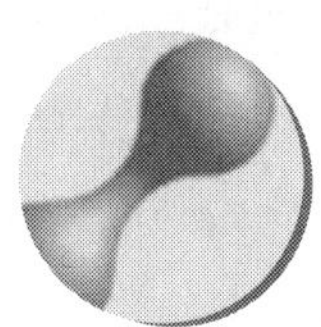

IT'S ALL ABOUT THE OS

- Get grounded in OS basics
- What you need to know about Windows
- Update on Apple's MacOS
- Fast facts about Linux, UNIX, and other alternatives
- The secrets of working in multiple systems

It doesn't matter what computer you own or why you own it; the operating system is the most important part of the deal. And though Microsoft Windows still dominates the desktop market, there are a number of good, viable OS options, including UNIX, Linux, and the don't-you-ever-count-me-out Mac OS.

The remaining chapters of Part II offer a few "how to" basics for the OS biggies and plenty of tricks for matching each OS to your computing style. This chapter quickly profiles each of the big-player operating systems, compares their major strengths and weaknesses, and gives you a good look at just how well these OS gladiators get along in issues of file-swapping and platform compatibility.

OS BASICS

Nothing doesn't matters more in your computer than its operating system. The OS is a program that runs every other program on your computer, and no general-purpose computer (like your PC) can operate without an OS.

The operating system does the following:

- It manages memory assignment and other behind-the-scenes activities that keep multiple programs and operations running while you work.
- It manages all the communication between you and the computer, by relaying instructions based on your mouse clicks and keystrokes.
- It also manages all the communication between your software and hardware, so your devices know how to respond to your program commands.
- It stores all the files on your system and keeps them orderly and accessible.

The operating system provides the platform your other applications run on, so the type of OS you have determines what kind of applications you can run.

Although they do similar things, all operating systems are not alike. Windows, Mac, Linux, UNIX—each does business in its own way. You might use different OSes at home, work, and play. For example, you might run Windows XP on your home computer, but you also keep a Mac handy for graphic design and Photoshop. At work, your business relies on a UNIX platform, so you play around with Linux. Whether this profile fits you or not, it pays to know something about all the big OS players. You might need—or want—to get up close to a new OS soon. The following sections give you a nodding acquaintance with the systems you're most likely to meet.

How the GUI Got the OS Groove Going

You used to get an operating system the same way you got a car engine: You bought the machine and lived with the system it came with. Until the mid-1980s, that system was some dreary version of DOS; then, GUIs (graphical user interfaces) came on the scene. The GUI gave the OS a "face," and suddenly, people knew and cared whether they were interacting with a Windows or Mac OS.

A CLOSER LOOK THROUGH WINDOWS

If you wanted to use Microsoft Windows (maybe even if you *didn't* want to use Windows), you have, so this section isn't introducing you to a stranger. Windows is everywhere and Microsoft takes a lot of heat for being the "evil empire" of computing, due in part to the massive popularity of the Windows OS.

The Windows family of operating systems sports well-designed GUIs, multitasking capabilities, built-in Internet support, easy hardware plug-in and software installation tools, and ever-improving security features.

This book isn't big enough—heck, few libraries are big enough—to list all the reasons Windows is or isn't a great operating system, but Windows works better now than it ever has. Microsoft seems to be resolving that business/consumer OS schizophrenia that in many ways divided the product's potential for so long.

Put the Bite on Bits

A microprocessor's bit size—16-bit, 32-bit, 64-bit, and so on—determines how much information it can process at one time. Companies design operating systems to take advantage of a microprocessor bit size, and that's why you describe an OS by bit size. Early software applications were linked to bit-size, too. Microsoft released Windows 95 with some 32-bit features, but kept 16-bit source code so users could continue to use their old Windows 3.1–based (16-bit) apps. NT arrived as a true 32-bit OS, so it was a beefier system from the beginning. Windows XP is slated to release a 64-bit version in late 2001.

The Business End of Operating Systems

In mid-2001, IBM announced a new operating system designed to help large mainframe computers compete with the smaller servers that dominate the market for online business. Dubbed z/OS, the system deals out resources quickly to handle high-demand crunches when thousands or even millions of users need attention. The new technology also adjusts resources to the lightest workloads. More importantly for non-business users, z/OS advances the use of 64-bit infrastructure—twice that of the 32 bits most folks are used to. Where the mainframe goes, the PC may follow. Keep your ears open for news about this business behemoth of a system.

The 9x Version of the Story

Windows 95, 98, and Millennium Edition (Me)—collectively known as Windows 9x systems—were born to be consumer operating systems. Microsoft spent a lot of time designing graphical icons, point-and-click commands, simple file management and search tools, and other user-friendly features specifically to make its Windows operating system approachable and easier to use.

Windows 9x systems also incorporated a number of hardware and software compatibility features to help users keep old programs and hardware going. But these systems weren't fast, secure, or robust enough for heavy-duty business workouts. Compatibility trumped reliability in the consumer-side Windows releases. Windows 98 was plagued with frequent crashes and problems that resulted from trying to be Mr. Easy-to-get-along-with. As a result, many people stuck with 95.

Get Down to Business with NT

Microsoft designed NT and its successor Windows 2000 (which is really NT 5.0) for people who need a workhorse system. Windows 2000 doesn't crash often; if a program crashes, the OS just keeps on going. You can leave 2000 running constantly—something you wouldn't want to do with Windows 98. Security in 2000 is rock-solid, requiring every user to sign on with an individual password.

Even though 2000 rides on NT, this OS was Microsoft's first step toward "marrying" the consumer and business OS. 2000 boasts improved navigation features, more wizards to walk users through installations and other processes, and enhanced window and menu features. For all that, 2000's beefier nature requires more hardware and system resources than many home users want to pony up. In other words, NT was (and 2000 is still largely perceived as) a business OS.

Becoming XPerienced

Microsoft sees Windows XP, released in 2001, as its real-deal merged business/consumer product. You can buy it in both Home and Professional versions, and the home version replaces Me. Built around the more stable Windows 2000 kernel (or core), Microsoft designed Windows XP to handle the digital media users pump through their systems these days. Microsoft touts Windows XP as the one OS for home and business, offering stable, secure operations and cutting-edge capabilities for ripping CDs, e-mailing photos, handling instant messaging, and so on.

Windows XP also offers remote diagnosis and troubleshooting capabilities. You can open up your machine and say "AAAH" to a geeky friend or technician located far, far away to get the inside scoop on what's ailing your system. The Professional version of Windows XP does all this and more, with additional peer-to-peer services, improved code protection, and scalable memory and process support. TechTV will continue to keep tabs on Windows XP's development, so stay tuned.

Why Don't We Just Start Over?

This is a tip for business and home users alike. If you use 98 or better, you can upgrade to Windows XP, but a clean install or preloaded version works best. Back up all your data, and then make a clean break from your old system and start with a fresh installation of XP.

TASTE THE APPLE

In 1976, Steve Jobs and Steve Wozniak designed and built a wood-framed computer in the Jobs' family garage. Jobs and Wozniak had to sell their coolest stuff—a Volkswagen van and a programmable calculator—to finance those first 50 Apple circuit boards. (Will a retro "woody" iMac soon join the herb, mineral, and fruit-flavored versions Mac-ophiles have come to know and love?)

The Mac, Mac Plus, Mac SE, and Mac II ran on 32-bit processors, so they offered good speed and reliability even way-back-when. Apple's Mac OS made the first big splash with a GUI, and it quickly gained a reputation as a reliable, easy-to-use, low-maintenance performer. In 1994, the Power Mac came on the scene, powered by Motorola's PowerPC CPU chip, which used a reduced instruction set that was therefore much faster; in 1998, the release of iMac, with its bright colors and hip design, breathed new life into what had become a struggling company. By the end of 2000, Apple held about five percent of the U.S. PC market.

Hey, 9x Users...Do You Want XP?

If you have at least 128MB of available memory, run Windows 95, and want to upgrade your system for better security, and faster processing, maybe you should move on up to XP. This new Windows system seems easy to use and full of digital management muscle. BUT (there's the big but), if you're a home user running Windows 98, Me, or 2000 and you're satisfied with your system—including your hardware and peripherals—you might want to pass on XP for now. The feature improvements aren't dramatic, and you'll save yourself both disk space and a lengthy installation. Windows XP isn't a DOS-based OS, so older DOS-based apps and drivers don't function well—or at all—in the XP environment. Home upgraders, for example, might find that their trusty old digital camera or scanner drivers don't work in XP. Business might have trouble supporting both Windows and DOS-based apps. On the other hand, many businesses running 98 will find XP's greater reliability, networking, and security features worth the upgrade hassles. Microsoft will be busy ironing out backward-compatibility issues in the months ahead, so keep an eye on TechTV news for updates on XP developments.

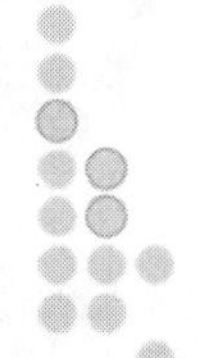

Getting Along

Today, the Mac has a loyal following of users, including some who claim they still work on machines they bought in 1986. Throughout most of its history, Apple has produced new Mac OS releases that remained infinitely compatible with all earlier Mac hardware *and* software. The Mac OS stayed simple to master, and users claimed they spent a fraction of the time Windows users devoted to installing and learning newer and ever-more-complex product "upgrades."

The Mac OS continues to be a favorite of graphics designers, musicians, engineers, and scientists, and Mac users exhibit fierce loyalty to their machines. If you ever want to see how deep Mac loyalty lies, drop in on a Mac versus PC discussion group (you can find any number of them by searching under "Mac discussion group" with any major search engine); Macophiles love their OS, and don't take kindly to "livin' in a Windows world."

The Big Apple: Mac OS X

In a move similar to the Windows XP professional/home product merger, Apple made major changes in its latest release, Mac OS X. Apple built Mac OS X on a version of UNIX it calls Darwin. Darwin is a rock-solid operating system that TechTV reviewers found to be very stable.

Mac OS X offers faster speed, greater cross-application compatibility, and a slick new user interface. When Apple unveiled Mac OS X, the system was unaccompanied by major applications able to take advantage of the OS's special features, though compatible apps started being released as soon as the operating system was available. In the meantime, a Mac OS X installation allows Mac users to boot into either a Mac OS 9.1 or Mac OS X environment, plus Mac OS X lets users run current Mac OS 9 applications under emulation. TechTV found Classic, as Apple coined it, a great idea for transitioning from Mac OS 9 to Mac OS X, but its incompatibilities with hardware and its slow performance were disappointing.

Apple Tech Info Library

Apple's Tech Info Library lists the compatibility issues you might be up against when you upgrade a Mac OS to a higher version. For that listing and lots of good troubleshooting advice, visit `til.info.apple.com`.

ARE YOU READY TO LEAP TO LINUX?

Lots of people think Linux is based on the UNIX operating system, but technically, it isn't. When Linus Torvalds wrote the Linux kernel while studying at the University of Helsinki in Finland, he based it on a UNIX clone known as Minix. Minix resembles UNIX, but isn't the same system. Torvalds designed Linux as a free OS that can operate on a variety of platforms.

Technically speaking, "Linux" refers only to the core or the operating system, the kernel. Through time, the term Linux has come to refer to the complete OS and associated applications developed by thousands of programmers from around the world.

Linux is a UNIX-like operating system that runs on many different types of computers, including those using CPUs from Intel, Compaq, Motorola, and Sun. You can find versions of Linux for your Alpha, Sun, Apple Macintosh, or PC. Linux is the core, or kernel, of the operating system, while the Linux operating system and its collection of software is properly known as a *distribution*. Red Hat and Caldera are just two of the popular Linux distributions available today.

Because Torvalds gave Linux source code away, any developer who wanted to could customize or work to improve the kernel. As a result, thousands and thousands of people from all over the world have dabbled in Linux, and have helped make it an incredibly sophisticated and powerful OS. Today, you can still download Linux for free, or buy it on CD for a nominal fee.

Linux offers a number of advantages to those users who are interested in tinkering with their OS source code. You don't have to pay royalties or licensing fees to use it, it runs on almost any CPU, and it doesn't support the feature-creep that pushes the users of most other operating systems into a never-ending upgrade spiral. If you know how to edit program code, you can dig in and customize with your operating system; you control Linux—it doesn't control you.

What's Open Source All About?

Open-source programs, including Linux, UNIX, and FreeBSD, are programs with source code that is freely available and accessible to the public. Open-source programs are certified as such by the Open Source Initiative (OSI). The Open Source Initiative holds that software is best developed when it is developed by all. Under OSI licensing standards, chief among them the general public license (GPL), code can be modified, improved, redistributed for free, and under certain circumstances repackaged and sold in the commercial market. You learn more about the Open Source movement in Chapter 11, "Living the Good GNU/Linux." You can find more information about the OSI at www.opensource.org.

What's in a Name?

Many folks don't even realize that when they speak of Linux, they might be talking about something else altogether. The term *Linux* refers just to the kernel of the operating system—the core of the OS that contains boot commands. Few people have any need to download and work directly with the source code of the Linux kernel. More often, users mess around with a Linux *distribution*, which is a complete Linux system of installation and running commands, mostly made of a collection of GNU code. (GNU stands for "GNU's Not UNIX," and you can learn a lot more about GNU by visiting its site at www.gnu.org.) So, what you refer to as Linux might really be a GNU operating system built on the Linux kernel.

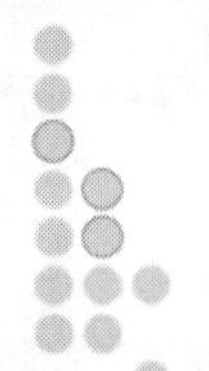

This is Not Everyone's OS

Not to rain on anyone's "It's free! It's free!" parade, but every distribution of Linux isn't the right OS for every user. Most Linux distributions work great for developers and anyone running a network, but you have to be relatively techno-savvy to install and run them.

Despite the number of applications written for Linux, don't think of this OS as being similar to Windows or Mac OS. Some Linux distributions don't have a GUI, and leave you SOL (sorta out of luck) if you rely on friendly icons and pick-and-click menus to help find and issue commands. Linux was designed as a command-line system. To use it successfully, you should be able to communicate with the OS in its language—not yours. (In Chapter 11, you learn where to find third-party GUIs for your Linux, so don't fret if your distribution came GUI-less.)

Linux Can Take You to UNIX

If you plan to learn the UNIX OS (the operating system that underlies most of the Internet) start with Linux. Linux shares enough with UNIX to help you learn to function in a less GUI-centric OS world. You'll find many distributions of Linux, but if you're prepping for UNIX, go with Red Hat. The Red Hat distribution is relatively easy to install, and it has just about the most complete toolset of any Linux distribution. You learn more about Red Hat and other Linux distributions in Chapter 11.

The Many Faces of Linux

Linux comes in many flavors, called *distributions*. The term "Linux" only refers to the kernel. As different developers and vendors add their own commands, software, installation, and customization support to the Linux kernel, different distributions of Linux become available. Occasionally, the kernel itself is updated—at this writing, the current kernel is 2.4.7.

Here are some of the most common current Linux distributions:

- Slackware Linux (`http://www.slackware.com/`) appeals to power users and those moving from the mainstream UNIX world. Most Linux gurus claim that Slackware acts the most like UNIX. It's also regarded as the distribution of choice for programmers and software developers who must support UNIX platforms. The first commercial Linux distribution, it's still one of the most popular.
- Red Hat Linux (`http://www.redhat.com/`) attracts beginning users and those not familiar with UNIX. It contains a detailed and easy-to-follow installation routine. The 7.1 release features a bevy of core program updates including the new 2.4 kernel, XFree86 4.0.3, better multi-processor support, and support for "hot pluggable" devices.
- Caldera OpenLinux (`http://www.caldera.com/`) Desktop 2.4 includes a host of tools for setting, deploying, and managing your Internet desktop.
- Debian GNU/Linux (`http://www.debian.org/`) stresses the use of Free Software Foundation (`http://www.fsf.org/`) tools in its release.

- S.u.S.E. (`http://www.suse.com/`) is a major player in Europe. It's also noted for advanced tools for configuring Linux and X installations.
- TurboLinux (`http://www.turbolinux.com/`) from Pacific HiTech offers support for the latest kernel version.

You can find an up-to-date list of Linux applications, tools, and utilities at `www.linux.org/apps/index` or at `lwn.net/current/dists.php3`. For information on distributions, visit `www.linux.org/dist/english.html`.

GO ALL THE WAY WITH UNIX

You can think of Linux as the son of a clone of the UNIX system. Linus Torvalds took care not to base Linux directly on licensed UNIX source code, which allows Linux distributions to stay free—developers don't have to pay license fees. But Linux displays its close kinship with UNIX in many ways. UNIX is really a kernel that developers use as a foundation for UNIX distributions. Sound familiar?

Bell Labs created UNIX back in the 1970s as a powerful development tool and system platform. Because developers based it on the C programming language, UNIX stayed small and flexible, and it ran on any system that had a C-compiler—and most systems did. UNIX was also cheap, because antitrust laws prevented Bell Labs from marketing it as a full-scale product. Many universities still use UNIX, which also powers most of the Internet.

Breaking UNIX Down

UNIX might seem like a hard-to-get-your-arms-around monster of a system, but actually, it contains three easy pieces:

- **The kernel:** The core of any UNIX system, the kernel contains the boot, memory management, data transfer information, and other functions that you don't have to mess with when you use an operating system.
- **The shell:** Any time you log in to a UNIX system, you land in the shell. The shell supplies you with a prompt (usually in the lower-left corner of your screen) where you enter commands. The shell passes your commands on to the kernel.
- **The file system:** As in other operating systems, the UNIX file system stores and organizes the information in your system so you can find and use it.

Beyond these main components, resemblance between the UNIX family members can be difficult to spot. Every computer manufacturer can create its own version of UNIX.

Don't Fear UNIX

If you think UNIX is a hard-to-use system you never want to meet, don't forget that UNIX is the founding father of the new Mac OS X release. Its UNIX roots make the new Mac OS the most flexible, powerful, and usable Mac system ever. With all of that UNIX power come some limitations, of course. Mac OS X isn't compatible with some older Mac software and hardware. But every time you fire up that shiny new Mac OS, remember that you're talking with UNIX. Expect OS heavy hitters like UNIX and Linux to grow more user friendly as time goes by. At the same time, user skills increase as the systems evolve into friendlier platforms. So don't shy away from UNIX—it's not just for geeks anymore!

Today's Most Exciting Flavors of UNIX

New distributions of UNIX continue to bring it closer to user-friendliness, but right now it still works best as a workstation product. Since AT&T splintered in the mid-1980s, the UNIX world split into two main camps: the Bell labs' UNIX version, known as System V, and the version created at the University of California at Berkeley, known as BSD.

System V probably is the more popular of the two UNIX versions, but from a user's perspective, the two systems look very similar. They have slightly different file structures, and they respond differently to certain commands. But if you can use BSD, you can use System V. Linux contains elements of both System V and BSD in its make-up.

EMBRACE DIVERSITY AND PROMOTE COMPATIBILITY

So, with all the operating system diversity out there, is it possible for users to just get along? Right-out-of-the-box systems don't always "click" with each other. But every system vendor knows that users aren't involved in exclusive relationships with their OS of choice these days. Many work on multiple operating systems, and an even larger group of computer users share files between systems.

Every software developer knows that to make it in this computing universe, a product has to get along with biggie platforms such as Windows. Plenty of patches and products exist that help smooth the bumps you encounter while working with multiple operating systems. The following sections list some of TechTV's favorite products and features for bringing all your systems together.

What's POSIX?

Because UNIX was such a powerful (and inexpensive) system when it launched in the 1970s, many developers tinkered with it to produce different UNIX-based systems. In the mid-1980s, the X/Open Company came up with the idea of creating an open UNIX system, complete with standards and guidelines. Industry experts came together to devise the Single UNIX specification, and that spec includes a requirement for POSIX (Portable Operating System Interface for UNIX) compliance. The POSIX standard defines how UNIX interfaces should function, so developers can port code from one UNIX system to another by recompiling the source code. Linux, as a clone of UNIX, is POSIX compliant.

Beaming Info Across the Platform Galaxy

You've finally decided to use your IrDA (infra-red data) port to beam your business card to another PDA, but there's a problem. You use Windows CE and the other PDA doesn't. Never fear, Scotty! With the help of a download, you can beam away to other PDAs, even if they don't live on your platform's planet.

Peacemaker (`http://conduits.com/ce/peacemaker/`) lets you beam from your Windows CE PDA to almost any other PDA, and it works for handheld computers as well. The personal version of Peacemaker is free; the professional version costs $14.95. SyncTalk (available at `synctalk.com`) is another great cross-platform beaming tool. It's compatible with several platforms, including Windows CE and Palm OS. The Companion version of SyncTalk is free, but it works only for a limited time. If you like the free trial, you can buy a full version for $29.95.

Run Windows in Linux

If you decided to switch to Linux, you probably struggled with the idea of walking away from all your Windows apps. The good news is that you don't have to! Among the companies vying for this compatibility market, VMware (`www.vmware.com`) has become the standard for running virtual PCs under Linux.

Virtual machines (operating systems) in a VMware environment are called *guest systems*. Your primary machine is the host. VMware has host releases of its software for both Linux and Windows NT. You can run multiple guest systems simultaneously, which you can display within windows or as full screens. Get the full specs and download the software at `www.vmware.com`.

VMware offers a Virtual Computing Environment that allows you to run Windows and Windows apps on a host Linux machine in a nearly native state. VMware doesn't involve any kind of environment emulation, so your apps run as they were meant to run—not in the "mirror world" model you would get from a more artificial OS environment.

VMware lets you test drive Linux before making a full commitment to switch. Linux beginners like VMWare because it's easy to install, doesn't require partitioning the drive or learning a lot of command-line entries, and it lets users do all their hardware configurations and installations from Windows.

Don't Expect WinLinux to Be a Painless Path to Linux

WinLinux is a Linux system that installs directly on your Windows PC. Although WinLinux can help you switch from Windows to Linux, it has a few inherent problems. One of these is a tendency to corrupt shared files. Because WinLinux 2000 and Windows work so closely together, if you make a mistake in one of them, you feel it in both. If you enter a wrong command, you might have to reinstall Windows before you can tap back into either operating system. So take care and don't treat WinLinux like a "simple solution." Although it's an elegant product, it's better used as an introduction to Linux. When you get serious about making the switch completely, get a full Linux distribution, such as Red Hat or Caldera.

Pack a Spare

When you experiment with any new OS—or even with a virtual environment, such as VMware—you can benefit from loading the new system on a spare PC or separate hard drive (if you have one). Everyone crashes or breaks something when they first learn a new OS—that's part of the learning process. But you don't want to lose a system to learning. Think of that spare PC just as you think of a spare tire. If one system goes flat for a while, you can keep going on your other system until you have the time and resources to get the other back in action.

Run Windows Programs on a Mac

You can run Windows programs on a Mac, but you need special software and it can be somewhat slow. Virtual PC 4.0 by Connectix lets you run Windows 2000, Me, and 9.x, Windows NT 3.11, DOS, and Red Hat Linux on your G3 or G4 Mac. Virtual PC 4.0 also gives you access to PC networks, and it lets you share files between your Mac and a PC.

Learn more about Virtual PC at `www.connectix.com`.

Get the Compatibility Picture

Don't think you can resolve every compatibility issue between Mac and OS platforms with a virtual environment or PC emulator software. Graphics display still suffers in the translation, as graphics created on a Mac will display slightly darker on Windows OS. If most of your viewers also use Macs, this issue doesn't represent a big problem. But if you really need to cater to users of both platforms, adjust your graphic design to accommodate this shift.

Run Mac Programs on Windows

Emulators, Inc. produces one of the fastest Mac emulators for Windows, SoftMac. SoftMac offers drag-and-drop file support between Mac and PC disk volumes, improved network and file-sharing support, and—even better—the support for Windows XP and Athlon processor speed optimizations, so you don't draw dust while you're waiting on your system to transfer data.

What an Emulator Does in Your Machine

An emulator is software that runs between the computer hardware and operating system and the program. Its sole purpose is to translate all the info flowing through your OS into the system's native language. On a PC, a Mac emulator must run all the programs, and it also must run the sound system, file system, and networking functions. That's why even the best emulators feel slow. If you're working with a program that's already slow, you can expect molasses-like speeds from the emulator. It's like listening to a translation versus hearing your native tongue. You can get the job done, but it takes time.

Run Linux on a Mac

Mac users, rest assured that you have plenty of Linux distributions to choose from. Unfortunately, most require destructive partitioning. When you make a new partition on a Mac, you wipe out all the existing data in that section.

This problem isn't a factor when you run Linux on a Windows PC, simply because you don't have to reformat a PC partition to run Linux. The reason? You can use the FAT32 version of Linux; because it operates in a native Windows file system, FAT32 Linux can run right in your PC. Unfortunately, no company has released an HFS Linux version yet.

Here are some of the Macintosh Linux distributions you can choose from today. Expect this list to go through frequent changes.

- **Debian (`www.debian.org`):** Debian GNU/Linux 2.2r2 features a streamlined and polished installation, automatic network setup, an easier (compared to previous releases) software selection process, and a simplified configuring tool for the X Window System.
- **SuSE (`www.suse.com`):** This company's Linux 7.1 PowerPC edition supplies the latest Linux operating system and more than 1,000 assorted applications for Mac users.
- **MkLinux (`mklinux.org`):** Close to Red Hat and works for NuBus, but isn't the full Linux kernel. The users maintain MkLinux—Apple doesn't support it.

Beginning in the summer of 1998, development work on MkLinux transitioned from Apple and OSF to a community-led effort. Upgrades to the kernel software are available from the `globegate.utm.edu` FTP server. The kernel upgrades available from globegate are generally known as the GENERIC kernels. A brief history of the community's efforts can be found in the Development section of this Web site on the Kernel Information page. Instructions for obtaining kernel sources directly from CVS are located on the CVS Information page.

The MkLinux Developer's Release 3 is available both on CD-ROM and by FTP. Apple's MkLinux FTP site appears to be gone, but check the mirrors for the complete DR3 release.

- **LinuxPPC (`www.linuxppc.org`):** This one has a fast installer and comes with a graphical partitioning tool.
- **TurboLinux (`www.turbolinux.com`):** The PPC version includes TurboDesk, a functional, easy-to-use desktop.

Not Every Linux Distribution Will Work on Every Mac

Be sure when you look for Mac Linux that you choose a distribution that's specifically made for your firmware. Not every distribution will work on every Mac. Check out MKLinux's (`mklinux.org`) list of distributions, and look through its FAQs for information about compatible firmware releases for each distribution.

Windows File Sharing in Linux

Even though you can run FAT32 Linux in Windows, you might need some help with your file-sharing and networking tasks. Samba, now in version 2.2.0, is an open-source software suite that provides file and print services to Windows clients. Before you can use Windows networking in Linux, install the Linux Samba software package, available at Samba.org (`ftp://ftp.samba.org/`). Samba is freely available under the GNU General Public License.

LIGHTNING ROUND Q&A WRAP-UP

Which version of UNIX is better for my PC, FreeBSD or Linux?

FreeBSD is an advanced BSD UNIX operating system. At this point, for most purposes, Linux and BSD work equally well. Neither one is necessarily better than the other, so make your choice based on your own preferences and what kind of support is available to you.

If you're surrounded by BSD lovers, go with BSD because you'll get more help from your peers. If you're surrounded by Linux users, use Linux. If you're all alone, choose Linux because you'll find more books and Web sites to help you. But remember, truly portable UNIX software runs on both platforms just fine.

What is a command line, and why does Mac OS X have one?

The command line lets you tell your OS what commands you want it to perform. Long before the GUI gave us buttons, icons, and other user-friendly interface options, the blinking cursor of a command line was the only method of telling your system where to go. Apple turned its back on command-line functions when it brought Mac users the GUI. But, as we learned in Linux, the command line equals power. Today, the command line is an optional way of interacting with the Mac system, thanks to Mac OS X. Mac OS X builds on the FreeBSD version of UNIX, and you can use that command-line access to take advantage of the full power of the OS. Don't look down on this feature—use it for all it's worth (and it's worth a lot).

How can I get files from my Mac partition to my Linux partition?

Three options:

- **Online storage:** Send the files you want to transfer to an FTP site or an Internet site offering free space, such as `freediskspace.com`. Then retrieve the files with your alternate partition.
- **Zip drive:** If you have a Zip drive, copy the files to a Zip disk that's been PC-formatted.
- **The Linux way:** Linux can load extensions for many alternative file systems, including Mac HFS, into a kernel using kernel-loadable modules. The HFS module joined the main Linux kernel distribution late in the 2.1.x series. When loaded, it allows you to read and write HFS disks under Linux as if they were native to Linux.

  HFS has been the native file system on the Apple Macintosh since the Mac Plus was released in 1986. Linux does not support the older MFS (Macintosh file system) or HFS Plus, the space-saving formatting option introduced with the release of Mac OS 8.1. If you want to use this module, you'll probably need to reformat your Mac's hard drive into the HFS file format.

CHAPTER 9

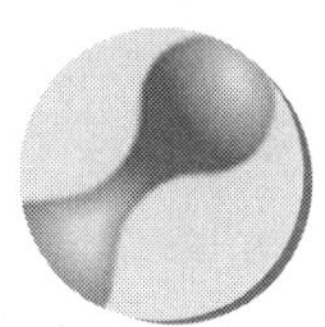

WINDOWS WORK

- Make Windows work faster
- Make Windows work better
- Make Windows work your way

Microsoft has gone through billions of dollars (and tons of pizza) to create that Windows platform everyone's so fond of bashing. Say what you will, Windows is the world's most widely used—and yes, popular—operating system. Because Windows is such a big and beefy OS, it's hard to know all the tricks for getting the most out of every Windows feature.

No one at TechTV claims to know every Windows trick and shortcut, but the combined Windows savvy at TechTV is pretty amazing. This chapter highlights TechTV's favorite Windows tips, tricks, and shortcuts. From showing off underrated powerhouse features to feeding your need for speed and unmasking techniques for tweaking the system as you like it, this chapter brings you the best of TechTV's Windows wizardry. Enjoy!

SPEED UP WINDOWS

Every Windows release boasts more power than the last. Unfortunately, all that muscle can bog down your system, unless you use Windows' built-in tools for keeping things clipping along.

Get to the Desktop Faster

When you have six programs running and need to get to your desktop, you could go through a long series of "minimization." Get instant access to the desktop by adding a desktop toolbar to your Windows taskbar. Besides giving you quick access to all desktop icons right from the taskbar, the toolbar adds Start menu-style navigation to My Computer, Recycle Bin, Network Places, and other folders that might be located on your desktop.

To add the desktop toolbar in Windows 98:

1. Right-click on an empty space on the taskbar.
2. Select Toolbars, Desktop; the desktop toolbar appears on your taskbar.
3. Slide the desktop toolbar as far to the right as possible so only the word "Desktop" is visible, as shown in Figure 9.1. It takes up very little space on your taskbar!

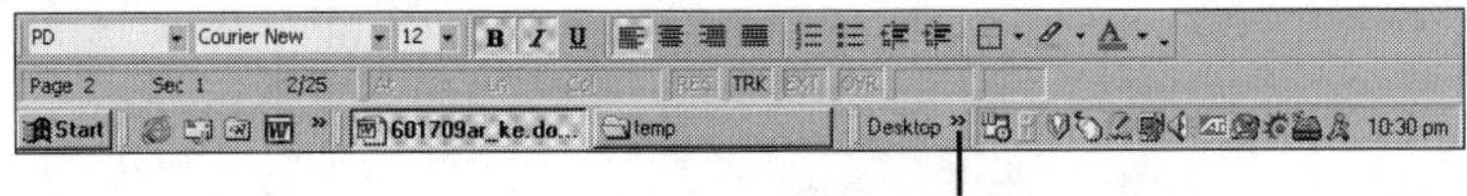

Figure 9.1

Click the chevron to the right of the word "Desktop" to access the desktop toolbar.

4. Click the chevron (double-arrow icon) beside Desktop to expand the desktop toolbar list; then, you can choose My Computer or any other folder, file, or application you need, as shown in Figure 9.2.

Faster Disk Access

Desktop shortcuts get you quickly into frequently used documents, programs, or hardware devices. Shortcuts are a great way to access disk drives or CD-ROMs. Here's how to put a disk drive shortcut on your desktop:

1. Double-click My Computer on your desktop.
2. Right-click the disk drive you'd like to make a shortcut for and select Create Shortcut from the menu.
3. Choose Yes from the pop-up window that asks if you'd like to have the shortcut placed on your desktop, as shown in Figure 9.3.

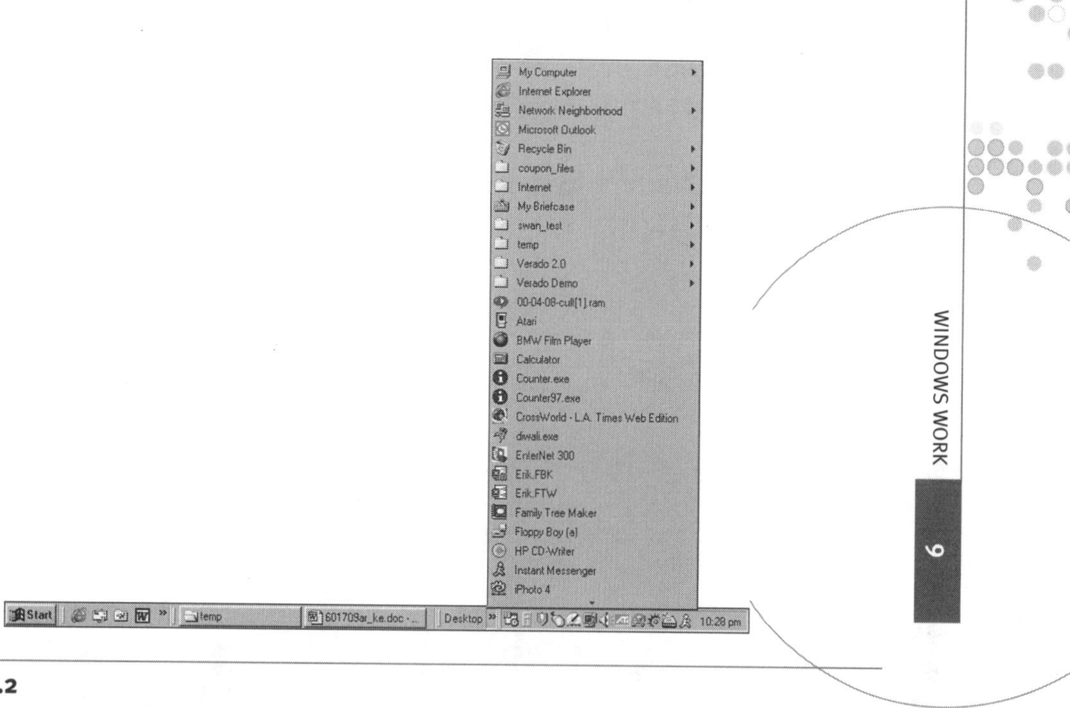

Figure 9.2

Clicking the chevron reveals the desktop toolbar list.

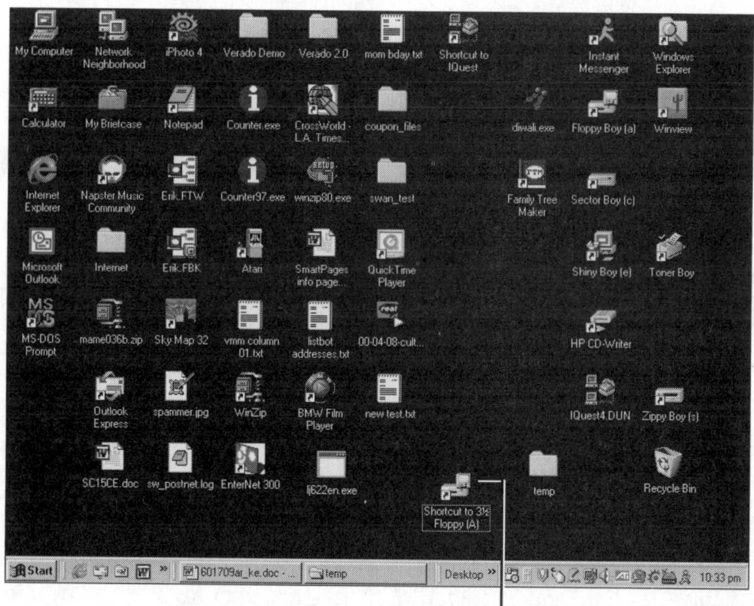

Figure 9.3

For quick access to other drives, place a shortcut on your desktop.

4. Continue to create desktop shortcuts for as many drive letters as you have (or want to shortcut, anyway).

Create a Shortcut to the Send To Menu

Send To is one of Windows' best-kept secrets. The Send To command, shown in Figure 9.4, can kick-start several Windows features. For example, it allows you to bypass file associations and open documents in any program. You can customize it with program executables, devices, and removable storage shortcuts of your choice.

Right-clicking any document in Windows brings up a menu that includes the Send To command.

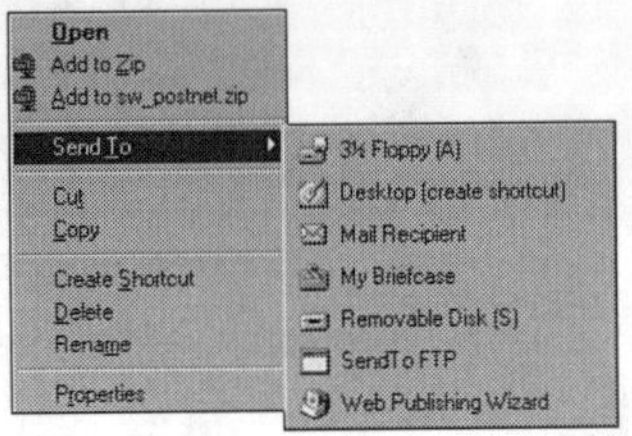

Figure 9.4

Use the Send To command to transfer files or programs to other devices, programs, or media.

Don't Mess Around in that Windows Folder!

Don't delete or play with any of the files or folders within the Windows folder unless you know what you're doing. The files in your Windows folder are essential to your system, and mucking about with them can create huge headaches for you—and your tech support rep.

Start the process of creating your personal Send To menu by creating a shortcut to the menu itself:

1. Double-click the My Computer icon, and then click the icon of the drive where Windows is installed (usually C:/).
2. Double-click the Windows folder.
3. Right-click the Send To folder and select Create Shortcut.
4. Now, right-click the shortcut you just created and choose Cut. You just cut the folder.
5. Double-click the Send To folder to open it, and then right-click anywhere in the folder window and choose Paste To. Paste the shortcut inside the Send To folder, and you're finished (see Figure 9.5).

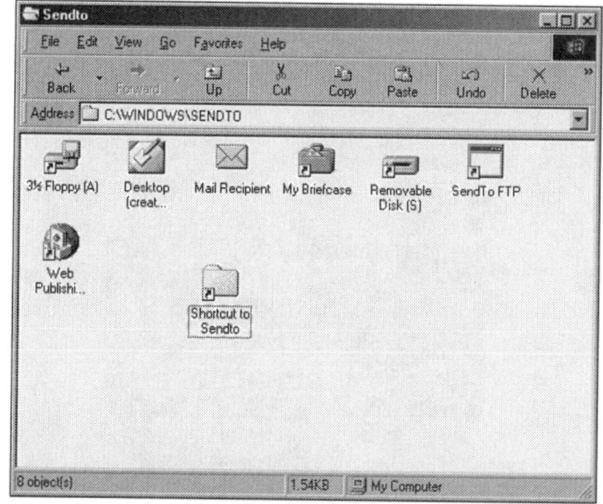

Figure 9.5

Create a shortcut to Send To and place it in the Send To folder.

Now, customize your Send To menu however you choose.

Print Fast with Send To

Send To does more than give you fast access to other Windows docs and features. You also can use it to send documents to the printer without having to open them first. Here's how to add your printer to the Send To menu:

1. Click the Start menu, and then choose Settings, Printers.
2. Right-click your printer's icon inside the Printers folder and select Create Shortcut from the menu.
3. Windows asks if it's OK for the shortcut to be placed on the desktop; click Yes.
4. Find your new printer shortcut on the desktop, and then right-click it once. Choose Cut.
5. Open My Computer from your desktop and select the drive where Windows is installed.
6. Open the Windows folder and double-click the Send To folder.
7. Press Ctrl+V to paste the new printer shortcut inside the Send To folder.

Windows XP Puts the Pedal Down

The much-ballyhooed 2001 release of Windows XP promises to be one of the fastest versions yet. XP was designed with media in mind, and the OS screams through media-related chores in a hurry. This version of XP embraces Media Player the same way Windows 98 folded Internet Explorer into its system core. With fast speeds and an integrated Media Player, XP might be the OS heard (and watched) 'round the world.

Now when you want to print a document without opening it, right-click it within Windows and select Send To (see Figure 9.6). Choose your printer from the menu and you're done.

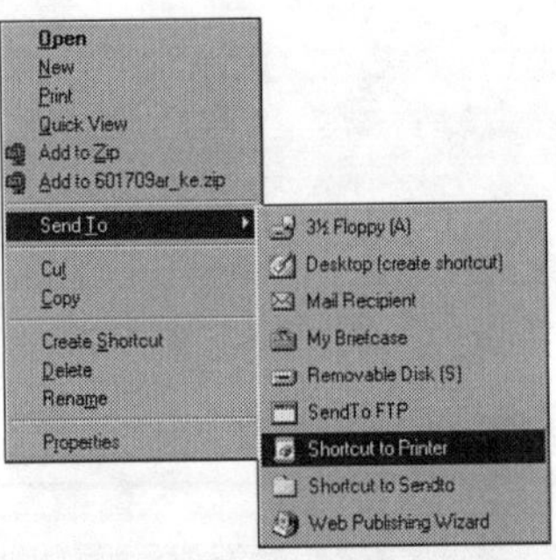

Figure 9.6

A document may be printed without opening it simply by right-clicking it within Windows, selecting Send To then selecting your printer.

Delete Words Fast

This tip can work in any Windows program that lets you type—not just your word processor. You know that you can delete a word by highlighting the entire word and pressing Delete, right? But you also can use TechTV's faster way to say "buh-bye." If the word is to the left of the cursor, press Ctrl+Backspace. If the word is to the right of the cursor, press Ctrl+Delete. Voila! No more backspacing character by character or highlighting to delete a word. Not an earthshaking act, but little things mean a lot when you're talking about trimming your typing time.

Find Files Fast in Windows

Have you ever downloaded a program, only to find you didn't notice where you saved it? Ever lost a copy of a crucial document or resume? Chances are those lost treasures still exist on your hard drive. Don't waste precious time guessing where your files went. Here's the fastest way to run a Windows search:

1. Choose Start, Find (or Search, in Windows Me), and then select Files Or Folders.
2. In the Name field, type the name of the file you'd like to find and select My Computer in the Look In field (see Figure 9.7). If you don't know the file's name, open the Date Modified tab and search for all files created or modified during the last day. (In Windows Me, check the Date check box, and then select your options from the drop-down list that appears.)
3. Choose Find (or Search) Now. A list of all the files on your computer containing the same text appears.

   If you still don't uncover the missing file, refine your search this way:
4. Keep the same information in the file name and location or date fields.

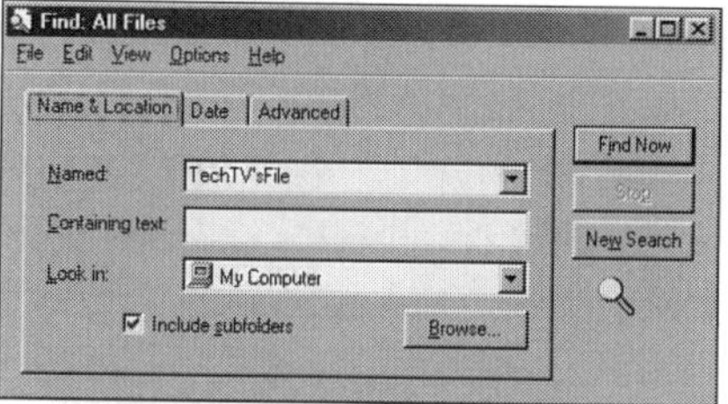

Figure 9.7

Use the Find or Search feature to find misplaced files quickly.

5. Select the Advanced tab. In the Of Type pull-down menu, choose the type of file extension you're looking for, as shown in Figure 9.8. (Or in Windows Me, check the Type check box and choose the file type from the drop-down list.)

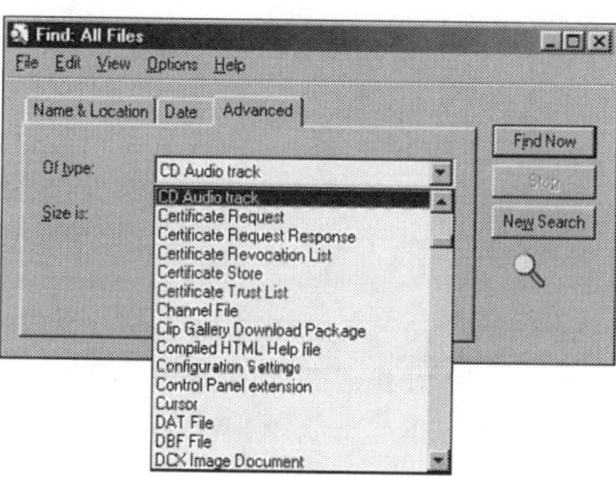

Figure 9.8

To further narrow your search (or find), use the Type pull-down menu (or Type check box and drop-down menu in Windows Me) to search for a particular extension.

6. Click Find Now (or Search Now) to bring up a list of all the files that fit the new (and old) criteria.

Defrag Those Drives

Is your PC slower than molasses in January? Do your files take forever to open up? The more you use your computer, the more scattered files become as they get rewritten to your hard drive. The TechTV reviewers recommend that you use Windows' Disk Defragmenter to tidy up your disk. This app reorganizes the data on your drive, which improves the drive's performance, reliability, and speed.

Use Disk Defragmenter when you can afford to be away from your computer for a few hours. Start the program and walk away; the utility runs by itself. If you use your computer often, run Disk Defragmenter about every three months.

1. Click the Start button, and then choose Programs, Accessories, System Tools. Click Disk Defragmenter.

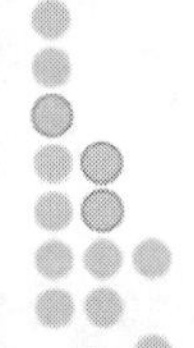

2. Select the drive you'd like to defragment and choose Settings to open the Defragmenter Settings menu, as shown in Figure 9.9.
3. Check the Rearrange Program Files So My Programs Start Faster and Check Drive For Errors options, then choose OK, and then choose OK again to start the process.
4. For a graphical representation of how it works, press the Show Details button.

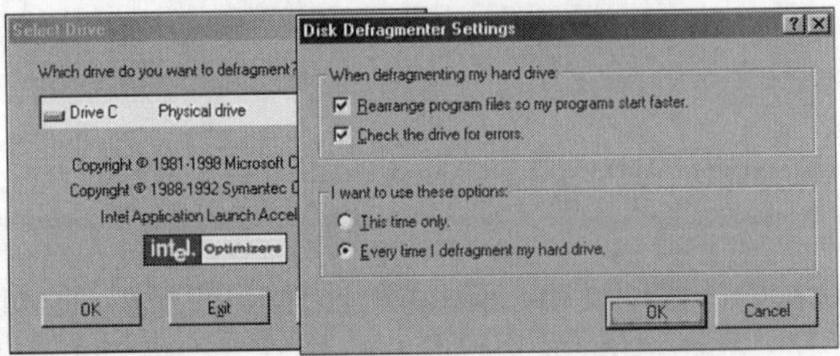

Figure 9.9

Speeding up your disk drive often is as easy as using disk defragmenter to clean house on your hard drive every three months or so.

MAKE WINDOWS WORK BETTER

In computing, faster is almost always better. But faster isn't the *only* kind of "better" you can get out of your Windows OS. In this section, you learn some of TechTV's favorite ways to make Windows work more efficiently, with fewer errors. These utilities and periodic maintenance routines encourage Windows to be all that it can be.

Run ScanDisk

If you've ever had a power shut-down, or if you accidentally turned off a PC without going through the required protocol, you know about ScanDisk. This program detects—and fixes—hard-drive errors that sometimes occur after an improper shutdown. You can use ScanDisk any time to find and delete files that aren't associated with any particular program and no longer have any business cluttering your system.

1. Click the Start button, then choose Programs, Accessories, System Tools, ScanDisk (see Figure 9.10).
2. Under the type of test, click Thorough. Uncheck Automatically Fix Errors if you want to have a chance to tell ScanDisk how to repair errors it uncovers.
3. Click Start to begin scanning your hard drive.

Don't panic if ScanDisk finds bad clusters. For a closer look at cluster errors and what they mean, skip ahead to the first Q&A in the "Lightning Round Q&A Wrap Up" section at the end of this chapter.

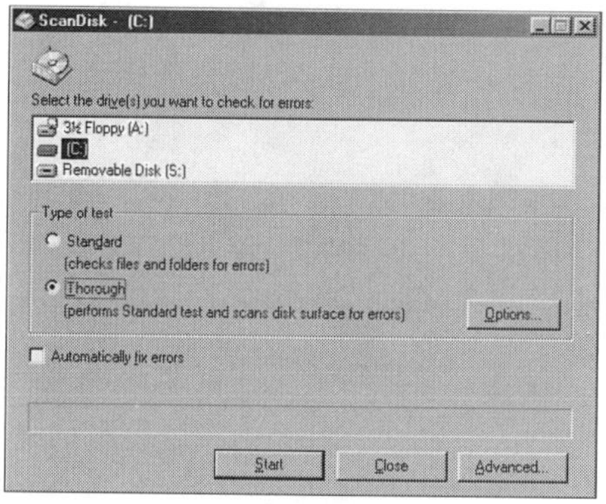

Figure 9.10

A thorough ScanDisk periodically or after any improper shutdown often will help unclutter your system and make your computer run more smoothly.

Troubleshoot Windows with the System Information Application

Tech support calls can suck up both your time and money. To spend "quality time" with tech support, open the System Information application before you call. This information helps the support tech find out what's troubling your system—fast.

To open the System Information tool (available in Windows 98 and higher versions), click the Start button, and then choose Programs, Accessories, System Tools, System Information. The display varies among Windows versions, but in general, the System Information is organized into three categories:

- **Resources** displays hardware-specific settings, such as DMA, IRQs, I/O addresses, and memory addresses. The Conflicts/Sharing view identifies devices that are sharing resources or are in conflict. If you have trouble with a device, it might show up here.
- **Components** displays information about your Windows configuration. This category determines the status of your device drivers, networking, and multimedia software. It also gives you a comprehensive driver history, where you can see what changes have been made to your components over time.
- **Software Environment** displays a snapshot of the software that's loaded in computer memory. The tech can use this information to check version information or to find out whether a process is still running.

Windows Me divides system information into five areas; in addition to the three above, it includes Internet Explorer and Applications.

Save Energy by Giving Your Hard Drive a Nap

Windows gives you lots of ways to take control of your system, and that includes customizing its power settings. Save electricity and cut down on wear and tear on your hard drive by adjusting the drive's power settings.

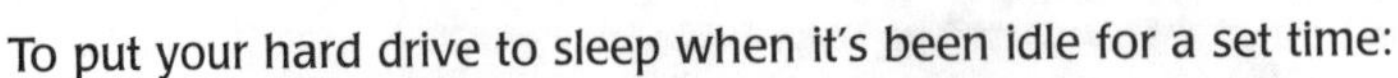

To put your hard drive to sleep when it's been idle for a set time:

1. Open your Start menu and choose Settings, Control Panel, Power Management (or Options).
2. In the Turn Off Hard Disk option, select the amount of time you want your hard drive to "idle" before it goes to sleep (see Figure 9.11).
3. Choose Apply to make it official.

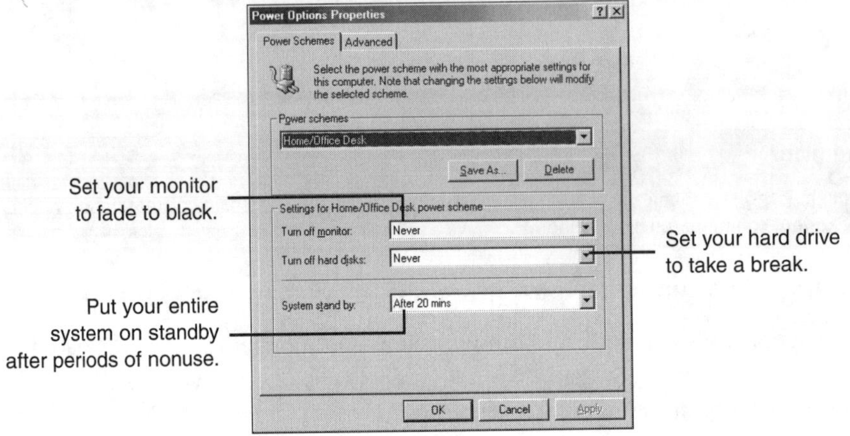

Figure 9.11

Power management can help conserve energy by turning off your computer's various components after a certain period of inactivity. These periods can range from 30 minutes to five hours.

Now, whenever your hard drive sits idle for that amount of time, it will power down and take a nap until you put it to work again. All that resting will help your drive live longer, and it will help you keep more of your money (sorry, MegaMonster Power & Light, Inc.).

Install New Programs on Your Palm with Windows

If you use a PDA that runs Palm OS, you can team it up with Windows for some fast-action, powerful functions. One of the many blessings of this tag-team is that you can use Windows to install new programs on your Palm.

First, go to a Web site (such as `www.palmgear.com`) and download a Palm application. Then install it like this:

1. Open your Palm desktop application from your PC.
2. Choose Install.
3. Browse to where you saved the downloaded file.
4. Select the file and choose Open.

5. Repeat steps 1 to 4 for any more files you want to install. You can install many programs at once.
6. Press Done and then OK.

The next time you synch, your programs will be installed on your Palm device. Depending on the model of Palm handheld you own (PalmPilot Professional, Palm III, Palm V, Palm VII, Handspring Visor, and so on), the process for doing this varies slightly. Follow the instructions that came with your handheld machine.

Stop ISP Disconnect in Windows

You're making a last-minute bid on the Louis XIV commode, and you need to grab your Antiques Price Guide to make sure it's worth the $49.95 you plan to offer. When you return, you find your ISP has decided that you didn't need that connection any longer and booted you offline. By the time you reconnect, some guy in Phoenix has snagged your commode and is laughing all the way to the Antiques Roadshow.

You might be able to nip those dial-up disconnects in the bud by changing the idle time in Windows. Here's how to do this in Windows 98:

1. In the Start menu, choose Settings, Control Panel, Internet Options.
2. Open the Connections tab.
3. Click the Settings button, and then choose Advanced.
4. Uncheck the Disconnect If Idle For (blank) Minutes box, as shown in Figure 9.12.

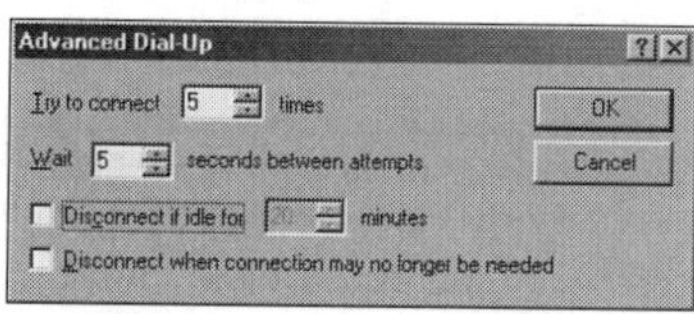

Figure 9.12

If Windows is causing you to be disconnected, uncheck the Disconnect If Idle for X Minutes box in the Internet Options window of your Control Panel.

When You're Doing Windows with Your Palm...

The Windows-assisted app installation for Palms is a nice feature, but don't let the devil rest in the details. These tips help you hold up your end of the process:

- Remember that many Palm OS files end in the file extensions .prc (Pilot resource file) and .pdb (Pilot database file).
- Use Winzip to unzip the program.
- Remember where you save the file on your PC after downloading it.

Now you've done what *you* can do to stop the ISP disconnects. But this won't work if your ISP is doing the disconnecting. Lots of ISPs will boot you off for an idle connection—whether you want them to or not.

Find Hidden Icons in Your .DLL Files

Icons help you work faster by giving you easily recognizable gateways to your files, folders, and programs. You might not know it, but you have hundreds—maybe even thousands—of well-designed (and useful) icons stashed in hidden files throughout your OS. Here's how to find them:

1. Launch RegEdit and drill down to HKEY_CLASSES_ROOT\dllfile\DefaultIcon.
2. Double-click on Default in the right pane.
3. Delete the entry in the Value data box, and type **%1** in its place.
4. Click OK, close the Registry, and reboot.
5. Use Find to search your computer for all DLL files (type in ***.DLL**). Select Large Icons from Find's View menu. Each .DLL file that contains one or more icons will display the first one as the icon for that file. Write down the files that contain icons and the names of their folders.

You can assign any of these icons to shortcuts. Right-click on the shortcut, select Properties, and click the Change Icon button under the Shortcut tab. In the dialog box that opens, type the path and file name in the File Name box. All icons in the DLL will display in the Current Icon window. Choose the one you want and click OK.

Mining for Icons

You can find hidden icons in most .exe files; you'll even find vintage Windows 3.1 icons in PROGMAN.EXE and PIFMGR.DLL. You can use these icons for any shortcut you'd like. Any bitmap file can serve as an icon, and it doesn't have to be moved, resized, or renamed. From within any shortcut's Change Icon dialog box, click on the Browse button, select All Files from the Files of Type box, and double-click on the BMP file of your choice.

MAKE WINDOWS WORK LIKE YOU DO

Sometimes the changes you want to make in your Windows OS are all about you. It's your system, after all, so why shouldn't you call the shots? This section helps you tweak Windows to make it reflect your [choose one] fun/quirky/down-to-earth/power-mad way of doing business.

Restart Windows Without Rebooting

If you ever need to restart Windows, but don't want the hassle of rebooting the entire computer, this is the tip for you. To restart the Windows operating system without a time-sucking reboot, follow these steps. (Sorry, Windows Me users, this tip won't work for you):

1. In the Start Menu, click Shutdown.
2. Check Restart.
3. As you click OK, hold down the Shift key.
4. Continue holding Shift until you see the words, "Windows is now restarting."

Create a Halfway House for Unwanted Programs

Besides Windows, your new PC probably came with a word-processing program, a spreadsheet program, an Internet browser, and a financial program. It also might include "bonus" programs, like card makers and games, that you won't ever use. You don't need unwanted programs cluttering up your PC and stealing precious memory. Still, you hate to uninstall all of them before you know whether you'll want to use them.

So, stash 'em, don't trash 'em. Create a folder called Miscellaneous and treat it like your junk drawer or vegetable bin. Let the stuff sit there for a while, and *then* get rid of it.

1. Open Windows Explorer.
2. Choose File, New, Folder.
3. Name the folder and press Enter.
4. Drag any unfamiliar programs into the new folder.

If for some reason you decide you want to haul a program out of the Miscellaneous folder, just open the folder in Windows Explorer, left-click the program, and drag it to the appropriate spot (such as Programs or Accessories).

Uninstall Programs the Right Way

Don't get rid of programs by deleting their folders. You'll gum up your Windows Registry and end up with a sloooooooow system. When you want to zap a program, use its uninstall utility or the Windows Add/Remove program feature. To use Add/Remove Programs, open the Start menu and choose Settings, Control Panel. Click the Add/Remove Programs icon; choose the Install/Uninstall tab and search for the program you want to remove. Select it, then click the Add/Remove button. If the program doesn't appear in the list, try Norton's CleanSweep utility (`www.symantec.com`). It'll get rid of the program and reclaim your space!

Kill That Windows Logon Screen

If you're the only one who uses your computer, you don't need to mess around with that logon screen every time you boot up. Follow these steps to eliminate the need to enter your name and password (this tip doesn't work if you use Windows NT, Windows Me, or use profiles):

1. Open Control Panel, and double-click the Network icon.
2. In the Primary Network Logon, choose Windows Logon.
3. Press OK to go back to Control Panel.
4. Double-click the Passwords icon and open the Change Passwords tab.
5. Click the Change Windows Password button, and then type your current password in the Old Password text box.
6. Leave the New Password and Confirm New Password boxes blank, and click OK.
7. Open the User Profile tab and be sure the All Users Of This PC Use The Same Preferences And Desktop Settings box is selected. Click OK.

When you restart Windows, you should be free of the logon screen.

Don't Take Properties for Granted

If you never investigate the Properties dialog box in Windows, you pass up an important source of info about what's going on in your system. The Properties pop-up box gives you important details about any file on your computer. The General tab shows you when the file was created, who modified it last, what type of file it is, and so on—but don't stop there. Look through every tab, so you know what kind of information you can access about a given file. To view Properties, right-click on any file you'd like to explore, then choose Properties from the menu.

Build Your Own Taskbar

Your taskbar can do more than just help you sort out open windows and apps. You can make the taskbar look and work the way you want it to. Here are some ways to build your own super taskbar.

Want to Customize the Face of Your Windows Properties Display?

The system properties of your computer probably includes a logo or graphic from the manufacturer. You can use a cool little utility called OEM Logo Changer 1.3b (downloadable at `www.geocities.com`) to replace the graphic with one of your choice. Your replacement graphic must be a bitmap image with a maximum size of 180×114 pixels. Go on and have some fun!

Want to add a Links menu to your taskbar, so you can launch your browser to your favorite news or e-mail page? Would you like to add an Internet address bar? You can have a start-style menu of your desktop on your taskbar, or even add icons to quickly open your favorite local folders. Your taskbar's contents are limited only by your imagination. To add more components to your taskbar (again, Windows 98 and 95 only):

1. Right-click on your taskbar and point to Toolbars.
2. Select an item in the pop-up menu to add it to your toolbar.
3. Repeat for as many elements as you want to add.

Can't see all the components of your taskbar? You can make it bigger. Here's how:

1. Mouse over the top edge of the taskbar until you see a double-headed arrow. If your taskbar is at the bottom or top of the screen, the arrows will point up and down. If your taskbar is on the left or right, the arrows will point left and right.
2. When you see the double-headed arrow, click and hold. You then can drag the taskbar up (down, left, or right depending on the location of the taskbar) to make it bigger.

Now you have more room for all that stuff you added to your taskbar!

KEEPING ON TOP OF THE OS SITUATION

PART 2

LIGHTNING ROUND Q&A WRAP-UP

My computer was running a surface scan and there were about 22,656 bad clusters. What does that mean?

Your computer stores the data on your hard drive in units called *clusters*, and each cluster holds a minimum of 4KB (kilobytes) of data. ScanDisk checks your clusters for errors. If it finds even one bad sector in a cluster, it marks the entire cluster as unusable. It can't read any of the data on the cluster, and it can't write any data to the cluster.

Your clusters can have two kinds of errors: soft errors and hard errors. Soft errors happen when the magnetic signal on the drive is weak or the format is messed up. You can fix soft errors by reformatting the hard drive. A hard error isn't so fixable. It results when your hard drive has some kind of physical damage, such as a scratch or bump. You can't fix hard errors; you just have to stop using the drive.

A few bad clusters are no big deal. Follow ScanDisk's recommendations for fixing them, and your system should function just fine. But if your disk has 22,000 bad clusters, that means you cannot use a substantial portion of your hard drive. Skip the ScanDisk fix and use a heavy-duty diagnostic and correction program called SpinRite (at `www.grc.com`). If you're still under warranty, send the computer back to the manufacturer and have a technician look at it to determine whether or not your drive has a serious problem.

I admit it—I'm getting older! I can't see small icons in Windows, but I'm not willing to lower my screen resolution to blow everything up. Any way I can bump up the size of icons without giving up resolution?

This is a great Windows feature for people who like to have the maximum screen resolution without having to worry about going blind from reading small text on icons. Give your eyes a break and make your icons larger by following these directions:

1. Choose Start, Settings, Control Panel.
2. Double-click the Display icon and select the Effects tab in the Display Properties dialog box.
3. Under Visual Effects, place a checkmark in the box next to "Use large icons."
4. When finished making your changes, click Apply and then OK to exit. Watch your new icons appear before your eyes.

CHAPTER 10

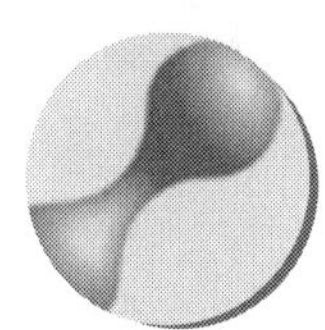

MAXIMIZE YOUR MAC OS

- Improve any Mac's performance
- Take on OS X
- Boost Mac power and speed

Oh, that mighty Apple! Mac lovers are true blue (or ruby red, sage green, snow white, graphite grey, and so on) to their favorite operating system—and with good reason. The Mac OS has always been easy to learn, easy to use, and easy to maintain. On top of that, Macs are versatile, powerful, and fun to work with.

But don't let those cheeky good looks fool you. Macs aren't toys. Mac's latest operating system—Mac OS X—proves to be Apple's fastest and most powerful system yet. In anyone's world, Mac is a force to be reckoned with. In this chapter, you learn some of TechTV's favorite tricks for using one of its favorite operating systems. Get good news about working with a variety of Mac versions, special advice for Mac OS X first-timers, and a final group of Mac techniques that are all about power and speed. Prepare to think different (as the ads say), and work that Mac!

MAKE GOOD TIME WITH ANYONE'S MAC

Most Mac applications are compatible with every earlier version of the Mac OS. In fact, some folks started the 21st century happily working away on Macs they bought in the 1980s (if only a car held up that well). This section highlights Mac actions that work with pre-Mac OS X systems, so you vintage Mac users (or "users of vintage Macs") can keep on keepin' on.

Stop Talkin' (to) Trash

Are you tired of engaging in a "Do you really? Are you sure?" dialog with your Mac Trash feature? By default, the system asks you whether you're sure you want to erase items when you empty the Trash. To say "YES, already!," and turn off this feature, do this:

1. Click the Trash can to select it.
2. Under the File menu, select Get Info.
3. Deselect the "Warn before emptying" check box.

If you find yourself accidentally throwing away files, you can always go back and reset it to bug you again, just like old times.

Want To Be Sure Your File Won't Get Trashed?

The best way to be sure you don't lose that important file is to lock it. Just click on the file, choose Get Info from the File menu, and click the Locked box at the bottom left. Not only will the Trash refuse to delete the file, but the system won't even let you change the filename. Now that's protection!

And While You're Shutting Things Up...

The first thing you might want to do when you break in a Mac is to turn off the voice that reads pop-up windows. If you've heard all you want to hear of that droid's voice, here's how to shut it up:

1. Go to the Apple menu and select Control Panels.
2. Select Speech.
3. Click on the pop-up menu that says Voice.
4. Move down to Talking Alerts.
5. Uncheck both boxes.

If you don't mind the talking alerts but hate the current voice, you can choose another one in the Voice pane of the Speech control panel. (When you tire of that voice—and you will—you can go back and kill it, too.)

Get Rid of Any Desktop Icon

You don't have to put up with icons you don't want, like, or need. To eliminate (well, at least cover up) an item's desktop icon, take a snapshot that includes some of your background pattern and replace the offensive icon with it.

1. Go to the desktop and press Command+Shift+3. (You'll hear a camera shutter sound if you have your speakers on.)
2. Open SimpleText, go to the File menu, select Open, and choose the snap you just took (it's on your hard drive, labeled Picture 1, if it's the only shot you've taken).
3. In SimpleText, select a very small amount of your desktop background color and pattern.
4. Go to the Edit menu and select Copy.
5. In the Finder (desktop), click to select the file or folder icon you want to eliminate.
6. Choose Get Info from the File menu.
7. Click on the upper-left box with the icon and paste (Command+V) the copied color.

Now, the Finder will use the bit of copied color as the icon and your file or folder appears on your desktop as just a floating name.

Use Mac OS 9.1 Keyboard Shortcuts

You can learn keyboard shortcuts by reading the menus in your Mac system. If you want the shortcut short course, though, here are some obscure but oh-so-useful 9.1 keyboard shortcuts:

- **Command+Delete:** Send the selected file or application to the Trash.
- **Command+Option+O:** Open a file or folder while closing the Finder window that contains the file.
- **Any letter key:** Takes you to the first file or folder in a Finder window that begins with that letter. To be more accurate, type the first few letters of the file name.
- **Command+Shift+3:** Snaps a picture of your screen and stores it on your hard drive as Picture 1, Picture 2, and so on.
- **Command+Click window title bar:** Displays a pop-up menu showing the file path of the selected folder's location.

Ready to Dance to iTunes?

At MacWorld Expo 2001, Apple debuted iTunes. The CD-writing features work with the CD-R in the Power Mac G4/466, G4/533, and G4/667 as well as a long list of third-party CD burners (check the list at `www.apple.com/itunes/compatibility`). iTunes can organize your playlists and convert your files to MP3. What's more, it's free (for now, anyway)! Download your copy at `www.apple.com`.

MAKE MAC OS X YOUR OWN

Mac OS X represents a brave new world for Apple aficianadas (and aficianados, too). Mac on the outside, UNIX on the inside, this Mac OS is fast, strong, and more media-savvy than any of its predecessors. This section presents some of TechTV's best tips for new Mac OS X users. You'll also find a few not-so-well-known tricks that might be news even to world-weary Mac OS X pioneers.

Say Yes to iTools

When you install Mac OS X, say yes when it asks whether you want to set up an iTools account. Apple introduced the iTools suite of online tools with Mac OS 9; the suite includes a free Mac.com e-mail address, a browser content filter for kids, and 20MB of free Internet storage in iDisk. After you create your iTools account, mount your iDisk by choosing iDisk from the Go menu. You can copy files to it, but you'll also find some tools already inside. The software folder, for example, lets you access a number of useful programs from Apple and other vendors (don't worry; none of this software counts toward your 20MB of free storage).

Make Friends with the Command Line

Mac OS X is based on FreeBSD UNIX, which gives Mac OS X the capability to multitask, use multiple processors more efficiently, and accommodate multiple users. To take full advantage of Mac OS X, you need to come to terms with the UNIX that lies within—and that means learning to use the command line.

Don't Have a Fatal Experience in the Terminal App

Take care when you're in the Mac Terminal application. You can do a lot of damage to your system in the Terminal—damage that no one can undo. To be safe, don't log on as root if you plan to tinker with system configuration files. And make copies of any files you plan to change, so you have a backup if something goes wrong.

First, find the Terminal application in Mac OS X (it's in the Utilities folder of the Applications folder). When you get comfy in the Terminal, try these helpful commands you can run in the command line of Mac OS X:

- **Telnet** allows you to access other computers on the Internet with command-line access. Enter the command **telnet** followed by the name of the remote machine you want to log in to (for example, type **telnet remote1**). This command works only if the machine you try to log in to is running a telnet server.
- **Kill** stops out-of-control applications, or just kills the dock. To use it, run "ps -u" first, so you can get a list of the processes that are running. Note the process ID number of the application you want to kill, and then type **kill*processidnumber*.** To verify that the kill command worked, run "ps -u" followed by the process ID number.
- **Who** lets you find out who is on your system. If you simply use the command "w," you can find out what they're doing and how long they've been on.

- **Tar** makes archives of documents or opens up .tar files. Tar is an archive tool used within Linux (think of it as the StuffIt of the UNIX world). The generic syntax for tar is **tar [options]** ***filenames***.
- **Compress** reclaims hard drive space by compressing specified files. To use compress, type **compress*filename***. The compressed file has a *.z extension, so you can identify that it's in a compressed state.
- **Cp** lets you copy files the UNIX way. To use this command, type **cp*filedestination***, where *filedestination* is the drive or storage medium to which you want to copy the file.

Find Out What Your Mac Is Made Of

You should be able to handle Mac OS X if you have a G3 system. If you have an older model with a G3 upgrade card, it might not support the new OS. Even if you meet the minimum system requirements, your system might not run Mac OS X with any sort of reasonable speed. Apple says you need at least a 400 MHz processor and 192MB of memory if you want to operate Mac OS X at peak performance.

To find out what's under the hood of your older Mac, go to the Apple menu and open About This Computer. Click once on your hard drive icon, then choose Get Info from the File menu. Get Info shows you what kind of processor speed and how much RAM your machine offers, as well as how much hard disk space you have available.

In Mac OS 9, go to the Apple menu and select the Apple System Profiler for a comprehensive look at your hardware, software, and firmware.

Your Favorite Mac OS 9 Features in Mac OS X

Many folks go gaga over Mac OS X—after all, it's the first Mac OS rewrite since the Mac was released in 1984. Most Mac users quickly discovered that the Mac OS X user interface performs differently (or should we say different) than the good old Mac they were accustomed to. To keep the best of the old with the rest of the new, use these tweaks. These changes are only cosmetic; they leave you with full access to all of Mac OS X's raw power.

Ready to Move to Mac OS X?

Mac OS X requires a G3 machine or better with 128MB of RAM and 1.5GB of hard disk space. iMacs, iBooks, and G4s of any type will do. G3 PowerBooks made before September 1998 will run Mac OS X as well. If you have a G3 desktop system, chances are it will support Mac OS X, but check Apple's Mac OS X Web page to be sure (www.apple.com/macosx).

The first thing to change is the Mac OS X Dock. The Dock holds minimized windows and stores shortcuts to apps, files, and folders. This new widget has its uses, but you don't need to see it all the time. Here's how to slide the dock out of the way when you don't need it:

1. Open the Dock Preferences window by choosing Apple menu, Dock, Dock Preferences.
2. Check "Automatically hide and show the Dock."

Why "See You Later," and Not "Goodbye"?

So why shouldn't you ditch the Dock altogether? Because it's great to have the Dock available in case an application gets temporarily stalled (or does something funky to stall the user interface). If that happens, you can use the Dock to switch to another application and keep working while Mac OS X sorts out the mess.

Now, the Dock's there when you need it, and gone when you don't. How about fixing Mac OS X's Finder windows? They don't behave like their Mac OS 9 counterparts. For example, when you open an item in a window, the contents of that item open up in the same window rather than open a new window.

You can change the Finder's behavior on a window-by-window basis by clicking the clear button at the far right end of a window's title bar (or pressing Cmd+B or choosing View, Hide Toolbar). If the Toolbar is hidden, double-clicking a folder in the window opens a new window. If the Toolbar is visible, the current window switches to display the contents of the folder you're opening.

Get to the Root of Things

Because Mac OS X has BSD UNIX as its underlying operating system, it has all the features of a true UNIX OS—except for one thing. The root account is disabled by default. The login you create when you install Mac OS X is an administrator account. That gives you most of the capabilities that a root account would have, but it doesn't turn over absolute power. To totally control your system, you need to log in as the root. To turn the root account back on, follow these directions:

1. Go into Applications, Utilities folder, and select the NetInfo Manager application.

Make Your Mac As Solid As a Brick House

Because it runs atop BSD UNIX, Mac OS X has a very capable built-in firewall. Unfortunately, turning on and configuring the firewall is a job for a UNIX expert—unless you use BrickHouse. This free script lets you easily turn on Mac OS X's built-in protection (download your copy at `personalpages.tds.net/~brian_hill/brickhouse.html`). BrickHouse is a shareware product, so pay the $25 if you decide to keep and use it.

2. Select Security from the Domain menu and click Authenticate.
3. After you enter an administrator password, select Security from the Domain menu again and click "Enable Root User."
4. Assign this account a secure password.

You should continue to use your normal user account most of the time. When you do need to get to the root account, you'll be glad you activated it.

Pin Your Mac Dock Where You Want It

Apple doesn't tell you about two features of the Mac OS X Dock: First, you can move the Dock to any edge of the screen. Second, you can pin its point of origin to either end of the edge, or you can center it. Both of these features come in handy for making the Mac Dock work the way you want it to, but neither of them arrives activated in the release version of Mac OS X.

Turn on these features with a free program called Docking Maneuvers by Austin Shoemaker (find it at `homepage.mac.com/isleep`). To move the Dock, control-click on the divider between applications and documents in the dock, and then select your preferred orientation. The selection won't "stick," so you'll have to do it each time you restart.

IT'S ALL ABOUT POWER AND SPEED

No matter how much you appreciate your operating system's personality and sense of humor, what you really want in a steady OS is power and speed. In this section, learn TechTV's techniques for pushing the Mac OS envelope. From transferring favorite features from an older version to tweaking the OS for maximum speed, the following tips will help you get the most from your Mac OS—every day, every way.

Create a Power Key in Mac OS 9

If you love your Power Mac G4 but miss using the power key on the keyboard for shut down, this is the tip for you. You can get the power key action back by creating an AppleScript. Here's how:

1. Launch the AppleScript editor from the Apple Extras folder.
2. Type the following four simple lines:

```
tell application "Finder"
activate
shut down
end tell
```

3. Save the script as a Classic applet.
4. Go to the Keyboard control panel and click the Function Keys button.
5. Assign your new script to a function key.

Now, you can shut your computer down simply by pressing that function key. That's a fast, easy, and elegant Mac tool you've just created!

Stop That Processor Cycling Slow Down in Mac OS 9

Does your slot-loading iMac or second-generation Power Mac G4 slow down when the mouse isn't moving? If so, the reason might be the Energy Saver features in your system. To eliminate this particular slow-down scenario, Apple suggests you turn off the Allow Processor Cycling option in the Energy Saver control panel. Here's how:

1. Open the Energy Saver control panel.
2. Click the Advanced Settings tab.
3. Uncheck Allow Processor Cycling.
4. Close the control panel.

Auto-Start Programs in Mac OS X

Mac OS 9 users are familiar with a little folder called Startup Items that's located in the System Folder. Any alias in Startup Items opens automatically when the system starts up. Mac OS X doesn't have a Startup Items folder, but you can still get files to autolaunch when you boot up. Here's how:

1. Open the Login system preferences file.
2. Click the Login Items tab.
3. Click Add to add items.

If you don't want to see the program launching, just click the Hide box. And if your Mac has multiple users, each of you can have your own set of startup items.

Looking for Location Manager?

Are you Mac OS 9 users wondering where the function went in OS X? Don't worry, it's still there. To find it, open System Preferences and select the Network item. Next, click Location, and then drop down and select New Location. When you press the Save button after you've named a location, you assign to that location all the network settings you choose. You can choose the location from the Apple menu to automatically change settings.

Boost Your Mac's RAM

It's not hard to install more RAM in your Mac, but you do need to be sure you get the right sort of RAM for your computer. EveryMac.com (www.everymac.com) delivers the specs on Mac systems, including information on pricing, compatibles, and upgrade cards. Click through to the listings to find your system, and you'll get the skinny on what's up in your Mac—fast and easy (see Figure 10.1).

Don't Give Your System Static!

Before you open your computer, ground yourself, so you can drain off any static charge between you and your system. Static electricity won't hurt you, but it can fry your computer chips. The best way to protect your chips is to use a grounding strip—you can find one at almost any electronic store for just a few dollars. If you can't find one, touch a metal part of your computer's case to discharge any static *before* you touch anything inside the machine.

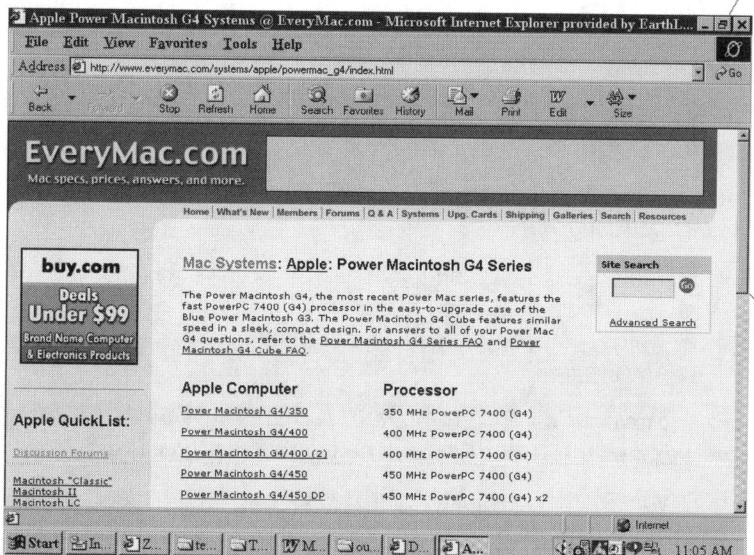

Figure 10.1

EveryMac.com can tell you how much RAM you can install, what type of RAM you need, and a few dozen other useful specs on your Mac system. It's worth your while to pay a quick visit to this site *before* you buy RAM, so you're sure you get the right goods for your system.

When you have your DIMM (Dual Inline Memory Module) or SIMM (Single Inline Memory Module) RAM, install it like this:

1. Open your computer case (your manual will come in handy here).
2. DIMM slots are black and have tabs at each end. Insert the DIMM upright. Release the tabs and gently push the DIMM into place. The tabs should snap up, lock, and hold the memory into place.

   SIMM slots are white and have clips at each end. Insert the SIMM at a 45-degree angle and gently tilt it up until it's upright. The clips should snap into place and hold the SIMM firmly in its slot. If it wobbles or seems uneven, release the clips and try again.
3. After you add the RAM, turn on your Mac. It should recognize the new memory automatically. Again, if you run into any glitches, check your manual for any exceptions to this basic installation technique.

LIGHTNING ROUND Q&A WRAP-UP

Can I customize my Toolbar in Mac OS X?

You can add icons to that handy Toolbar at the top of the Mac OS X file browser to make it your own. Drag the files and folders to the Toolbar and drop them there. Here's a step-by-step for adding specialized buttons and functions to customize your toolbar:

1. Click the Desktop, click the View menu, and select Customize Toolbar.
2. Drag the icons you want to the Toolbar.
3. Drag the ones you don't need off at the same time.
4. Click Done when you're through.

Entourage has become agonizingly slow on my Mac. Any ideas for troubleshooting this slowdown?

If your Entourage is slow, you might need to rebuild the program's database. To do that, hold down the Option key as you launch the application. Start with Typical, which compacts the database. If that doesn't work, back up your files and try Advanced.

I want to upgrade my RAM to 128MB. I currently have 64MB, 66 Mhz SDRAM. Can I mix it with 100 Mhz RAM and accomplish the same results?

RAM is your Mac's workspace. Your CPU takes data off a drive (typically the hard drive) and temporarily stores it in RAM. Mixing RAM with different speeds can be tricky. Always check your motherboard manual, your computer manual, or other spec source before adding RAM. Although the combination you're considering should work, not all RAM combos do, so you need to check before you mix RAM.

SDRAM synchronizes itself with your CPU's motherboard speed (bus speed). Even if your computer has a 66 MHz bus, you can install higher-speed RAM. The 100 MHz RAM you're proposing will slow down and work just fine.

CHAPTER 11

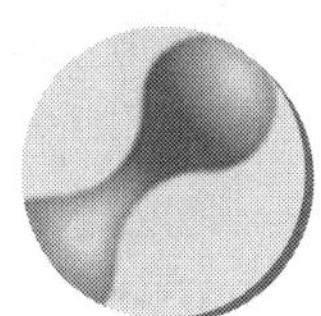

LIVING THE GOOD GNU/LINUX

- Step through a GNU/Linux installation
- Tweak your GNU/Linux setup
- Keep GNU/Linux healthy

GNU/Linux is a brave new world, but it isn't for everybody. This isn't your huge, well-padded, comfort-ride sort of operating system. GNU/Linux is designed for users who crave power, speed, and performance—and who want to be able to pop the hood and poke around in the engine once in a while, too.

Lots of people are just approaching the "experimental stage" of their GNU/Linux relationship. So, this chapter begins by walking you through a basic GNU/Linux installation. If you've been thinking about using GNU/Linux, look at how simple the install can be. Those of you who are up and running in GNU/Linux can skip the first section and move right into the later info for customizing your GNU/Linux ride, along with TechTV's best advice for routine system maintenance and troubleshooting.

MAKING THAT FIRST GNU/LINUX INSTALLATION

If you've decided to give GNU/Linux a test-drive, you might be confused by the variety of GNU/Linux distributions that are available and a bit skittish about the installation process. Well, don't be; the information in this chapter walks you through the process—painlessly.

Under the surface, every GNU/Linux distribution is basically the same. Applications designed for GNU/Linux run on any distribution and work the same way. Commands that perform certain tasks (such as file management) or that configure the system are executed the same way from distribution to distribution. The differences show up in the installation process, the applications that you install, the level of technical support, and the extra programs and utilities that work with each specific distribution.

When choosing a GNU/Linux distribution, consider how you will use the operating system, its ease of installation, and the availability of technical support. Several Web sites offer help selecting a GNU/Linux distribution:

- Linux Headquarters, at `www.linuxhq.com/dist.html`, provides a short review of the popular GNU/Linux distributions and links to the distributions' Web sites.
- Linux Links, at `www.linuxlinks.com/Distributions`, also lists GNU/Linux distributions with links to each distribution's Web site.
- The Linux Documentation Project has a HOWTO at `www.linuxdoc.org/HOWTO/Distributions-HOWTO/index.html` that provides detailed descriptions of the most popular distributions, along with links to Web sites and mailing lists.

After you have downloaded a GNU/Linux distribution from the Internet or have purchased a set of CDs, you're ready to start the installation. Before you begin, read and reread the installation instructions for your particular distribution of choice. Keep in mind that every GNU/Linux distribution is slightly different, so don't be put off if your distribution instructions aren't quite the same as the instructions in this chapter. The general installation is similar in all GNU/Linux flavors, so the information here can help any first-timer get started.

Don't Be Afraid of GNU/Linux

Don't be afraid of installing and using GNU/Linux, but remember to look before you leap onto this OS bandwagon. Although TechTV doesn't necessarily recommend GNU/Linux for casual home users, if you're running a network, you should know about it. Before you take the GNU/Linux plunge, answer these questions: Do you know how to partition your hard drive? Can you find your way around your BIOS? Are you comfortable setting up user accounts? Do you know how to write scripts or edit configuration files? Are you attached to a GUI, or can you find your way around a computer in a text-only environment? If you can answer "yes," then you should be right at home in the GNU/Linux world. If not, you might want to reconsider the move.

Getting Ready for the Install

Installing GNU/Linux used to be a…well…challenging experience. That was then and this is now. Newer distributions of GNU/Linux are much easier to install, and they do a good job of reading your system hardware specs and recommending options. That said, you should get your Linux ducks in a row before you launch into the installation. Here are TechTV's recommendations for your pre-Linux prep:

- **Know your system:** Although most modern GNU/Linux installs automatically detect your hardware configuration, you'll need to know what's in your machine if you hit a snag. At a minimum, you should know the names of your monitor and your graphics accelerator, what graphics chip you have on your video board, the amount of video memory, and what native resolutions and color depths it supports. And if you *really* want to be prepared, be sure you know the preferred refresh rates for your monitor.

Your Hardware Lists Are Waiting

You'll find hardware information in the documentation that came with your computer. If Microsoft Windows is installed on the computer, you can print the Device Manager list from the System Properties dialog box. To be sure you have hardware that is compatible with GNU/Linux, read the hardware compatibility list at the Linux Documentation Project (`www.linuxdoc.org/HOWTO/Hardware-HOWTO/index.html`).

- **Get some written guidance:** GNU/Linux documentation and an independent guide to GNU/Linux installs will be your best friends during installation. Most GNU/Linux distros—downloads or purchased CDs—include documentation. Go for a beginner's guide, such as *The Complete Idiot's Guide to Linux*, as your "book companion" during the installation.
- **Choose your distribution:** You have a world of distributions to choose from. TechTV reviewers recommend a version of Mandrake for first-timers because the installations are so simple (`www.linux-mandrake.com`). Mandrake is based on the oh-so-popular Red Hat distribution, but it's served up with the user-friendly KDE GUI (and you can find great user information and resources at the Red Hat support site). Read more about KDE and other GNU/Linux desktop environments in "Choosing a Desktop for GNU/Linux," later in this chapter.
- **Decide how you're going to boot:** If you're installing it on a machine with Windows or another operating system, you'll either need to make some partitioning decisions regarding the hard drive or add a second hard drive to the computer before you start. Windows must be installed on the first partition of the first hard drive before you install Linux. Then, you can install Linux on the second partition or the second hard drive. This way, LILO and GRUB, the two Linux multi-boot managers that allow you to choose which operating system to use, can easily find both operating systems. Another option is to install GNU/Linux as the sole operating system on the computer. Most folks say you're better off starting with a Windows-free system.

- **Begin the partitioning:** Whether you're going multi-boot or not, you'll need to partition your hard drive. At minimum, create a boot partition in the first 1024 cylinders, a swap partition, and a native partition. You also might want to consider a second native partition in which user files can be stored. Some GNU/Linux distributions will nondestructively partition a hard drive during the installation. If your distribution doesn't do this, several commercial programs let you partition without losing data. If you're still relatively new to partitioning, you should try Partition Magic (`www.powerquest.com`).

Don't Forget to Scan and Defrag That Disk

Before you partition a hard drive that contains Windows, run Scandisk and the Disk Defragmenter.

It's on TechTV

If you just need to update your Linux kernel, you don't have to go through an entire distribution installation. If that's the case, we have the how-to on that process all lined out for you. Visit `www.techtv.com`, and search on "Screen Savers: Update the Linux Kernel." In that article, we walk you through the four simple steps of kernel updating, and give you important sidebar info that can keep the process simple *and* effective.

Installing GNU/Linux in Seven Simple Steps—Really!

Ready to install GNU/Linux? Let's check on that: Do you have your installation boot disk? How about the manual and HOWTO pages for that distribution? And is that beginner's GNU/Linux guide we recommended lying close at hand? And you've researched (and written down) all of your system and hardware information, too, right? Okay, then, you *are* ready to install, so let's go:

1. Boot up for the installation and get into BIOS: Try pressing F1, F2, or the Delete key during startup. Or look for a "Click X now to change system settings" message. We like installing GNU/Linux from a bootable CD, so we don't have to hassle with an installation boot disk first. If your BIOS is willing, make your CD-ROM the first boot device, the floppy your second, and the hard drive the third stop (that option is under Advanced Setup in some BIOS setups, and BootTK in others).
2. Answer the distribution installer's questions (and there are plenty of questions). What language would you like? What keyboard do you have? Do you want a two- or a three-button mouse? Which time zone do you live in? If you can't answer those questions, you need to go back and do more research. The questions get more difficult, too: Are you installing a workstation or server? (You're probably installing a workstation.) Is the computer attached to a network? What desktop

environment do you want to use? (TechTV pros recommend KDE.) Read the distribution manual as you go along.

3. Create your accounts. Note the "s" on the end of that last word; GNU/Linux is a multi-user environment, so you'll need to create more than one user account. The Root account is assigned to the person responsible for system administration tasks. The Root account can do anything on the system, from setting up accounts to erasing things that shouldn't be erased. You won't want to do your daily computing in the Root account, so create at least one "daily use" account, as well. And if more than one person will be using the system, create an account and password for each user.
4. If your GNU/Linux install hasn't detected the graphics card and monitor in your system, it will ask you to tell it what it's talking to. Grab that pre-install system inventory you pulled together, and give it the info it asks for.

Get Your GUI

If your distribution skips step 4, you will need to run a configuration utility after the installation to set up the graphical display system so that you can use KDE, Gnome, and all the cool GUI applications. Refer to the distribution installation manual for help with the graphics configuration.

5. Get your X Window configuration out of the way. Your GNU/Linux distribution probably has identified your graphics hardware, and all you have to do is click the Test This Configuration button. If the autodetection didn't work, though, you'll need to enter the specs that describe how you want your monitor to run. Again, use the information you put together before the install. But don't skip the configuration test; otherwise, you might find yourself in command-line mode trying to configure X Window so you can see it.
6. Hurry up and wait. Most installs take about 30 minutes to an hour, and you spend a good part of that time waiting for files to copy from the installation CD. You can spend this time reading over your GNU/Linux guide, right? When the Installation is Complete message pops up, the copying's over. Remove the installation CD.

What's X Window?

X Window is the GUI shell that accompanies most GNU/Linux distributions. A window manager, such as KWM for KDE or Sawfish for Gnome, mates with the X Window System, which serves as a low-level interface between the hardware (video card, mouse, and so on) and the Linux kernel. In other words, the X Window System shell acts as a translation layer between the command line and a window manager. The window manager dishes up the actual GUI to the end user. The window manager is responsible for controlling the look, placement, and display of program windows.

7. Reboot your new GNU/Linux machine. You'll see a long line of text scrolling up the screen. When it stops, you should see a text-based login prompt (localhost login:) or a brightly colored desktop with a login screen.

Don't Forget to Remove the Install CD!

After you configure X Window during your GNU/Linux installation, don't forget to remove the installation CD before you reboot. If you don't, instead of booting into your new GNU/Linux install, you'll run the setup all over again. Sounds like something you'd never forget, but take it from the TechTV pros, lots of folks have.

Congratulations, you've installed GNU/Linux! When the text prompt comes up, type your username, and then your user password. After you log in, type **startx**. That launches the window manager or desktop environment you selected during the installation; now you're ready to roll. If your installation displays a login screen, use the menus to select a window manager or desktop environment, and then type in your username and password.

WORKING GNU/LINUX YOUR WAY

If you have GNU/Linux up and running on your machine, you probably are looking for information on how to make it run as efficiently as possible. You've come to the right place. GNU/Linux is an incredibly well-developed OS, because lots of developers have spent lots of time tinkering with this code to make GNU/Linux distributions as slick and powerful as possible. In this section, we share our favorite GNU/Linux tips. Although some of them require you to edit some of the system files, no overt geekiness is necessary to use these tips.

Set Your GNU/Linux Startup for X Windows

The default installation of some versions of GNU/Linux drops you into a command-line shell when it starts up. You type **startx**, and you enter the X Window System GUI. If you're comfortable modifying the system files, though, you can skip the start-up command line and launch directly into X Window after you launch GNU/Linux and log in to your user account. To modify the files, follow these steps:

1. At the command line, type **su** and log in as root.
2. Use a text editor (such as Emacs, Vi, or Pico, for example) to open the /etc/inittab file.

   Notice the following lines close to the top of /etc/inittab:

   # Default runlevel. The runlevels used by RHS are

   #   0 - halt (Do NOT set initdefault to this)

   #   1 - Single-user mode

```
#     2 - Multiuser, without NFS (the same as 3, if you do not have networking)
#     3 - Full multiuser mode
#     4 - Unused
#     5 - X11
#     6 - Reboot (do NOT set initdefault to this)
# id:3:initdefault:
```

3. Change the **3** in the last line (**id:3:initdefault:**) to the number that corresponds to X11 mode (5 in our example, which is a Red Hat system).
4. Save the file and restart. You will be presented with a graphical login screen where you can supply your username and password. When your login is verified by the system, you should boot automatically into the X GUI.

Choosing a Desktop for GNU/Linux

You can choose from a lot of different window managers for GNU/Linux (a window manager is an application that controls the windows, icons, and other cute tricks that put the "G" in GUI). To make your GNU/Linux experience even more enjoyable, you can add a desktop environment. The two most popular are Gnome (GNU Network Object Model Environment) and KDE (K Desktop Environment). Both of these apps are free, and they're made up of source code that is licensed under the GNU General Public License (GPL), meaning that anyone can contribute to their development. That also means that these GUIs have been through a thorough working over, and you can find plenty of information and support resources for them online.

Tried the Linux PDA?

In May 2001, Agenda Computing released the industry's first handheld Linux devices—the VR3 and VR3R. The VR3 is about the same size as a Palm V, and Agenda Computing says it will run three to four weeks on two AAA batteries. The monochrome touch screen displays 16 shades of gray at 160×240 resolution. The VR3 is powered by a 66MHz 32-bit NEC VR4181 MIPS processor with 8MB of RAM and 16MB of flash memory. The VR3 comes with all the applications you would expect in a PDA, including Contacts, Schedule, E-Mail, and so on, and an impressive number of games. This handheld has some room for improvement; the screen isn't very sensitive, so entering data can be difficult. And the VR3 is underpowered, so launching and running multiple apps can be a painfully slow process. On the upside, though, the VR3 includes a serial cradle to synchronize data with several apps (including Microsoft Outlook), and—at $250—its price is right.

KDE (shown in Figure 11.1) is arguably the most popular GNU/Linux desktop; it's mature, stable, and packaged with a lot of GNU/Linux distributions, so it's undergone plenty of debugging and tweaking. KDE has a very Windows-like presentation, so it makes a good "easing over" application for former Windows users. But KDE can be a memory hog, so don't opt for this desktop if you don't have plenty of memory to spare.

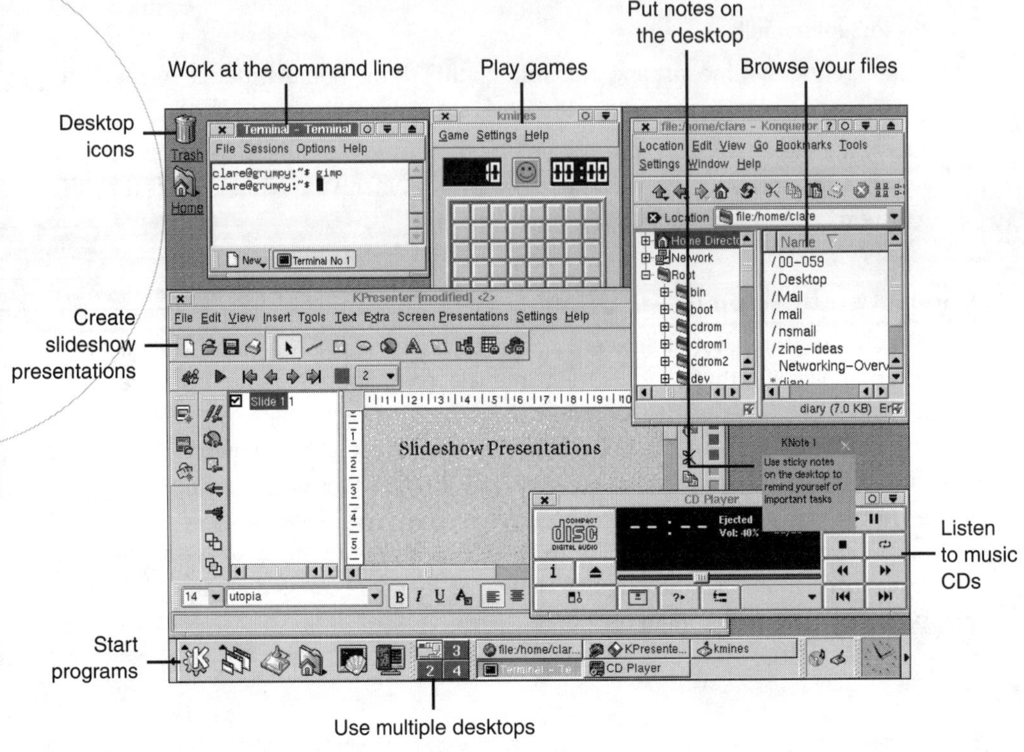

Figure 11.1

The KDE desktop is packed with a variety of applications.

Gnome (pronounced "gah-nome" and illustrated in Figure 11.2) is a very cool desktop that's also an easy learn for most Windows users. Gnome was designed under a Common Object Request Broker Architecture; as a result, objects within different applications running in Gnome are compatible. So if you want to open a spreadsheet in a text document, you shouldn't have any problems.

But don't think your options are limited to KDE and Gnome. These are the two most popular desktop environments, bundled with many distributions, but remember that choice is what drew you to GNU/Linux in the first place. To read about and get a look at some of the many other desktop environments you can choose for your GNU/Linux computer, visit Window Managers for X (`www.plig.org/xwinman`). There, you'll find complete descriptions—and even screen shots—of a long list of window managers and desktop environments.

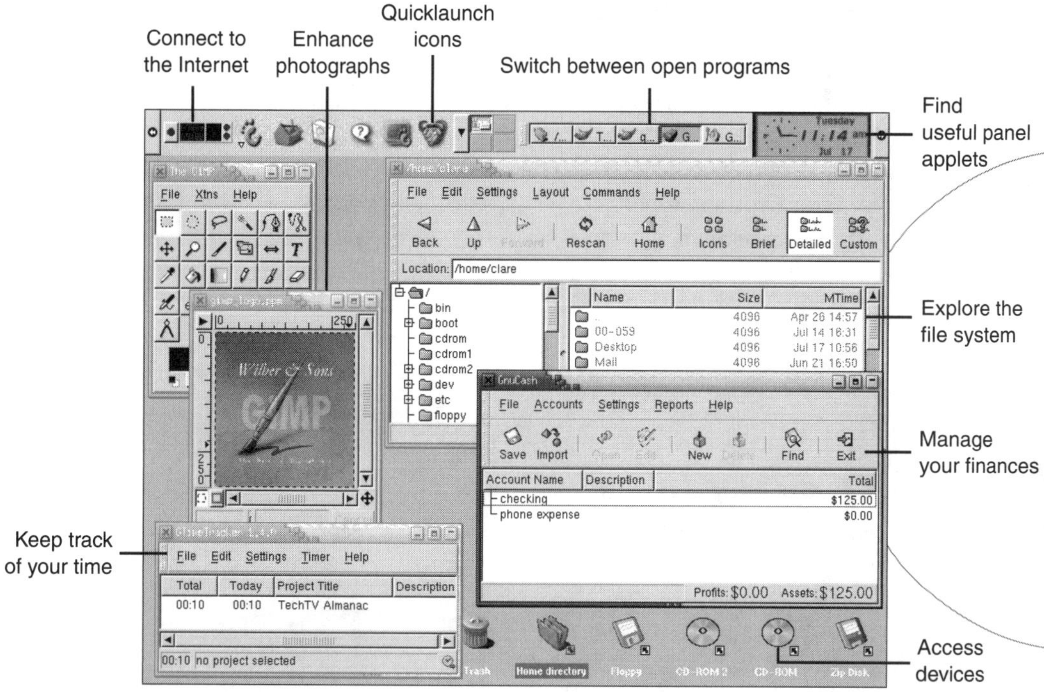

Quicklaunch icons

Connect to the Internet

Enhance photographs

Switch between open programs

Find useful panel applets

Explore the file system

Manage your finances

Keep track of your time

Access devices

Figure 11.2

You can easily customize the Gnome desktop to suit your computer style.

Jazz Up Your Desktop

Although there's a lot to love about KDE, the default installation of the desktop is pretty boring. And TechTV's reviewers aren't alone in thinking that, either—lots of Windows users who migrate to GNU/Linux yawn over KDE's fonts and background selection. But you can

Where Are Those Linux Drivers?

Finding drivers for Linux can be a time-intensive task. Unless a peripheral manufacturer creates a Linux driver for its products, it's left up to the GNU/Linux community to create and support device drivers. This means that if no one has felt the need to create a Linux driver for a product you want to use, you might be out of luck. Things are starting to change, though. Some companies, such as Creative Labs (`http://www.americas.creative.com/`), are offering Linux drivers for their products. But that won't solve all of your problems now; if you're embarking on a Linux driver hunt, our best advice is to start with sites such as `redhat.com`, `Freshmeat.Net`, `Linuxapps.com`, and any of the Linux newsgroups. Good luck!

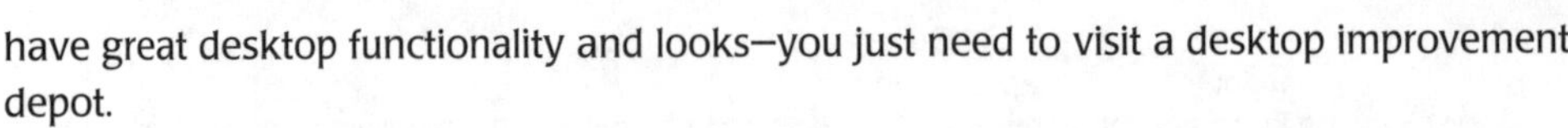

have great desktop functionality and looks—you just need to visit a desktop improvement depot.

To find just the kind of desktop redecorating, go to `www.themes.org` (see Figure 11.3). That site offers a number of window managers and themes for desktops, including KDE, Window Maker, and Enlightenment, to name just a few. So, if your desktop is achingly dull, you have no one to blame but yourself! Use a themes.org solution, and get happy with your desktop environment.

Figure 11.3

Themes.org offers desktop environments for KDE, Window Maker, LiteStep, and more. You can use the themes from this site to make your GNU/Linux desktop look just about any way you'd like.

Share Securely Over a Network with Samba

One great way to learn a lot about GNU/Linux is to work with Samba. Samba is a software suite licensed under the GNU General Public License that provides file and print services to SMB/CIFS clients, so it lets you share your Windows files in GNU/Linux. Samba's one of the best programs out there for use with GNU/Linux, but you need to be careful when you're customizing it for file sharing. Be sure your customization takes into account specifically what you want to share and with whom you'll be sharing it. And don't forget to set up password protection. Set up share security, so that each user has to input a password for each individual share. That's a lot more security than you get with simple user-passwords.

Reset Your Root Account Password

It happens. Time passes and you forget your root password. Don't sweat it. You can change your password. Here's how:

1. Start your computer and, at the LILO prompt, type **linux single**. Your machine starts in single-user mode.
2. Type **passwd** and enter the password that you want for your root user. A message appears, saying "All tokens updated successfully."
3. Shut down and restart the machine. When the machine restarts, log in as root with the new password.

KEEPING THINGS SAFE AND SECURE IN GNU/LINUX

GNU/Linux is an incredibly versatile and useful OS, but that doesn't mean it lets you turn your back on safety. In this section, we share our favorite techniques for keeping your time spent with GNU/Linux safe and secure.

Stay Safe While Surfing the Internet

One of the joys of GNU/Linux is that it provides a vast assortment of programs that protect you from the wired world. You'll find programs that filter spam from your e-mail, track activity between your modem and the Internet, and keep your e-mail private. Many of these programs are very small, and some work from the command line. Be sure to read the help documentation before you start using any program.

Surf Safely with a User Account

Never, never, never browse the Web when you are using the Root account. If someone does gain access to your computer, they will have complete access to every file and program installed. Always use a regular user account when connecting to the Internet.

Several GNU/Linux applications let you see exactly what is going back and forth between your computer and the wired world. To monitor your PPP connection, give wmnet a try. If you want to see what is going in and out of your Ethernet device, check out kdevmon. These tools allow you to measure your speed. If you want to see the route that your request for a Web page travels from your computer across the Internet to the server where the Web page resides, use Xt. Xt shows a graphical display of the traceroute on a picture of the Earth.

To keep prying eyes out of your computer while you surf, set up a firewall between you and the outside world. Many good firewalls for GNU/Linux are listed at `www.linux-firewall-tools.com`. Other GNU/Linux applications can detect when someone attempts to intrude on your computer to make an attack. One such program is Snort. Snort detects buffer overflows, port scans, CGI attacks, and more.

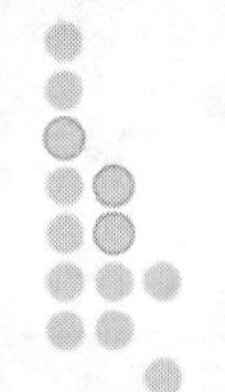

To keep people from snooping in on your e-mail while it's in transit, set yourself up with GnuPG. GnuPG is the free software version of PGP (Pretty Good Privacy). GnuPG encrypts e-mail messages and supplies you with a public key so that only authorized viewers can read e-mail messages that you send. To learn more about GnuPG, visit `www.gnupg.org`.

Spam in a can is a neat treat, but spam in your e-mail can be an annoyance. Several GNU/Linux programs will keep spam out of your inbox. SMTP-refuser allows you to reject mail from specific hosts and gives you the opportunity to send a message to the spammer. Some of the GNU/Linux e-mail programs include this feature.

Are you tired of banner ads and other junk showing in your Web browser? Junkbuster makes it easy to set up filters that destroy these ads before they are delivered to your computer.

Keep Your GNU/Linux System Healthy

You don't have to fly blind when you work in Linux. You can use some simple processes and system checks to keep tabs on what's happening in your GNU/Linux machine. Here are three ways you can keep your GNU/Linux system chugging along in good order:

1. **Use Top:** Run Top from the command line to get a good look at all the processes running on your computer (see Figure 11.4). If your system slows down, you can run Top to find out just what's behind that memory load. If you can find a runaway process that's sucking your system's speed, you can nip it in the bud and get your system back on track. (For more information on Top, see the second question in this chapter's "Lightning Round Q&A Wrap-Up".)
2. **Back up your configuration files:** Every GNU/Linux user should keep backups of important files, and the config files (like those in the /etc directory) are *really* important. If anything goes wrong with your GNU/Linux installation, you'll need backups of those config files to get things up and running again. The good news is that many text editors automatically back up any file you're editing. But you should do your own routine backup of your user files and of the /etc directory periodically, for safety's sake. Don't forget to back up on a removable media (such as a floppy or Zip disk), or a separate hard drive or partition, just to be sure your backup is available to you in case of a stall.
3. **Get familiar with Maintenance mode:** Maintenance mode, or single-user mode, lets you perform system maintenance without interruptions. You can access maintenance mode by typing **init 1** at the command line. If you want to reboot, you can access maintenance mode by typing **single** or ***kernelimagename*** **single** at the LILO boot loader prompt (*kernelimagename* represents the name of the kernel image that you assigned in your /etc/lilo.conf file). Press Enter, and you boot into maintenance mode.

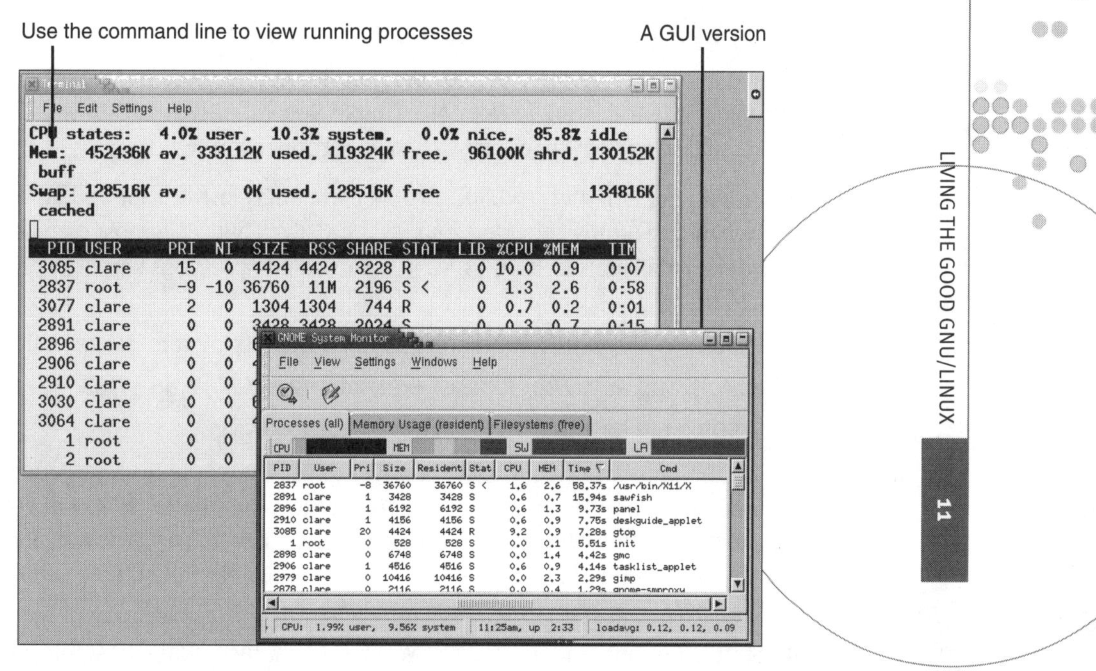

Figure 11.4

Top can be run from the command line or GUI versions that you might find easier to use.

Script Kiddies Infest GNU/Linux with Worms

According to security experts, GNU/Linux-damaging viruses are being pasted together from pieces of other programs by a growing group of low-tech, malicious hackers known as "script kiddies." Internet worms, such as the Ramen worm, infect Red Hat distributions. Although it isn't destructive, the Ramen virus sucks up a lot of system resources regenerating itself. A similar virus, called Lion, attacks GNU/Linux servers running a specific version of BIND (Berkeley Internet Name Domain). An infected GNU/Linux machine sends encrypted passwords to an e-mail account at China.com, where hackers can decrypt the passwords and gain root administrator-level access to a corporate network. Red Hat has made fixes for the Ramen virus available at its site (`www.redhat.com`), and a patch for the BIND flaw has been available from the Internet Software Consortium (`www.isc.com`) since January of 2001. But security experts warn that not enough people take the trouble to keep up with the latest patches and fixes to secure their GNU/Linux installations. Not a good idea—who wants worms in their system?

Getting Your Cable Modem to Work in GNU/Linux

You have a lot of cable modem providers out there to choose from, but how do you get your cable modem to work under GNU/Linux? Never fear—we can show you some simple steps for setting up that super-fast GNU/Linux connection.

1. Install your Ethernet card. Most cable companies install it for you, and most (depending on the provider) also install a 3Com NIC. The most common NIC for a home installation is 3C509B, so you should compile your kernel to reflect that NIC, and then….
2. Reboot. When your computer starts up, it will display a message similar to this:

   eth0: 3c509 at 0x220, 10baseT port, address 00 20 af a6 37 83, IRQ 5.

   3c509.c:1.16 (2.2) 2/3/98 becker@cesdis.gsfc.nasa.gov.
3. Get the paperwork your cable provider gave you (you got some papers, didn't you?) and find the list of information you need to connect to its network. This list should include DNS servers, how your IP is assigned (DHCP or static), and the gateway. If you don't have this information, look at your networking settings in Windows, or contact your cable provider.
4. Start Linuxconf, and go into Networking/Client tasks/Basic host information (as shown in Figure 11.5).

What Config Utility Does Your Distro Recommend?

If your GNU/Linux distribution doesn't use Linuxconf, consult the distribution documentation to see which configuration utility it recommends.

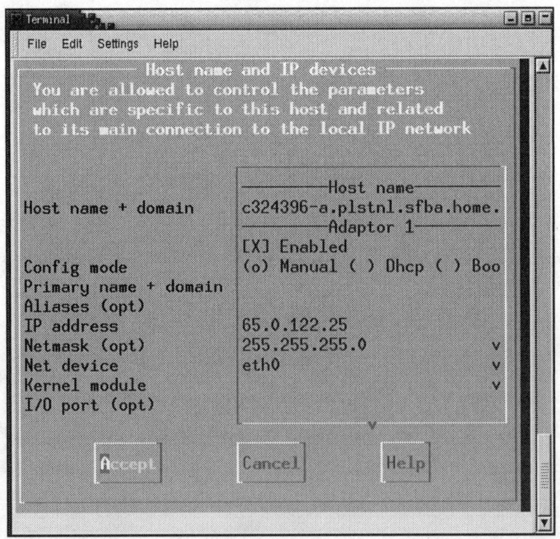

Figure 11.5

Use Linuxconf to set up the host information for your cable provider.

5. Enter the Config mode. Enter **Manual** if you have a static-assigned IP address, or **DHCP** if you have a dynamic-assigned IP address. If you don't know which one you have, ask your provider.
6. Enter the hostname. The cable will have listed your hostname on your information sheet—it'll be something like **c324396-a.plstn1.sfba.home.com**.
7. Type in the IP address *if* you entered **Manual** in step 5. It's a series of numbers similar to **65.0.122.25**. If you answered **DHCP** to the above, leave the IP address blank.
8. Set the Netmask to **255.255.255.0**, unless your instructions tell you to enter something else.
9. Set the Net device to **eth0** unless you have two NICs in your machine. If this is the second NIC, then set it to **eth1**.
10. Go to the nameserver specification section (shown in Figure 11.6), and set these items:

    default domain: Set this to the actual domain address, such as **plstn1.sfba.home.com**.

    nameserver 1: Set this as the primary DNS IP the cable provider gave you (for example, **24.4.0.26**).

    nameserver 2: Set this as the secondary DNS IP the provider gave you.

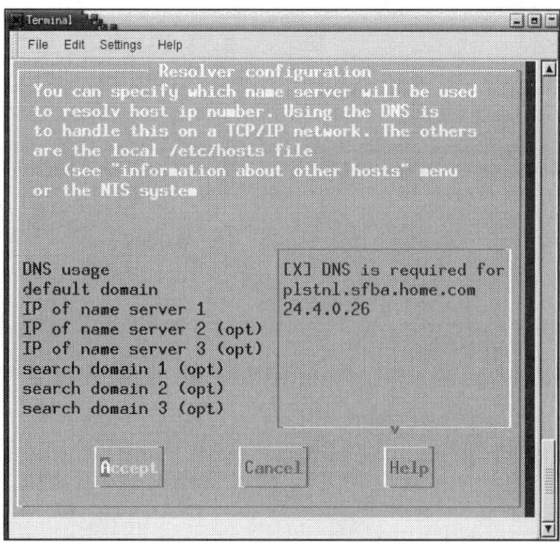

Figure 11.6

Provide Linuxconf with the resolver configuration information.

11. Go into the Routing and gateways section and edit these items:

    Default gateway: Enter the gateway address the provider gave you.

    Other routes: Select Add, and set the gateway as the IP address that the cable provider gave your modem. The destination is the gateway that you defined earlier, and the netmask is an optional setting.

12. Save everything and exit from Linuxconf.

How do you know whether your hook-up is a success? Just reboot your machine. All is well if, when it starts up, you see the message

```
Starting up eth0
```

LIGHTNING ROUND Q&A WRAP-UP

I have an old 486 running Red Hat Linux 6.0. I'm the only one using it, and it isn't online. I would like to boot directly to KDE, without entering a password. Can this be done and if so, how?

GNU/Linux (like all multiuser operating systems) has good reasons for requiring a password. First and foremost, when you start your system without a password you compromise security on that system. If you're on a network (including the Internet), people can enter your system freely and use it to hack other systems. In other words, unless you're on a standalone system, leave passwords on.

That said, you can get into a GNU/Linux system without using a password. You can use the single-user mode, for example, to enter your system without a password so you can modify scripts that don't work, reset the root password, and so on. To enter single-user mode, type **linux single** or **linux 1** at the LILO prompt.

To boot into single mode all the time (so you never have to use a password), follow these steps:

1. su to root and edit /etc/inittab
2. Change the runlevel command (id:3:initdefault:) to **id:1:initdefault:** (runlevel 1 is single-user mode).

This technique is useful (or advisable) only on non-networked machines. All network services are disabled and, on most Red Hat 6 systems, this startup leaves users with no X Windows access. That's probably because the start-up scripts aren't running. To get those services on track, you'll need to do a lot of shell script hacking. Check out the Linux Gazette for more info on that process (see the article at `www.linuxgazette.com/issue19/booting.html`).

I just started using my new 800MHz GNU/Linux machine. Occasionally, my system slows to a snail's pace. I can close programs or change the order of tasks, but I don't know what culprits are actually causing the slowdowns. How can I find out what tasks are dragging down my system resources?

There's one sure way to find out exactly what's causing your system to bog down, and that's by using a diagnostic tool called Top. Top works by reading information from the /proc filesystem, and then listing system resources and displaying a running account of processor activity in real time. Top sorts by memory use, shows you the most CPU-intensive tasks on the system, and lets you manipulate the system processes. You can even kill any process that's using up all your system resources.

Top is a standard feature of most Linux distributions, or you can download a really good GUI version from `ftp://ftp.gnome.org/pub/GNOME/stable/sources/gtop/`.

How do you set up a PPP connection on GNU/Linux?

A Point-to-Point Protocol (PPP) connection lets you connect your GNU/Linux PC to a PPP server, so you can access the resources of the network server to which it's connected. Or, you can make your GNU/Linux PC into a PPP server, so other computers can dial in and access the resources on that server or on your local network. Our experience has been that setting up PPP in GNU/Linux is relatively easy. The only major problem is the modem (or rather, the lack of a modem).

Some people who switch to GNU/Linux from Windows have a Winmodem. (The prefix "Win" means it's for Windows only.) A Winmodem is a modem without a UART (Universal Asynchronous Receiver Transmitter) or processor. Instead, it uses your computer's CPU to process the data. So far, drivers and software for Winmodems have been limited to the Windows OS. If you want to use PPP with GNU/Linux, check to see if your modem is a Winmodem. If it is, you'll need to replace it with a "real" modem (most external modems will do the job).

TechTV reviewers recommend X-ISP (`users.hol.gr/~dbouras/`), a dial-up networking tool for X Window. It uses the standard X-form interface, so it gives you a relatively anxiety-free PPP setup. X-ISP supports Linux 2.x (SuSE, Debian, Slackware, Red Hat), Sun OS 4.1.x, and Solaris 2.5.x, 2.6, and 2.7. You need to have X Window up and running. For more information, check out the Linux PPP How-to (available at `www.linuxdoc.org`).

PART III

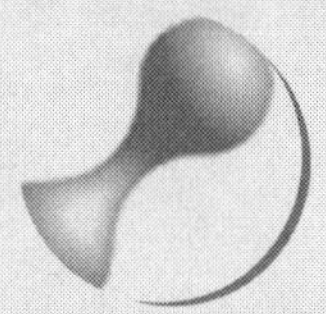

MAKING THE MOST OF SOFTWARE

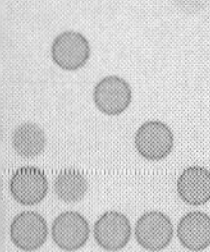

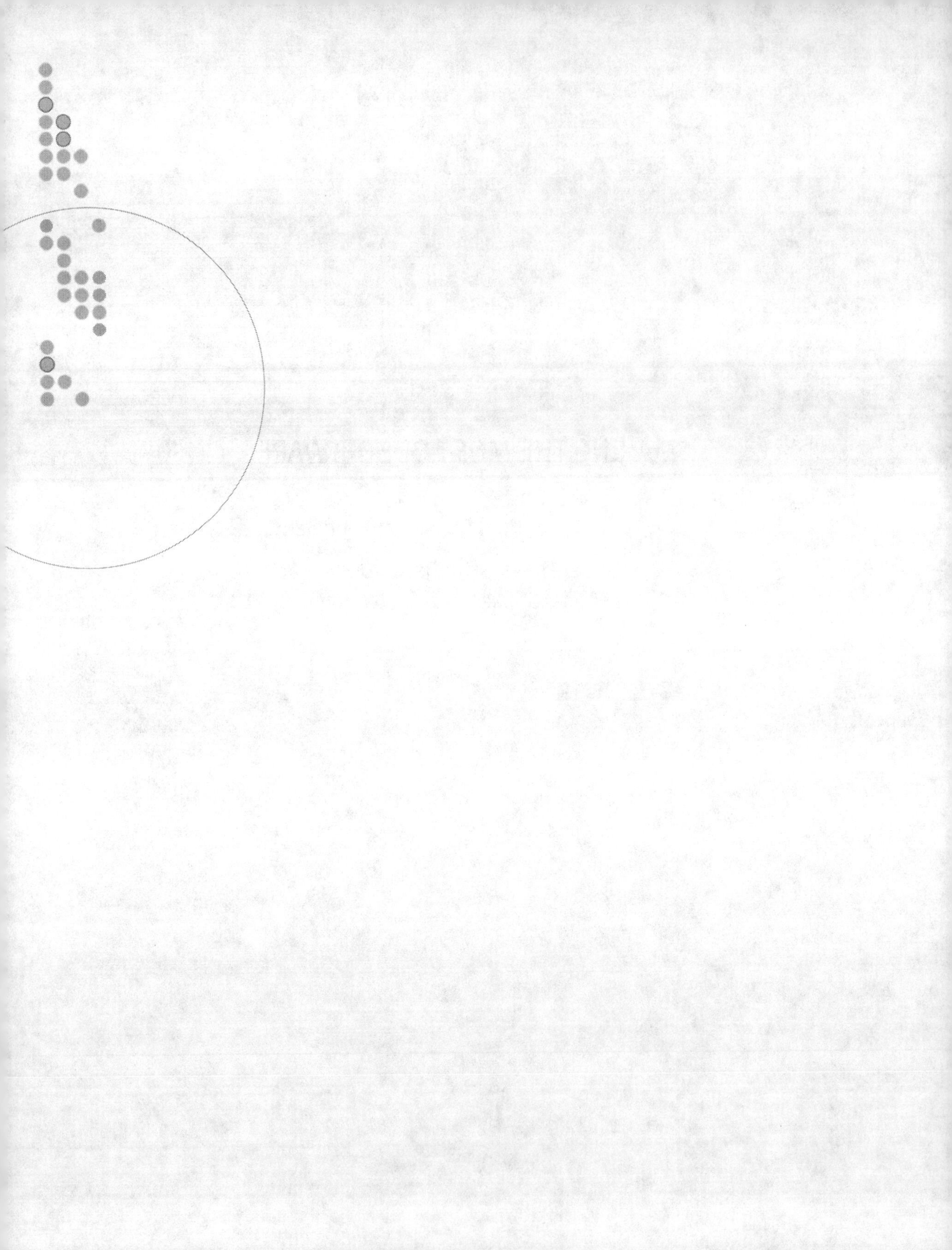

CHAPTER 12

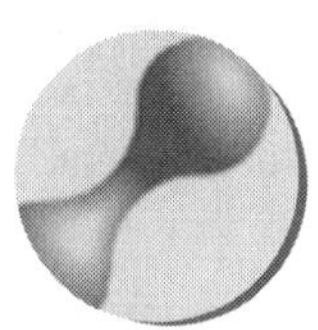

HARD FACTS ABOUT SOFTWARE

- Review the basics
- Go beyond the box
- Look ahead to a .Net world

These days, it doesn't pay to get attached to your software. Even operating systems update on an annual basis, putting every computer user in a non-stop upgrade mode. Although software upgrades are as much about revenues as they are about progress, software really does improve all the time. Most new releases are faster, more powerful, and easier to use than the versions they replace.

In this chapter, you find out what you need to know about software development, distribution, and delivery. What's the difference between buying a shrink-wrapped box-o-software and downloading the latest version from the manufacturer's Web site? And do you *need* to buy all that software, or would it be wiser to rent applications from one central source? If you gotta go for the upgrader's ride, why not sit in the driver's seat?

BACK TO THE BASICS

If you've ever felt that you couldn't get your arms around a piece of software, you were right! Even though it controls so much of what we do with our computers, software doesn't exist as a tangible "thing." Software really is just a set of computer instructions; a collection of magnetic bits, arranged in a pattern that sets off specific responses from a computer processor. Like the San Francisco fog that often drifts around the TechTV studios, software has a compelling presence, but it isn't permanent.

Putting a Face on Software

Programs are the software you're probably most familiar with. Every tool and utility on your computer is a software program, including your browser, word processor, MP3 manager, virus checker, accounting program, games—even your software installers and uninstallers. Programs communicate with each other to manage the functions of your system hardware and software. This communication takes place in a programming language, such as Visual C++, Basic, Pascal, Java, Perl, and (a TechTV favorite) Python.

Take a Closer Look at Free Software and the Open-Source Movement

When you discuss software in a crowd of developers, the topic eventually turns to the politics of the free software movement. Now, you might never get stuck—um, have the privilege of—talking to a crowd of developers, but the topic of free and open-source software definitely matters to you, too. Here's why.

The free software movement is all about making software freely available to anyone who wants it. Why is this a movement, and not a terrible business plan? First, because the free software followers believe that users should share programs they like with other users, and that selling software and preventing its free distribution pits users against users. Second, folks who develop and support free software can earn money by selling improvements to the software, products related to the free programs, and support services.

What About Firmware?

Now for the exception to every rule. System software is built right into a computer's hardware, so it's semi-tangible and semi-permanent. This type of software—known as *firmware*—is stored in ROM (read-only memory) and the BIOS in most PCs. Because it links with a computer's hardware, you don't get a new version of firmware every year. Instead, you keep the firmware you have until you update your computer (or its components).

Although many of the same folks who support free software also support the open-source movement, the two issues aren't identical. The term *open source* refers to software that is distributed freely in both source code and compiled format, with limited licensing restrictions. Developers and programmers can get in and tinker with the code as much as they'd like. Open-source software is certified by the Open Source Initiative (OSI), and you can learn much more about the certification standards by visiting the OSI site at `www.opensource.org`.

Sound like an operating system you may know and love? Linux is a prime example of an open-source product that works well—and it's safe to say that it has generated some good incomes, too. Followers of the open-source movement think it's downright wrong to keep code proprietary. Some compare it to refusing to list the ingredients on prepared foods or making a car with no dashboard controls.

Don't think of this as a lot of geek politics. The fate of the open source and free software movements will have a direct impact on the type of software you can lay your hands on and how much you'll pay for it. No matter which side of the fence you fall on, it's a good idea to follow developments in these issues.

It's on TechTV

Want to hear what Linus Torvalds, open-source proponent and creator of Linux, had to say to TechTV about the state of software today? You'll find an interview with Linus, along with more information and important links, at `www.techtv.com`.

Be Smart: Use Installers and Uninstallers

Installers and uninstallers are two of the most important pieces of software you use. Installers unpack and put away the files that make up any program you load and run on your computer. Above and beyond moving files from the source to your computer, installers also organize those files, pass important information about the files to your system (or Registry), and give you all the legal and oh-so-important registration information you must know about every program you install.

What Does Java Have to Do With It?

Programmers use Java, a network-oriented programming language, to create applications that can be downloaded from a network and run on almost any computing platform, using a *virtual machine*. True to its name, a virtual machine isn't a machine; it's a bunch of software that interprets instructions for whatever machine it runs on. Not only can Java run on any computer (with a virtual machine), it also delivers necessary software components, and it comes complete with built-in security features. Java is used a lot for Web-based content because it enables animation and heavy user interaction. Java might be the key to the ever-expanding world of ASPs (application service providers) by making software rental practical and affordable.

You've probably used an installer. If you have AutoRun set up on your machine, the installer usually kicks in the minute you load a software CD or floppy. When you download a program, you launch the installer by clicking a "start install" command button.

Because most installations send files to odd and obscure locations all over your computer system, it pays to go with a professional when you clean a program from your system. Uninstallers are the pros, here. They ferret out the odd little instructional files, icons, shortcuts, and other pithy bits the installer wove through your system.

If you don't get rid of that stuff, your computer's Registry, start menus, and so on think the program is still alive and well in your system. You run into system hangups and lingering options and icons, and those ghostly hauntings can get really annoying after a while. Worse yet, if you try to get in and strip out all of a program's files on your own, you might end up deleting a file your system uses to run other programs. Take it from TechTV; installers and uninstallers are your friends.

Don't make the mistake of believing you can get a program out of your system by deleting its directory. The traces will linger long after the most visible presence of that unwanted software is gone. If the program didn't come with its own uninstall package, get a third-party replacement such as CleanSweep (`www.symantec.com`) to track down and scour out all files associated with a program. If you use Windows, you also can use the Add/Remove programs option (shown in Figure 12.1) to uninstall most programs, but some folks say third-party utilities like CleanSweep do a more thorough job.

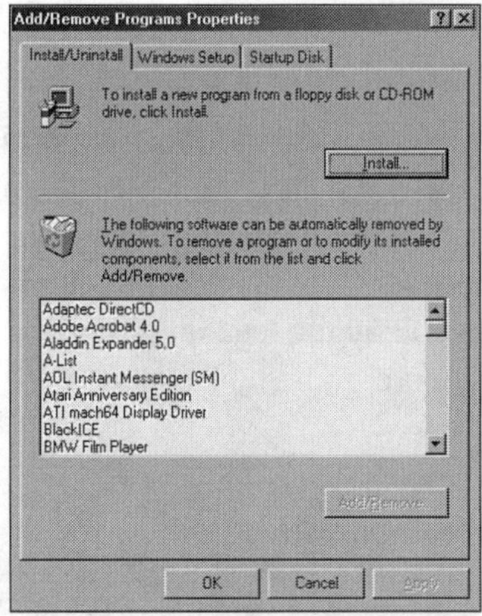

Figure 12.1

Use an install/uninstall program, such as Add/Remove Programs in your Control Panel, to safely put new programs on to or take programs off of your computer.

Don't Forget to Defrag

As you use your computer, files get spread out all over your hard disk drive. Your system slows down as it tries to track down the fragmented data it needs. When you defragment, you put all the files in one place, and that speeds up your disk access. You might think that a once-a-year defrag is adequate, but if you constantly add and delete programs and other data, you might need to defrag each month. That said, don't defrag more than you need to (your defrag program will tell you if a defrag is unnecessary). You'll wear out the disk and waste time, and there's a small chance that you could lose data in a defrag gone wrong.

Most Windows versions come with a built-in defrag program (find it by choosing Start menu, Programs, Accessories, System Tools, Disk Defragmenter). If you're using a Mac, you'll have to buy a defragmentation program, such as Norton Utilities (`www.symantec.com`).

In Search of an Installer

If you turned off AutoRun or if you're loading a program from a floppy disk, you might have to track down the installer yourself. Installers are easy to find. Search the program's directory for a file labeled install.exe or setup.exe. Double-click that file, and your install should be off and running.

LEARN YOUR SOFTWARE SOURCE

You can still buy most major software products in their shrink-wrapped state, but now you have other options. You can download software—and software updates—directly from the manufacturer or vendor Internet sites. Or, you can log on to the Web and *use* software without ever buying or installing it on your machine.

Check Out the Wares

So far, you've learned about software and firmware, but here are some "otherwares" you might run across in your software travels:

- **Freeware:** Software offered free of charge.
- **Shareware:** Software you can use freely during a trial period, after which you pay a registration fee to continue using the product.
- **Demoware:** An application "sample" that lets you test-drive a limited-feature model, to decide whether you want to pay up for the full-featured version.
- **Expireware:** Software (usually shareware) designed to "self destruct" after a trial-use period (determined either by date or number of uses).
- **Bloatware:** Software that hogs space on your computer system, usually with a lot of features that few people use.
- **Vaporware:** A software product that's announced but that never appears on the market. Companies might announce a non-existent product to gauge user interest or to undermine the success of a competitor.

Out of the Box: That "New Software" Smell

Shrink-wrapped software sets the gold standard for most computer users. When you buy a box-o-software off the shelf, you get the full monty, including installation instructions, user information, and registration and licensing documentation. Often you get a maintenance agreement that gives you access to a free or reduced-rate upgrade, should the product update within a given period of time (usually 12 to 14 months).

Any boxed software you buy contains licensing information that tells you how many computers you may install it on (usually just one) and the terms of use for that software license. If your software arrived pre-installed on or bundled with a new computer, find your software registration and licensing information in with all the other paperwork you received with the computer.

Save Software Dollars

Buying shrink-wrapped software feels good—you get the program and all its "fixins," and your registration and authentification numbers entitle you to all that lovely tech support. But the happy glow of new software ownership quickly fades when you discover that your neighbor bought the same accounting package for less than half of what you paid for it at the local Office Despot Software Department Store. Where can you track down good software bargains? How about online? After rebates, some of the software at these sites costs you zip—and that's a good that keeps on giving. Note these online software vendors that often offer bargains:

- Beyond.com
- Chumbo.com
- Egghead.com
- www.gotSoftware.com
- Outpost.com

Shrink-wrapped software offers advantages you won't find in its downloadable version. If your hard drive crashes or you accidentally delete a piece of your application, you have the shrink-wrapped product's disk to repair the problem. Sometimes you run into problems with your OS, for example, that require you to rebuild the system with a clean install. And installing from disks is usually quick, because you don't have to invest time in downloading the application.

Software Piracy Puts You in Dangerous Waters

If you think there's nothing wrong with "borrowing" software and running an unlicensed (and unpaid-for) version on your computer, you're wrong. Pirating software—just like pirating music, movies, or video—is a crime many developers consider just one step up from pick-pocketing. Ethics aside, using pirated software can be a bad deal for you, too. When you run unregistered, you can't use the manufacturer's tech support resources, and that can be a drag when you hit a glitch or have a question during a critical point in your program's operation. And if you're a business, watch out. The Business Software Alliance, in conjunction with major software manufacturers such as Microsoft, Apple, and Symantec, makes regular sweeps in search of pirated software in use in businesses. And even if you don't get caught in a sweep, let one disgruntled employee decide to blow the whistle on your little "software swaparama," and your company could be out thousands—maybe tens of thousands—of dollars. Save yourself time, worry, *and* cash, and pony up the price for the software you use. You don't want to end up in the brig, do you?

Download Programs from the Net

Of course you don't *have* to buy shrink-wrapped software. You can buy downloadable versions of most commercial software products, and the downloadable version might save you money. When you download an application, instead of installing the software from a CD or floppy disk, you save it to your computer, and then run the installation package. Downloadable software usually comes with registration and licensing information, which the manufacturer requires you to read and affirm. It's as legally binding as any fancy printed Certificate of Authenticity you might receive with a boxed product.

You don't even have to buy software over the Net—you can find tons of freeware and shareware available for the taking online. Freeware comes with no economic strings attached, while shareware lets you try before you buy. Search "shareware" and "freeware" with your favorite search engine to find places to download the programs. Some primo download sites include ZDNet Downloads, Free-Programs.com, and TUCOWS.com. (Chapter 13, "Get Those Gotta-Have Downloads: Apps, Utilities, and System Tweaks," gives you more TechTV insights on the best downloadable stuff on the Web today).

Don't Expect a Free Lunch

When it comes to freeware, you don't get everything for nothing. Most freeware comes with less documentation and user support than you get with commercial software. Some commercial products are beefier than their freeware competition. But if you're just trying out a new kind of software product, or you don't need high-powered, heavily supported programs, freeware and shareware can be the way to go.

You learned about the download process in Chapter 4, "The Good Life Online," so there's no need to repeat that information here. But you need to know more about downloading software than just how to do it.

What's a Competitive Upgrade?

You might run across discount offerings of "competitive upgrades." The idea is a simple takeoff of the upgrade discounts you find in many software packages. When you buy a new version of a word-processing product you already use, the company might offer a discount price for the new version; that's their way of rewarding a loyal customer. A competitive upgrade, on the other hand, is offered by a company hoping to win you over from another company's software. Company A lets you buy its product at a discounted rate if you're currently using company B's competitive product. You get the software at a less-than-MSR price, and the software maker gets a convert.

Earlier sections of this chapter hint at the downsides of downloading apps; the download can—depending on your modem, Internet connection device capability, and the size of the program—take a l-o-o-o-o-o-ng time. And if the download goes bad at any point in the process, you gotta start over. However, if you upgrade your software often, and you can handle the download time, using a downloadable product is a cheap way to enjoy a wide range of new and emerging software.

Dude, Where's My Program?

Don't panic if you download a program and can't get it to launch. You probably just left out a step. After you download a program, you still have to install it before it will run. You can run the install program by double-clicking its executable file (look for the EXE extension). If you didn't notice where you stored the file on download, do a search. (In Windows, go to Start menu and select Search or Find; on the Mac, open Sherlock or Find from the Apple menu.) Another option for installing the downloaded program in Windows is to use the Install feature of Add/Remove Programs. Find it by choosing Start, Settings, Add/Remove Programs. Open the Install/Uninstall tab, and you'll see the Install button. Click it and browse to find the executable file for the program you want to install.

Downloading Versus Uploading

Don't confuse the terms *downloading* and *uploading*. Downloading is when you copy files from the Internet to your computer; uploading transfers a file from your computer to the Net, like when you post a Web page.

Working in a Web-Based World

The brave new world of Web-based apps is quickly becoming a reality. Just as people jumped quickly on the car-leasing model that emerged a few years back, computer users are becoming interested in renting software rather than buying it. You've probably heard all about Microsoft's .Net strategy; well, software rental is a big part of what that strategy is all about. In fact, some analysts predict that within a few years, Microsoft will be thought of as an ASP (application service provider) with a sturdy foundation of software technology. As Gates goes, so goes the world, right? So, what does an ASP do, and why is it so wonderful? An ASP hosts software applications, making them available over the Internet to businesses—large and small—and individual computer users. For a monthly or per-access fee, users can access this off-site software and avoid the hassles of software ownership, such as maintenance, upgrades, support, and storage (some beefy apps suck up loads of system space).

Small businesses with few or no in-house tech staff find this option very attractive. If you're just launching a new venture, renting software and contracting for its upkeep rather than eating the purchase, installation, and support costs can make good economic sense.

For home users, several free Web-based applications have become extremely popular. You might be familiar with Web-based e-mail packages like Hotmail, but you also can find Web-based calendars, organizers, and diagnostic tools that are particularly attractive for anyone toting a PDA. You can't store much on a handheld system, so Web-based software is a natural for the mobile market. And, because the software resides on outside servers, you can access it from any computer.

Downsides to Web-world? Your modem and Internet connection speed play a huge role in your Web-based software experience. And if you use an application very rarely, paying a monthly fee might not be an economical route.

Want to Learn More About ASPs?

ASPs are such hot commodities right now that you can find lots of buzz about them in the trade. If you want to learn more about what ASPs are and what they do, check out `ASPscope.com`. There, you'll find information on industry trends, product availability, and late-breaking articles about new developments in all things ASP. The site's ASPmatch service can help you locate an ASP that's right for your business or personal operation, too.

LIGHTNING ROUND Q&A WRAP-UP

I just bought a new PC, and I want to transfer all of my old software to it. But I'm not sure I know how to find all those program files. What's the best way to make the switch?

First, your software license might require that you run the software on only one machine. If that's the case, you'll need to uninstall all the software files from your old machine, and then reinstall them on the new computer. If licensing isn't an issue, though, use LapLink (`www.laplink.com`) for a fast way to transfer files to a new PC. LapLink walks you through the transfer process and even includes cables to help promote rapid transfer speeds.

Isn't an installer just a glorified "copy" command?

Nope. Installers don't just throw a directory full of files on your computer. They locate files on an install disk, and then uncompress those files and move them to the destination you designated during installation (usually someplace on the hard drive). Installers also communicate "handling information" about the installed programs. If you use Windows, for example, installers give your Windows Registry information about storing and managing installed programs. Finally, installers clean up after installation and present you with registration information. You almost always have the option of using an installer, and I recommend you do.

I recently bought a used computer that came with Windows 98. I've run into a problem, though, and a message box keeps telling me to insert the Windows 98 CD to fix it. I don't have the Windows 98 CD, so how do I fix the problem?

We don't want to sound like Captain Bringdown here, but your last opportunity to fix the problem without spending more money came when you bought the computer. Whenever you buy a used computer, insist on getting the program CDs and/or registration and licensing permissions from the seller. In your case, the guy who sold you the computer can take the original CDs and install them on his *new* computer. That second installation breaks the registration and licensing agreement. You can try to contact the seller and request the CDs. If that doesn't work (and don't be surprised if it doesn't), we advise you to buy a new version of the operating system. In your case, you'll probably come out ahead anyway, because you can upgrade the OS.

CHAPTER 13

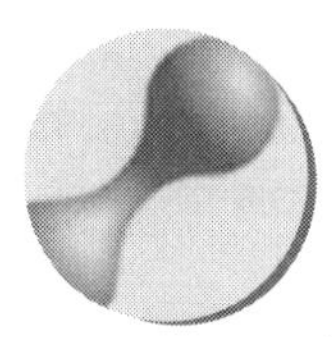

GET THOSE GOTTA-HAVE DOWNLOADS: APPS, UTILITIES, AND SYSTEM TWEAKS

- Tips and tricks for downloading
- Favorite downloadable system tweaks
- Great music, video, and animation tools
- Take care of business with downloadable tools
- Downloadables for work and play

If you'd love to get your hands on some cool new tools and toys, you need look no further than the World Wide Web. The Net is a treasure chest of some of the best downloadable music, video, and animation files, business applications, creativity tools, and cutting-edge "system helpers" you could ever hope to find. In this chapter, you learn about some of the best downloads on the Net—freeware, shareware, demoware, or pay-up-and-love-it software. Some of these downloads are classics, so you might already have them on your machine. But you can bet that you'll run across some goodies you've never encountered before—and will soon find hard to live without.

TIPS FOR PAINLESS DOWNLOADING

The Downloader's Shortlist of Sites

Here's a compact list of "can't-miss" download sites everyone should visit. You'll find something you like at each one.

- `ZDNet.com/downloads`
- `Tucows.com`
- `Download.com`
- `Jumbo.com`
- `SuperFiles.com`

Downloading isn't rocket science, but there are plenty of ways for a good download to go bad. As many a TV cop has said when questioning a suspect, "We can do this the easy way, or we can do it the hard way." Sitting through an endless download, experiencing a mid-point failure, or losing the file you just downloaded are just a few of the ways you can do it "the hard way."

For These Downloadables, It's All Good

Some of the software you learn about in this chapter comes bundled with Netscape or Internet Explorer, so you might already have it. Even so, visit the download site to be sure you have the latest version. Many of the files are freeware, shareware, or demoware, so even when you do have to pay, you can try before you buy.

Keep downloading clean and easy by following these simple tips:

- Create a separate folder for downloaded files, so you never have to wonder where they went.
- Use virus-detection software such as McAfee or Norton to avoid DTDs (downloadably transmitted diseases) and run it at least once a week if you frequently download from the Web.
- Don't get into a download until you've thought about the time it will take. This tip is especially important for dial-up users. A 5MB file can take more than 25 minutes to download over a 28.8 Kbps modem. Use a download calculator if you want to double-check download times (try the one at `www-sci.lib.uci.edu/HSG/AATimeCalc.html`).
- Go after popular downloads at off-peak hours (or, when you can, choose a download source where the hour is off-peak). You'll have better luck connecting and might get better download speeds.
- Only download files from reliable sites—you don't want to download an infected file.
- If the software tells you to close all your applications or restart your computer, take its advice.

For a step-by-step download "how to" and other basic type of info, see "Downloading Files" in Chapter 4, "The Good Life Online."

SYSTEM TWEAKS, PROTECTION, AND MAINTENANCE

The Web's loaded with downloads—free and otherwise—that can help you keep your system ticking along safely, securely, and efficiently. In this section you find a good sampling of Windows system tweaks (hey, even Windows lovers agree that the default performance leaves room for improvement). No matter what system you use, this section offers tools for securing your privacy, warding off marauding viruses, and cleaning up after not-so-complete uninstalls.

Don't Assume You're Alone Online

Don't assume that your downloading habits are nobody's business but your own. If you're one of the 14 million people who download with Netscape Smart Download, Real Download, or NetZip, somebody might be watching you every time you download, according to Internet privacy advocate Steve Gibson. These programs tag your computer with an ID and log every file you download from anywhere on the Internet under that unique ID. Even worse, the programs can capture and record your machine's unique IP address, and then create a detailed "profile" based on the Web sites you visit and the files you download. In late 2000, legislation in the form of a Spyware Control Act was before the U.S. Senate, but as of this book's printing, the act hasn't been passed. If you want to read more about this issue (and learn how you can protect your own downloading privacy) visit the Gibson Research Center at www.grc.com.

Here are some of TechTV's favorite Windows system tweaks:

- **X-Setup:** This collection of Windows system tweaks contains more than 500 separate ways to make your Windows system more like you want it to be. Use X-Setup to change the appearance of Windows or its software, specific hardware settings, Internet settings, network settings, or general system settings. The 6.0 version includes an automatic plug-in updater, so you'll always have the latest tweaks at your disposal. Get it at www.xteq.com.
- **Hare:** No matter what kind of Windows system you have—fast or slow, new or old—this tool will speed up the CPU time for the foreground application. In plain terms, that means your programs will load and run faster. Hare is relatively new on the scene, but early adopters have had good luck with it. Download it at www.dachshundsoftware.com.
- **MIE55SpeedUp:** Microsoft's Internet Explorer context menu can take five seconds to load. That's because the browser searches through a section in your system registry that contains a bunch of empty entries. Eliminate those unnecessary keys, and your browsing experience becomes much faster. That's what MIE55SpeedUp does. Download it at www.bluestarsoftware.de/html/english.
- **Cablenut:** Many TechTV reviewers say this is the best ISP optimizer they've ever used. Click through the suggested settings to double your online throughput. Running this baby takes only a few seconds. Download it at www.cablenut.com.

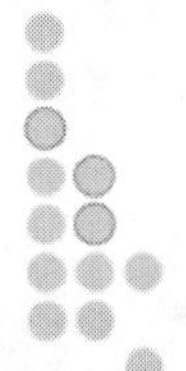

- **Diskeeper:** Yes, Windows' default defrag tool works, but it doesn't do the job Executive Software's Diskeeper does. This tool delivers scheduling and smart optimization features for all Windows versions, keeping your system running smoothly. Download it at www.executive.com.
- **For cleaner uninstalls:** Ashampoo Uninstaller 2000 probably is the most effective and efficient uninstaller we've come across—and we've tried a lot of them. Many uninstallers are half-magic solutions; even the mighty Windows Add/Remove Programs tool can leave behind unwanted files. But Ashampoo gets that program gone—all gone—and lets you use a wizard to choose unwanted software files from your Start menu, Program Files, Registry. Ashampoo also cleans up unwanted temporary Internet and duplicate files, and it even offers an installation tool to make sure you install things right in the first place. Try it free from www.ashampoo.com; if you want to keep it, you'll have to pay $10.
- **Windowblinds:** This ultra-cool utility makes Windows look like any OS you want it to—even Linux, BeOS or Mac. Use one of Windowblinds' hundreds of skins or create one of your own. Get this Windows system tweaker at www.windowblinds.net.

Tired of Windows-only utilities? These system tools work for all of us:

- **For essential anti-virus protection:** EZ AntiVirus, available for $19.95 at www.my-etrust.com, and Norton AntiVirus (free demo, $40 retail) are the essential utilities on any downloader's system. Both programs offer free virus signature updates, and that's a critical option. Without up-to-date virus protection, you have no protection at all.
- **For all-around system protection:** The Norton SystemWorks 2001 (www.symantec.com) is the best, all-around, total system protection program the TechTV reviewers have used. It costs just under $60, and it's worth every penny. In addition to Norton AntiVirus 2001, this package includes Norton CleanSweep 2001, Norton WebServices 2001, and Norton Utilities 2001.
- **For protecting your privacy:** PGP (www.pgp.com) is a freeware utility that is way too modest in its name (which stands for Pretty Good Privacy). PGP offers secure e-mail, file encryption, and peer-to-peer VPN support. Despite this program's name, it goes beyond "pretty good" to bring your system great privacy protection.

Download Wirelessly

Using the free utility PQA Updater, developed by PalmGear H.Q. and Pendragon Software (www.pendragon-software.com), you can download and install hundreds of files on the Net using your wireless handheld. You need approximately twice the amount of free memory space as the size of the application you are downloading for this to work.

1. Go to PalmGear H.Q. (www.palmgear.com) and search on "PGHQ PQA" to find and retrieve the necessary files.
2. Download either the .zip or .sit files, depending on whether you use a PC or Mac.
3. Unzip or unstuff the files and save them to your hard drive. Remember where you put them!
4. Install the PGHQ.PQA and PQAU.PRC files by double-clicking them and then clicking Done.
5. HotSync your wireless Palm, and then go to your Palm's Applications screen and tap on the PGHQ PQA icon.
6. Tap on the PalmGear H.Q. PQA Picks to see a list of downloadable files.
7. Tap on the file you want to install. The Updater asks you if you want to download the file.
8. Tap Yes. When the download finishes, Updater asks whether you want to install the file. Tap Yes.

Remember, 200KB is the maximum download. A PalmOS file that large would take almost 20 minutes to download on a Palm VII.

FEED YOUR INNER ARTIST: MUSIC, VIDEO, ANIMATION, AND MORE

Your computer puts a powerful creative force at your fingertips. Music, video, animation, graphics editing—whatever creative recreational activity you do, there's a download out there that can help you do it. These downloads are must-haves for listening, editing, and just generally messin' around with music. You can download these goods at www.zdnet.com/downloads or at the listed address (see the sites for full details):

- **MusicMatch Jukebox** (www.musicmatch.com) is not only the best jukebox program around, it does much more (see Figure 13.1). Use it to play and convert MP3, WMA, and WAV files, manage your music, and burn CDs. And this juke's got changeable skins and visualizations, so your music experience never gets boring. You can go for the free version, but we suggest that you pony up $20 for the Plus flavor; it offers faster encoding and burning, along with other functions not found on the freebie.

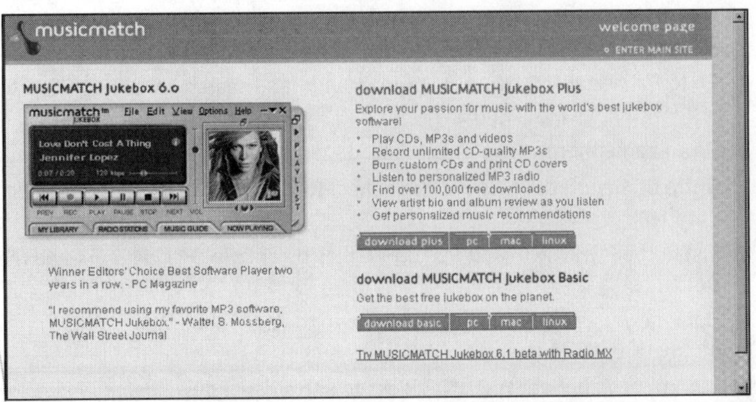

Figure 13.1

MusicMatch Jukebox is a must-have if you like to download music and burn your own CDs. Try the Basic model for no charge. If you like it, you might want to pay up for the added speed and functionality of the Plus version.

- **Gnutella** (`www.gnutella.wego.com`) is a file-sharing network that works much like its predecessor, Napster, in that members of the Gnutella community designate which files on their hard drives they're willing to share with everyone else in the community. Unlike Napster, however, Gnutella isn't limited to music files, but extends to images, videos, recipes, and other types of files, including software distributions. And the best "unlike-Napster" quality of Gnutella is that it doesn't have a central server for Hollywood or RIAA lawyers to shut down. To tap into the riches of the Gnutella network, you need a client such as LimeWire (`www.limewire.com`).
- **Winamp** (`www.winamp.com`) is a standard for listening to MP3s. It's free and customizable. You can switch the player's skins, visualizations, and plug-ins to change its color, design, and functionality. Play around with audio mixing, fading, control of your music via joystick, and other features.
- **Agent-MP3** is a great way to seek and capture MP3s. If your college or workplace banned Napster, you can quietly switch your loyalties over to Agent-MP3. This software cut its teeth on Usenet newsgroups—the sources we used to mine for music before Napster came along. And, like many good must-haves, Agent-MP3 is free.

Napster Smackdown

The whole Napster thing was too good to last, but no chapter about downloads should fail to pay homage to this file-swap behemoth. By helping millions of people exchange their favorite music files online, Napster helped broaden the world's musical horizons. After being targeted by a series of legal challenges and court-ordered content blocks, Napster is sadly reduced, but (for now) you can find its remains at `www.napster.com`.

- **MetaSynth 2.5 Demo** is a Mac-based supersynth—a software program that deconstructs pictures and renders them as sound. The program creates 400 simultaneous sounds, all without a soundcard. You can buy the full version of MetaSynth 2.7 from `www.uisoftware.com`. It's not for cheapskates, but it's well worth its $299 price tag. MetaSynth runs only on a Mac. If you don't have a Mac, could this be a reason to get one?
- **ER-Zero Drum Synth** isn't the only drum synthesizer program out there, but it's among the best and the easiest to use. No matter how new you are to the drum-synth world, you can handle ER-Zero. It does a great job of emulating the sound of Korg's ER-1 analog-modeling drum synth. Download this marvel free at `www.er-zero.tripod.com`.
- **Hammerhead Rhythm Station**, a six-track loop-sequencing program, comes loaded with TR-909-style drum computer sounds, a distortion effect, and sample reverse. This tool lets you import your own sounds (like the ones you make using the ER-Zero drum synth) and save your finished tracks as WAV files. Download this freeware gem at `www.threechords.com/hammerhead`.

And now, to bring more than music into the mix:

- **For streaming audio and video:** RealPlayer, Windows Media Player, and QuickTime are—and deserve to be—the standards for streaming audio and video on the Web (see Figure 13.2). All of these products are free, so try 'em all (you'll probably *need* to use them all, because the industry still hasn't come up with a streaming standard).

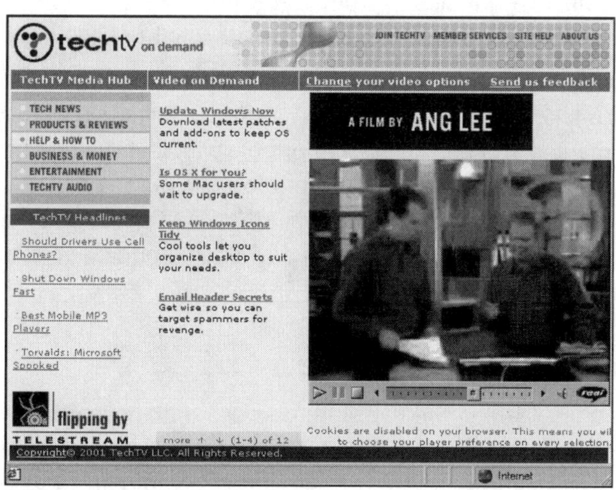

Figure 13.2

If you watch archived videos on the TechTV Web site, you can choose to stream them to a RealPlayer, Windows Media, or QuickTime Player program on your computer. All of these players are free downloads.

You Don't Have to Buy It

When you download RealPlayer, Real will try to trade you up to its Plus version. Don't feel like you have to pony up for Plus. The free player gives you just as good a picture, so why shell out the dough?

- **For watching animation:** We love Shockwave (and Flash Player (both available as free downloads at `www.macromedia.com/shockwave/download`). Use Shockwave to play games on the Web, and download the Flash Player to see most online animation. Both of these might have been installed with your browser, but check to be sure you have the latest versions (and don't miss the gaming downloads later in the chapter).
- **For browsing images:** The ACDSee shareware program costs $50, but it's worth all that and more. This program manager is a favorite tool at TechTV for everything from importing pictures from a digital camera or scanner to downloading snapshots from the Web.
- **For editing images:** What can we say? We like Paint Shop Pro, even though this shareware product sports a $100 price tag (still sizably less than Adobe Photoshop's $400 sticker price). Paint Shop Pro lets you edit and manipulate images so well that you'll feel like you'd spent your formative years in the darkroom. The image editors in the latest release are truly amazing.
- **For creating and sending video:** Video Capturix 2001 lets you record AVI movies and freeze images as BMP or JPEG files. Use this shareware to watch your videos in full-screen mode, automatically start recording when something moves in front of your camera, print directly from your video source, and more. Download it free from `www.capturix.com`, and pay $29 if you want to keep it.
- **For creating 3D animation:** Blender 3D modeling and animation software is for folks who take their 3D computer art seriously. You need to be committed to reading the manual and becoming comfortable with inverse kinematics and animated rotoscoping to make this product work for you, but the results can be stunning. This free software works on Windows, UNIX, and BeOS, and you can find it at `www.blender.nl/download`. You can download a printed version of the HTML user manual for $40 at the same site.

TOOLS THAT DO THE JOB

Life isn't all fun and games, but the right tools can make even the most tedious computerized jobs less awful. These downloads can help you tackle many of the mundane day-to-day chores you know and love. As before, you can download these files at `www.zdnet.com/downloads` unless an alternative address is listed.

- **WinZip** is a must-have for downloaders who work with a PC. WinZip not only unarchives and unpacks your downloads, you can use it to zip files for storage or to send as e-mail attachments. WinZip is free to try; pay $29 to keep it.

- **Stuffit Expander** from Alladin Systems (www.alladinsys.com) is a compression and decompression utility that's popular with Mac users. Stuffit comes with the Mac, but it's a free download for Windows, Linux, and Solaris. If you want to order the software in the box, it'll cost you $19.95.
- **Adobe Acrobat Reader** probably came bundled with your browser. You need this plug-in to view and print formatted documents online. The reader's especially useful for downloading and printing out tax forms or documents.
- **Capture** is a handy little tool for capturing screen shots, brought to you by the good people at AnalogX. Use Capture to take screen shots of windows or of your desktop, and then save the captured image as a bitmap. This program is free at www.analogx.com. While you're there, check out the other freeware downloads, too.

Don't Forget That You're Taking Up Space

When you work with programs that capture and save bitmap files to your system, don't forget how hefty those files can be. If you plan to maintain access to a lot of bitmaps, take advantage of compression programs (like WinZip), Zip directories, and removable storage media.

- **NoteTab Lite** is a Notepad replacement utility that you can download free from www.notetab.com/download.htm. This utility is essential for HTML editing and programming.
- **CuteFTP** is THE user-friendly FTP program. CuteFTP is as good for first-timers as it is for those of you who have done the downloaded via FTP thing a time or two. Try it free by downloading a shareware version from www.cuteftp.com. To keep it, pay $40.

WEB WORK (AND PLAY)

These downloads make your Web life better, faster, easier, and more entertaining. You already have some of these jewels; others are destined to become your newest best friends.

Unless another address accompanies the listing, you can download these files at www.zdnet.com/downloads.

- **For browsing the Web:** You can always count on the classics, and the classic Web browsers are Internet Explorer and Netscape Communicator. These browsers are free, slick, and ultra-functional. Use the latest versions if you want the best features.

Keep Your Eye on Opera

One of the Net's newest contenders in the browser wars, Opera, is now available free of charge at www.opera.com (if you want the ad-free version, you have to pay a still-modest $39). Opera is fast and lean, but it isn't slim on performance. Use Opera's streamlined version of the ICQ protocol to chat it up with friends while you browse. Right now, Opera only works with Windows, but watch for this browser to branch out to other OSes soon. Then, who knows—it might shove one of the Big Two off the TechTV favorites list!

- **For chatting with friends:** AOL Instant Messenger and ICQ are both free chat programs owned by AOL. Either product lets you create a Buddy List and notifies you when one of your "Buds" comes online. ICQ lets you chat via video or share real-time game playing. Another chat favorite, Odigo (www.odigo.com), is the self-proclaimed "world's best instant messenger," and it delivers on its claim by offering compatibility across ICQ, AIM, and Yahoo! Messenger—three of the biggest platforms.
- **For cleaning your visual landscape:** Popupkiller 3.12 is one of the best ways to help say NO to the of the biggest annoyances on the Web—pop-up ads. Popupkiller 3.12 monitors all browsers that you have open at a given time, and lets you choose which ads to kill. Download a master list of pop-up ads that fellow Web surfers have compiled and merge it with your own list. It's free from www.davecentral.com.
- **To avoid getting caught in your slack attack:** Boss! is a must-have download for anyone who does non-work–related Web surfing on the job. If your boss walks by your open-air playpen while you're looking online for a new job, writing a short story about your lousy supervisor, or playing Solitaire, minimizing won't completely hide your window from view. But Boss! can; just tell Boss! what software you want to keep strictly hidden and at the strike of a hotkey all evidence vanishes from your screen. When the boss takes a powder, hit the key again, and you're back in business—sort of. This free job-saver is available at www.rohitab.com.
- **For simul-surfing multiple pages:** Katiesoft is a fantabulous multi-tasking piece of freeware that lets you surf four Web pages at once. Katie also supports other apps, so you can view the Web, Napster, your e-mail, and that Excel spreadsheet you're working on, all at the same time. The view is small, of course, but you can maximize any window you want to. Download Katiesoft free at www.katiesoft.com.
- **For redecorating your desktop:** Webshots re-wallpapers your desktop every day. Choose from thousands of photos in the Webshots archive and get a new photo automatically delivered to your desktop daily. Download the software at www.webshots.com.

All Utilities Are Apps, But All Apps Aren't Utilities

You hear the terms "programs," "software," "utilities," and "applications" tossed around quite a bit. All these terms are sort of similar, but those last two (in particular) aren't necessarily the same. Utilities are specialized programs that perform specific tasks, such as computer resource management. Although utilities are applications, their specific functionality means they're usually smaller than beefy, Swiss-army-knife apps like Word and Excel.

- **For finding out if you're psychic:** Do you want an expert opinion on your psychic skills? Then check out ESP 2.0. This simple program uses the standard Zener Card test, in which you try to choose the correct cards more than 20 percent of the time to qualify as a second-sight sorta person. An ESP meter tracks your paranormal progress. The 30-day free trial should give you plenty of time to get in touch with your sixth sense. Get it at `download.cnet.com`.
- **For chronicling your life online:** The Journal is for anyone who wants to record the daily events of life and prefers a keyboard to one of those Harriet-the-Spy, green-marbled comp books. The great thing about this download is that you can record more than just your soulful scribblings—the Journal also lets you store images and multimedia clips on its electronic pages. Try it free at `www.filefarm.com`; keepsies cost $35.

Make Visual Basic Shareware Work

Sometimes, shareware developers write their programs in Visual Basic (VB) and forget to bundle in the files you'll need to make them work. You'll recognize this problem if Windows says its missing files like these:

VB40032.DLL

MSVBVM50.DLL

MSVBVM60.DLL

These are Visual Basic runtime DLLs, and you need them in your computer's System folder to run VB-based shareware. You'll find these files at `www.Milori.com` and at the Microsoft Downloads Center (`http://www.microsoft.com/downloads/`). Windows tells you exactly which file you need, and most VB DLL files use the last two digits to signify version. For example, VBACV20.DLL means the Visual Basic Application Converter V2.0 DLL.

LIGHTNING ROUND Q&A WRAP-UP

I hear a lot of people talking about using FTP for downloading. What is FTP, and how would you use it?

FTP stands for File Transfer Protocol. It's a series of protocols or rules that define how to transfer files across the Internet. FTP's a very popular way to send files across the Net, and lots of people use it as a downloading tool.

To use FTP, you need client software that lets you access the FTP server storing the files you want. Even older operating systems like Windows 95/98 came with a command-line FTP client, and most Web browsers also have FTP functionality. But you'll probably find FTP-ing easier if you use a shareware or freeware FTP client. For more info on a TechTV favorite, refer to the earlier information on CuteFTP (see "Tools That Do the Job," earlier in this chapter).

I am just getting into MP3s and was wondering if you could give me some information about them. What is the difference between running an MP3 from stream and downloading an MP3? Also, when I run an MP3 from stream, it tends to cut out while the song is playing back.

Streaming is the process of watching or listening to media files that are stored on a computer other than your own. You request a media file from the remote location and it's sent to you in data packets. Your system stores these data packets in a buffer; the media file begins to play as soon as the buffer collects the minimum amount of packets required.

Downloading is the act of physically transferring and storing a media file to your computer. To download media files, such as MP3s, right-click on the link to the MP3, and choose Save As. This brings up a dialog box asking where you'd like to save the file on your PC. You need plenty of available RAM for fast downloading, though; 32MB or less will leave you waiting a long time for the downloads to finish.

Typically, MP3 compresses a CD track at a ratio of 11 to 1, and at that ratio, the MP3 sounds almost indistinguishable from a CD. But the compressed size of the MP3 is manageable—you can download and store it on your hard drive.

Streaming MP3 is best if you have a cable modem or DSL; otherwise, you experience skipping and stuttering as the data slows down. Before you begin streaming, choose a speed that matches your modem. In your case, you need to use a format with a lower bandwidth. The best bet for you is to download—rather than stream—MP3 files (or upgrade to a cable modem or DSL).

I have MP3s associated with Winamp. I tried to change the file association so I could open the MP3s with MusicMatch Jukebox. I followed the instructions to the letter. The MP3s kept opening up in Winamp. I tried again, thinking I missed a keystroke, but no luck.

This is a case of Winamp hijacking your music files so they will automatically open in Winamp instead of the player of your choice. Even though Winamp is a great program, sometimes you want to use MusicMatch or RealPlayer. Here's how to fix this problem:

1. Choose Ctrl+P from the Winamp preference menu.
2. Choose Setup.
3. Choose file types.
4. Uncheck MP3.
5. Uncheck "Register types on Winamp startup."
6. Choose Agents.
7. Uncheck "Enable Winamp agent."
8. Uncheck "Maintain file association."

Now, you're back in the MP3 driver's seat.

PART IV

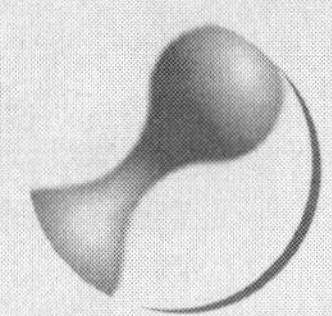

COMPUTING FOR ALL IT'S WORTH

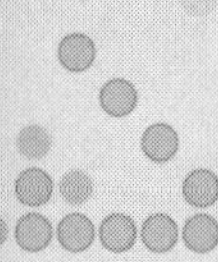

CHAPTER 14

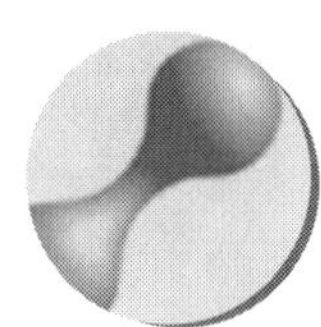

CHECK IN ON HOME AUTOMATION

- Ready to cross the automated home threshold?
- Check out the state of the home automation art.
- Tie it all together.

In the past few years, you couldn't walk through the annual Consumer Electronics Show (CES) and other tech conventions without bumping into the next, best thing in home automation software, hardware, and systems. In case you haven't attended CES for a while (and you forgot to watch TechTV's CES coverage or haven't caught it on `www.techtv.com`), this chapter can bring you up to speed on all things auto-home. Here, you get a wide-angle look at home automation and an update on what's here and what's near in this technology.

YESTERDAY'S TOMORROWS: THE COMPUTERIZED HOME

When you think about home automation, what comes to mind? Thumbprint-recognition door locks, music and light settings that follow you from room to room, and online-accessible security cams that let you see who's knocking on the front door of your home while you're miles away at work? Or are you dreaming of that little sliding panel in the kitchen wall that slips aside to reveal a steaming hot made-to-order shrimp curry accompanied by a chilled Chardonnay?

Just because that little-sliding-door thing isn't ready for prime time, don't give up on your other dreams for a smart home. Home automation technology encompasses a collection of products and services that dish up communications, entertainment, security, convenience, and information systems—and much of it is available right now. The field of home automation gets bigger and better all the time. And you don't have to be Bill Gates to afford *or* use a smart home system.

Deconstructing Smart Home Systems

Home automation systems come in a number of packages. Most involve some combination of software and hardware, with a dash of communications systems and wiring thrown in. Because smart home setups can run anywhere from $40 to $400,000, no single system is representative of the entire technology. But in general, most home automation systems include these basic components:

- **Energy saving/environmental controls and devices:** HVAC (heating, ventilation, and air conditioning) controls, including thermostat controllers, lighting controls (such as wallplates, switches, dimmers, and panels), thermostat programmers (see Figure 14.1), central vacuum systems, plumbing systems (leak detectors, shut-offs, and so on), pool and spa automation, and central air filtration controls, automated drapes and shades, and motorized windows.

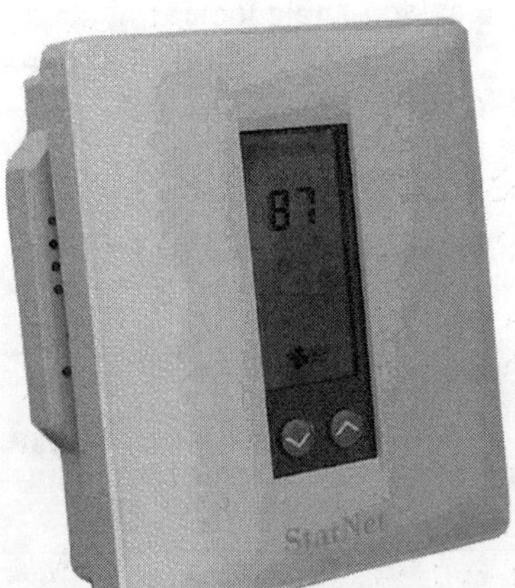

Figure 14.1

Energy-saving devices, such as this programmable thermostat (available for $127.95 at www.smarthomeusa.com), are one of the more inexpensive ways in which to make your home "smarter."

- **Entertainment devices and programmers:** Audio devices such as in-wall speakers, all-weather outdoor sound components, jukebox software, surround-sound systems, controllers for programming televisions, DVD, VCRs, and other infrared devices.
- **Communications components:** Home networking software and systems, always-on Internet access in every room, and in-home communications systems such as room-to-room intercoms and front door cameras, as shown in Figure 14.2.

Figure 14.2

Be sure you know who is knocking at the door with a weatherproof surveillance camera. This model from `smarthomeusa.com` is priced just under $70. Remember, you also will need to buy a monitor to view what the camera sees!

- **Security systems:** Room-to-room netcam monitors, wireless and wired-in security systems, whole-house monitoring services, motion detectors, and heat, gas, and smoke detectors.
- **Wiring and cabling components and power line carriers:** Any structured wiring and cabling system, connectivity products, surge protection, UPS, and plug-in protectors.
- **Whole-house controls:** System controllers, panels, touchscreens, remotes, and automation software (see Figure 14.3).

Most of this stuff isn't *new* new; home automation hardware devices such as switches, dimmers, timers, and netcams have been around for some time. And home automation systems don't have to be expensive, either. For less than $50, you can get a kit from X10 (`www.x10.com`) that lets you control several lights or home appliances through a PC interface. If you're willing to spend slightly more (around $200), Omnipotence Software will sell you its flagship ECS system (`www.omnipotencesoftware.com`). ECS does everything from regulating your home's climate controls to answering your phone to telling you when your child or Chihuahua roams outside the "secure zone" you've established.

Think Big When It Comes to Internet Connectivity

If you think of smart-home products as being geek-boy toys, think again. Continuous Internet connectivity might seem like a luxury today, but not long ago people laughed at the notion of ever *needing* to use the Internet, an idea that doesn't seem laughable at all, today. As the electronic gadgets, controls, and technologies converge in our homes, central access and control becomes more essential. Not only can you use the Internet as a form of remote control, but Internet connectivity in every room provides instant access to news, information, entertainment, and communication with others in and outside your home. That's why the Internet plays such an integral role in most new smart home designs. So, even if you don't lust after non-stop Internet access today, chances are strong that it's destined to become a bigger part of your tomorrow.

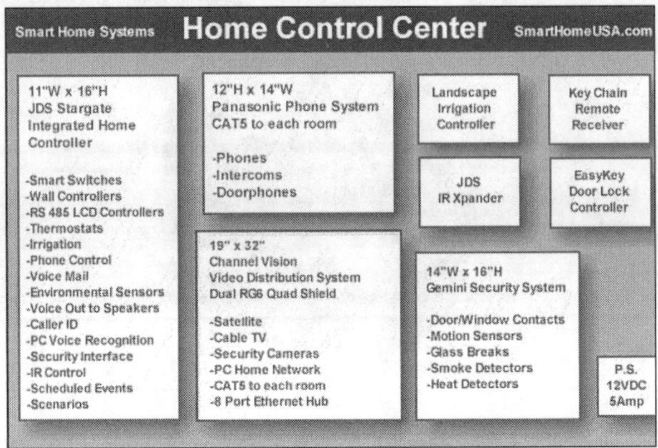

Figure 14.3

A home control center brings together all the elements of a smart home. One look certainly demonstrates that a fully automated home requires careful planning and the necessary financial resources to make your dream a reality.

What Home Automation Can Do for You

Basic smart home systems are pretty simple—like a series of devices connected through your home's electrical wiring system. You can install a central controller and use it to control your HVAC, home security devices, lights, water heater, VCR, and so on. Add a software component and broadband Internet connectivity, and you have a truly automated home, with expanded control programmability, remote control access, and maybe even high-level interactivity options such as voice-command recognition.

Depending on what system you buy, home automation can do a lot for you:

- "Speak" programmed phrases at specific event triggers (so your home system will greet you with a "hey, your majesty, welcome home!" when you walk in the door).
- Let you log on from the office, and respond to your remote controls to adjust the thermostat and raise the temperature of the hot water heater when you're getting ready to head home.
- Check your e-mail and issue automated responses.
- Deliver a prerecorded message to specific callers.
- Send infrared commands to control devices such as your TV, VCR, and stereo through your computer.

- Let you use netcams and remote access to get a visual check of your home's interior and exterior while you're away. (So you can find out that your kid is eating four packages of Ding Dongs after school, or catch your neighbor secretly using your backyard as a bacon-grease disposal site).
- Announce, play, and record TV shows as they air.
- Remind you of upcoming events and important dates.
- Monitor your home for fire, flood, or the arrival of visiting in-laws.
- Create macro "environments" of specified temperature settings, light levels, and entertainment offerings, and serve them up at voice command, timer, or touch-screen triggers.

Whether you want security, all-over, always-on Internet accessibility, or simple home appliance control, home automation offers a solution for you.

You'll See a Lot of X10

If you poke around in the world of home automation, you run across the name X10 all the time. X10 is a company that produces home automation software and other products, but it's also the name of a home automation protocol that lets you control plugged-in devices through your electrical system. X10 technology is actually a "communication language" that works through the existing AC wiring in your home. The devices can talk to each other and a central switching station or be controlled by your computer.

Other vendors supply devices that use the X10 protocol, so all X10 devices aren't manufactured or distributed by X10 the *company* (`www.x10.com`).

THE HOME AUTOMATION PRODUCTS SHOW

The TechTV reviewers have seen a lot of home automation systems, software, and hardware, so they know that the market's loaded with good products. This section won't try to cover them all, but it does give you a good sampling of the home automation wares you can buy and some links to their sources.

Go Window Shopping

You can find all sorts of information about home automation technology, products, and developments online or any magazine rack. Start with Home Automation Times (`www.homeautomationtimes.com`) and Electronic House (`www.electronichouse.com`). Both of these publications—print or online—offer auto-home how-tos, product information, catalog links, and coverage of latest developments and news in the field of home automation.

Systems and Gadgets

The Pioneer Digital Networked Entertainment (DNE) system is a home network tied together with FireWire (large-capacity cable). At the heart of the product lies a server with voice recognition capabilities and a 27GB hard drive. You take it from there, attaching your TV, DVD, CD player, telephone, home LAN, Internet access, PCs, wireless viewing devices, microwave, coffee machine, and so on. Control the whole she-bang with voice commands, thanks to the VR server. This cool system might not be available at your local mega-computer-doodads store just yet, but you can learn more about it at www.pioneerelectronics.com.

Calculate the True Cost of Those Shiny New Internet Appliances

Internet appliances are gaining popularity, especially with those who are interested in Web surfing and e-mailing but don't want to use (or configure) the computer for other chores. Internet appliances give you Web access without the oomph of a full-service computer, so they stay relatively small and easy to use. And many of these devices are advertised as "free." Unfortunately, those "free" systems can be pretty expensive. You're usually asked to pay monthly connection fees, and sign a contract to stick with an ISP for a given period of time. Add it all up, and you're paying $600 to $800 or more for a machine that only connects you to the Internet. For $500, you can get an inexpensive computer system that will give you the same Internet access and let you choose, drop, and otherwise lose your ISP at will.

You also might want to look at Home Systems Plus's Aegis Home Management System (www.hsplus.com). It controls lights, temperature, the entertainment system, and the gas fireplace. This system uses your home's existing lighting, security, and thermostat setup, bringing all of them under the control of a wireless, handheld touch-screen. Set up whole-house programs of your choice (such as "gone fishing," "coming home," or "hit the hay") and set them off with a touch of a button.

Don't even want to touch a button? Fine. The IntelaVoice Wall Switch from VOS Systems (www.vossystems.com) is just what you're looking for (from your prone position there on the sofa). Turn lights on, off, or set them to dream-date dim with your spoken commands. Isn't saying "dim the lights" classier than clapping?

And here's that Internet access you've been looking for: 2Wire's HomePortal 1000 (www.2wire.com). This residential gateway works with a DSL connection to deliver Internet access, networking, telephony, and firewall protection in a single box. In other words, this all-in-one setup will have you living large in the home automation universe. 2Wire promotes this system's easy installation and operation. The whole deal costs $200 to $400, depending on the model.

Don't Forget to Password Protect

If you use any software—including home automation software—that requires you to leave a computer on and running during your absence, you open up security gaps in your system. Whenever your PC is up and running, it's vulnerable to off-site hackers and intruders. Use good firewall security, and don't forget to password protect your system software to help ward off unauthorized system access.

Anyone looking for a DVD home-theater system without the fuss and expense of separate player and receiver components will appreciate the Panasonic SC-PM08 (www.prodcat.panasonic.com). This system's Dolby Digital and DTS decoding features give you a respectable home theater experience, although you might want to upgrade the speakers for a richer, low-end sound.

It's on TechTV

Find full reviews of many of the products mentioned in this chapter at TechTV.com. Search the product news and reviews and check out the latest industry offerings in Fresh Gear.

Check Out the Software Scene with HAL

One of the most impressive contenders in the crowded home automation software competition is Home Automated Living's HAL line of software (HAL 2000 and HALDeluxe). What puts HAL ahead of the field is its effective voice-recognition technology. With HAL's software, you choose the appliances or devices you want to network, and then install the appropriate interface for them.

The HAL interface, shown in Figure 14.4, is easy to use and lets you add as many devices as you want to control. For example, add a device called "living room lights"; then, without requiring the usual speech-recognition training process, the system can begin controlling that device in response to your spoken commands. Activate the system by calling its name (HAL or any name you choose), and then name the device and speak your commands. You can speak into a PC microphone, a properly interfaced home phone, or a cell or work phone.

Commands don't have to be simple phrases like "Turn on lights and dim them to 40 percent." You can issue complex commands, such as "Every Tuesday, Wednesday, and Friday, turn on the light at 6 p.m. for three hours." HAL also can pull information from the Internet and read it to you, so you can ask it for news, sports scores, or TV listings.

Eliminate Remote Bloat

Does your gadget-happy household overflow with remote controls? Those things seem to breed if you leave them alone together. Anyway, you can lighten your load considerably by replacing some of your remotes with an LCD-screen-equipped universal remote, such as the Sony RM-AV2100 Commander (www.sony.com). Like other offerings in this ever-expanding category, the Sony RM-AV2100 provides central control for all your AV components. Or maybe you'd like to turn your PDA into a remote. If so, download the free-to-try OmniRemote universal remote application (www.pacificneotek.com) onto your Palm. This app learns from other remotes and you can program it yourself. You'll have all those home devices eating out of your hand(held) in no time. See the site for full details.

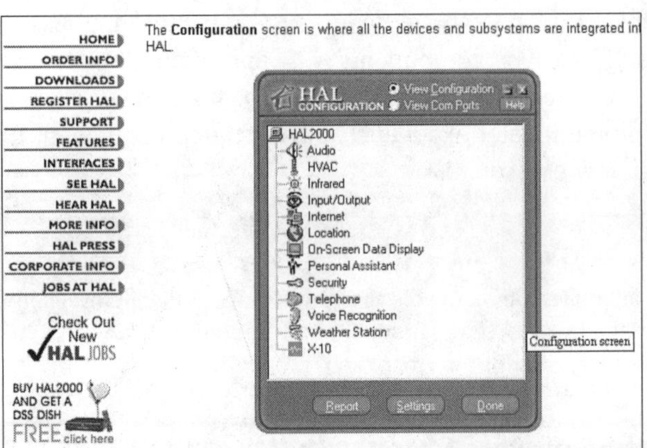

Figure 14.4

The Hal 2000 Interface (at `www.homeautomatedliving.com`) allows you to control almost any system in a smart home by manual or even voice command.

Go for the beefier HAL 2000 version, and you also can enjoy IR (infrared) equipment control, security, and HVAC support, along with telephony and personal-information management features. But even the pared-down HALdeluxe offers a lot of convenience, security, and control to the auto-home owner.

BRINGING IT ALL BACK HOME

Now, to bring together all the information on systems and products, let TechTV take you on a brief tour of a sample automated home. You can understand the power and appeal of this technology better when you see how it's integrated throughout the house. As in any model home, this showplace may boast features you don't want or need (or don't want to pay for). But this home tour doesn't require you to spend hours driving through an endless maze of new suburban developments, and no desperate real estate agent will follow you from room to room.

Check Out Your Spot on the Big Blue Marble

If all this talk of home automation makes you feel sort of futurific, take that sensation even higher by getting a look at your place from space. Using Microsoft's TerraServer site, you can search, browse, and zoom in on satellite imagery of over 60 countries (`www.terraserver.microsoft.com`). The TerraServer database offers imagery with incredible resolution—you can see objects as small as one meter. And the database updates constantly, so expect imagery to improve and coverage to expand. So make like a real space pilot and check out your corner of the planet from way up high. Then, let no one accuse you of missing the "big picture."

In addition to traditional phone and power wiring, this smart home has data, voice, and video wiring—the kind used in many new and custom homes. The nerve center of the smart home is in the garage; that's where Internet connectivity cabling is routed and the hardware components are stored.

In the kitchen, a Qubit Web pad serves up recipes, a menu planner, and access to online food shopping sites. A bar code scanner helps you put together your shopping list, and the home's Java-card technology lets you fill prescriptions online. The pharmacy electronically verifies your identity, and then accesses your health profiles. When you finish with the Web pad, store it in the refrigerator door where it's out of the way. The smart home's kitchen is fully equipped with smart appliances that automatically notify you and the repair service provider when they require maintenance.

Take a Virtual Smart-Home Tour Online

One of TechTV's favorite home automation technology sites is `www.smarthome.com`. From the driveway to the outdoor pool, this site offers a well-designed and informative tour of a palatial smart home, with close-ups and full descriptions of all of the products and features. Of course, this site peddles its wares, and some of them seem a bit over the top. Take the Critter Gitter motion detector in the backyard, for example; are we really supposed to believe the owners of this *casa* have to protect their corn crops from thieving animals?

There's more than convenience to this smart home. You might have seen the security cameras at the front door, but you probably wouldn't notice the driveway security sensor you tripped when you drove in. These security features might seem old hat, but they offer a few new tricks. The netcams can send images to your PC at work, and relay your visitor's voice to your cell phone. If you want to buzz someone in, do it from wherever you are, using your phone interface, a PDA, or by logging onto your home's system online from any computer with Net access.

In the media room, you see how this setup shines. All the media devices in this smart home are connected with Apple's blazing fast IEEE1394 FireWire technology. Add the set-top boxes and media components of your choice to create your dream entertainment center, and control it all with a master remote from the comfort of your chair or sofa. This really is a home, sweet home.

LIGHTNING ROUND Q&A WRAP-UP

You folks at TechTV talk about CES quite a bit—what is it?

CES is the Consumer Electronic Show, held every year in Las Vegas since 1967. This is the world's largest consumer electronics trade show. Retailers and manufacturers use CES as their opportunity to unveil all their cool new and soon-to-be shipped products. Remember the Laserdisc player? It was introduced at CES in 1974. In 1993, the mini disc debuted at the show. In 2001, the CES crowd boasted lots of digital audio radio (DAR) gadgets. Although the name says "Consumer," the show isn't open to consumers at all. That's why TechTV covers the convention so closely, so you can get a close look at the latest and greatest devices *before* they hit the shelves.

So, I need a firewall in my home automation system. What's a firewall and how does it work?

A firewall is hardware, software, or a combination of the two that prevents unauthorized access to or from a private network. Think of it as Internet customs and immigration. The firewall acts as an agent that checks every item entering or leaving the network. Each item must pass the right criteria to make it through. So, a hacker attempting to enter the network of California with a Florida orange would be stopped at the border. Firewalls come in three major types:

- A **packet filter** looks at each packet entering or leaving the network and accepts or rejects it based on user-defined rules. Packet filtering is fairly effective and transparent to users, but difficult to configure. In addition, it is susceptible to IP spoofing.
- A **proxy server** (also known as **application gateway**) intercepts all messages entering and leaving the network. The proxy server effectively hides the true network addresses. Proxies forward messages between clients and servers by appearing to the client (that is, a Web browser) as a server and appearing to the server (that is, the Web server) as a client. Hence, the client talks to the proxies, which then decide whether to forward the communication to the server. It then contacts the server and forwards the approved messages to it. Proxies can handle complex protocols, which packet filters cannot, because they implement a complete set of a client and a server for each protocol. The drawbacks are slower performance and a limited number of supported protocols.
- **Stateful inspection** combines the speed and broad protocol support of packet filters with the security and complex protocol support of proxies. It inspects all the traffic, looking for security-related information, and uses this security-related information to make smart decisions regarding which traffic should be accepted and rejected.

In practice, many firewalls use two or more of these techniques together to protect systems. You can learn more about firewalls in Chapter 5, "Lock Down Basic Security."

I don't need home automation software to access my home PC from the road, do I? Are there any software products that let me connect to a home PC from a remote location?

If access to your PC is all you need, you can get it with a product called pcAnywhere from Symantec (`www.symantec.com`). The Windows operating system ships with a dial-up networking program, but it has problems. pcAnywhere gives you secure PC-to-PC connections through standard modems, ISDN lines, direct cable, and TCP/IP and IPX/SPX networks.

To use it, install pcAnywhere on two machines and designate one as a host (probably your home computer) and the other as a guest (designate your remote computer as the guest). After you configure the system, the guest computer can access files on the host computer, and you can transfer files back and forth between the two. You also can troubleshoot problems, modify settings, and even use programs installed on the host.

To use pcAnywhere, you have to leave your home PC turned on and connected to a modem while you're on the road. That means your home system might be vulnerable to hackers, so be sure your system software prompts for a keyword to discourage intruders.

CHAPTER 15

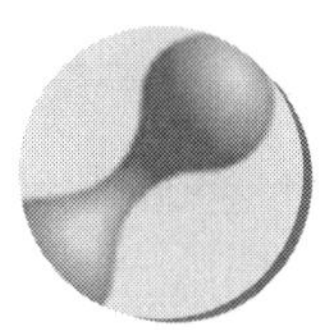

ORCHESTRATE YOUR PDA, CELL PHONE, AND WEB COMPANION

- Choose your weapons
- Lighten your load with hybrid devices
- Synch your devices

The consumer electronics industry has been busy coming up with devices to satisfy consumer demand for constant access to the Web, their phones, schedules, computers, televisions, dry cleaners, and so on. So what do you have in your mobile armada? You have a cell phone, of course, and a PDA (personal digital assistant) no doubt. You might have added a pager to that mix—and maybe an MP3 player, too. If these gadgets overload your back, arms, and briefcase, think what all of that info and access does to your brain.

In this chapter, you get TechTV's perspective on some of the best ways to sort out the mobile device dilemma. You get shopping tips for tracking down the best mobile devices and deals, and highlights from TechTV's expert reviews of the best mobile "hybrids." You also learn fast and easy ways to synch and link all your data and devices with your home and office PCs, so you can ride the communication stream without worry of going under.

MAKE 1+1+1 = 1 WITH HYBRID MOBILE DEVICES

Are you one of these folks who want it all, but don't particularly like *carrying* it all? If you're lugging around a pager, mobile Internet device, PDA, and a cell phone, we'd guess you're ready to do some doubling up. Maybe you want a cell phone/PDA combo, or a two-way pager with Net access. The market's cluttered with "franken-mobile," combination devices, and you have to sort through a lot of clutter to find the one that's right for you.

When you're considering a hybrid mobile device, look for one that's as good at multitasking as you are. Run devices through their paces so you can judge how they perform in every function. And give special attention to which function or functions mean most to you. The hybrid you choose should perform strongest in the features you use most. Here are some of the best options TechTV reviewers have found in the hybrid handheld market.

Keep Your Eyes on the Prize

Whether you're choosing a hybrid or a solo cell phone unit, don't forget the basic "must haves" of any phone you want to own. New phone set and carrier service plans spring up like mushrooms, so shop around to be sure you're getting the best deal of the day. And *always* check coverage and roaming options. Look for

- **Dual analog and digital modes:** Web-enabled services require digital mode.
- **Good performance:** Try before you buy.
- **Long battery life:** Never count on more than the manufacturer's *lowest* estimate.
- **Basic options:** Vibration caller alert and a headset jack for hands-free use make mobile life more convenient, safe, and courteous.
- **Form that fits function:** Look for a usable keypad, readable display, and manageable size.
- **Good, consistent coverage:** Ask for and check user recommendations to be sure this package will give you the service you need, where you need it.

Finally, plan to expand. If you think you'll need to use the phone as an on-the-road modem, be sure it has those capabilities.

Take the Internet on the Road with Your Cell Phone

On-the-road Internet access is a great way to keep up on e-mail, destination weather reports, stock market news, and the latest frightening happenings in Washington. If you travel with a cell phone, here's an option for taking the Net on the road with you.

First, choose a mobile phone that doubles as a data modem for dialing into an ISP. Add an optional data cable, and you can connect your laptop or PDA to the phone, giving you a data connection wherever you have service. This isn't a Web surfing tool, but you can certainly collect your e-mail and access basic information.

Connection kits cost $100 or more. Find a service provider that supports data calls. Data calls cost airtime, so this isn't an economical tool for surfing. Finally, expect sloooooow connection speeds. Most services support speeds between 9.6 and 19.2Kbps.

Got the patience for downloading e-mail at that speed?

You might have another alternative. Many mobile phones and service providers offer WAP (wireless application protocol) access for an additional fee. WAP is a text-only version of a Web page, optimized for devices with small displays, slow transmission speeds, and limited memory. (This is a simplified description of WAP, which does more than we can detail in this space.)

Don't ask WAP to deal with book-length e-mails or graphics-rich Web pages. If you just need basic e-mail handling and online news, weather, travel, and e-commerce, WAP does the trick. The ever-evolving WAP technology is still clunky. Prepare to take your time tapping through multiple menus and screens. Check the TechTV Web site (`www.techtv.com`) for more information on WAP.

The Standard Story

Getting the hippest, most advanced cell phone you can find won't guarantee that your device delivers top-of-the-line functionality. Wireless networks play a strong role in determining just how far cell phone functionality can go. Networks gain technical ground in such huge leaps and bounds that standards are now referred to in terms of evolutionary stages or "generations," labeled 2G, 2.5G, and 3G. Standards vary around the globe, with a handful of major players:

- **GSM** (Global System for Mobile Communications) is the world's largest wireless standard, encompassing Europe, parts of Asia, and the Americas.
- **CDMA** (Code-Division Multiple Access) is the major competitor for GSM in the States.
- **GPRS** (General Packet Radio Service) is a 2.5-generation technology that adds packet-based data access to GSM. This standard improves WAP with faster data speeds and always-on connections, and it's taking over Europe.
- **UMTS** (Universal Mobile Telecommunications System) will bring broadband speeds to GPRS.

The United States currently runs second-generation networks built around CDMA and GSM, with speeds reaching 19.6Kbps. Both standards are expected to go 3G soon, which will bring Internet access and broadband to the network, with speeds up to 2Mbps (that's faster than a T1 connection). No commitment on which standard will rule in the States, though, so there's no ETA on when this new and improved network will arrive in your cell-phone's universe.

Partner Up Your Personal Digital Assistant

PDAs provide a wide variety of functions for today's fast-paced lifestyles. Aside from the Internet functions described earlier, they help with some of the mundane aspects of life. Most PDAs come with features such as address books capable of holding thousands of contacts; a to-do list to ensure everything gets done; a daily, weekly, and monthly calendar to keep track of major events in one's personal and business life; and memo functions to capture those important thoughts before they are forgotten. If you want more than a personal organizer, just download one of the many programs available for use on PDAs.

Web sites, such as Palm, Inc. (www.palm.com), are a virtual shopping mall of ideas for ways you can use your PDA. Figure 15.1 shows one such PDA.

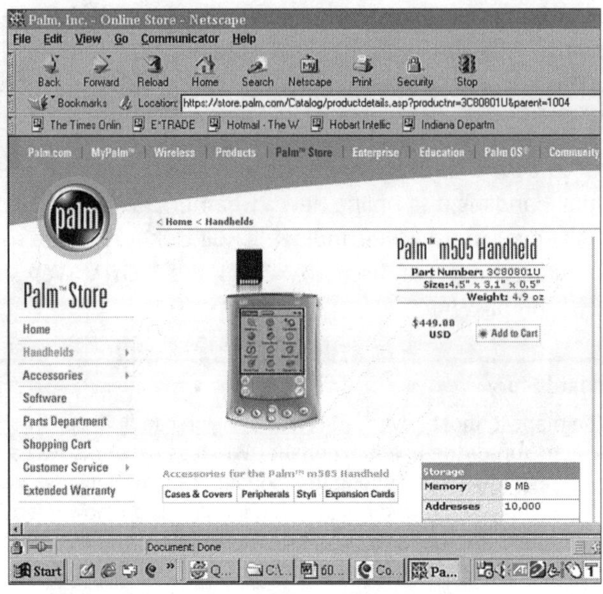

Figure 15.1

PDAs, like this Palm m505 Handheld, are becoming more popular. Aside from basic organizer capabilities, many are taking on new features and are fast becoming mini-computers.

Most cell phones offer basic PDA functions such as built-in phone directories, address and contact lists, and so on. But because most folks want their mobile phones to be small and flashy, few cell phones offer good screens. If you really want a good mobile display, a PDA makes a better choice than a phone. You can see more content at one time on the larger PDA screens.

Don't Overlook the Web Connection!

Choosing a PDA? While you compare costs, battery life, and other features, don't forget to check into Web connectivity, too. Most Palm and Windows-based PDAs connect to the Net by cabling through a digital phone or with a wireless modem, so you don't have to hunt up a phone jack when you want to get online. If your cell phone doesn't have modem capability, be sure the PDA you buy does. If a PDA doesn't come with a built-in wireless Web connection, you'll pay dearly to add one. Wireless modems can cost between $300 and $500, with monthly connection charges running $10 to $60.

An Alternative Online Route for Your PDA

For a non-WAP alternative, consider Cellular Digital Packet Data (CDPD). With CDPD modems, providers such as OmniSky (www.omnisky.com) and YadaYada (www.yadayada.com) provide Internet access for PDAs. CDPD delivers an always-on connection. It operates in the 800 to 900MHz range and transmits data in packets. This isn't a screaming solution; 19.2Kbps is the speed limit and all data is optimized for the PDA's limited memory and display. Although you won't think you're sitting in front of your desktop PC when using CDPD, it's a big step up from the WAP display in terms of usability and connectivity. Expect to pay between $150 and $300 for the CDPD modem and another $40 a month for service.

And now, on to the hybrid devices. Cell phone/PDA combos are becoming more popular all the time, and one of the best examples is Ericsson's R380 (www.mobile.ericsson.com), as shown in Figure 15.2. This smartphone is WAP enabled, offers a generous-sized touch-screen, and includes built-in calendar, address book, and e-mail features. The R380 also boasts handwriting recognition, voice dialing and answering, and even a voice note recorder. These hybrids cost about $600, but as time and technology evolve, you might see some "shrinkage" in that price.

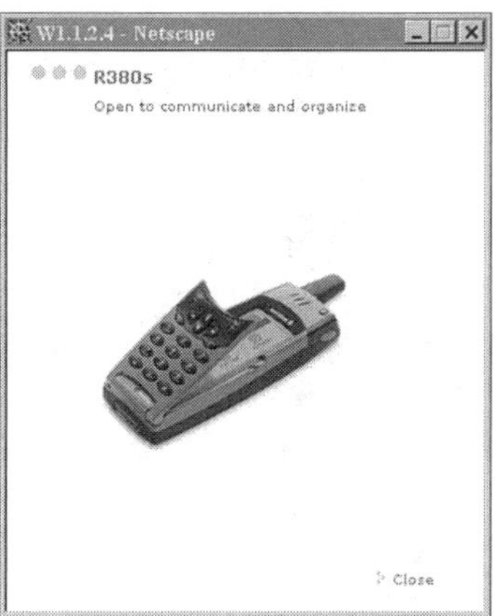

Figure 15.2

The Ericsson R380s is a "smartphone" that combines functions of a mobile phone with advanced communication features such as WAP, SMS, and e-mail. It also has all the other basic PDA tools.

The Packages Just Keep Shrinking

Mobile devices keep getting smaller all the time. Take Timex's new Internet Messenger (www.timex.com), which looks and feels like a typical sports watch. But the Messenger is actually a one-way text pager that can receive news, weather, stock reports, and other info from the Net. The smallest phone we've seen is the Motorola V.series 66 GSM (www.motorola.com). It weights less than 3 ounces, and measures in at 3.3∞1.7∞.8 inches with its lid closed. How much smaller can these devices go? Well, with developments in nanotechnology taking robotics to a molecular scale, who knows? LCD-screen eye implants, anyone?

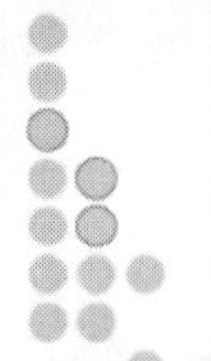

If you don't like dealing with tiny keypads and tedious stylus entry, consider a PDA-cell phone hybrid with an onscreen keypad. The small Samsung SPH-1300 (www.samsung.com) has an onscreen keypad with easy-to-see large numbers you can enter without a stylus. When you want to use the Palm-based PDA features, the keypad screen turns into a Graffiti pad for entering text. The device comes with the usual PDA features, plus voice dialing, memo, and speakerphone. The Samsung's 8-bit color display is one of the first in a PDA-cell phone hybrid, but you shouldn't consider it a why-to-buy for this device. The prototype TechTV received wasn't priced yet, but Samsung anticipates pricing at $350 to $500 (depending on your service provider).

If a Pager Is Your Main Pal...

If you want a two-way pager first, and a cell phone or PDA thrown into the mix, then the handheld market has some communicators designed just for you. Dual-purpose message devices bring cell phone and PDA features into the pager mix to give you a full range of communication tools in a small package.

Although the technology is developing rapidly, right now Motorola offers a couple of feature-packed, dual-purpose devices. Motorola's Accompli 009 and v100 (www.motorola.com) both have Qwerty keyboards to help eliminate the "tap trap" of so many handheld devices (see Figure 15.3). The top-of-the-line Accompli 009 includes full PDA features and a 256-color display, SMS (short message service), and WAP, among other applications.

Figure 15.3

The Motorola V100 has a wide variety of features including phone calling, text messaging, Internet service, and the new "Ping Pong" service so users can have access to AOL Instant Messenger Service.

All data services on the Accompli use the always-on GPRS standard. No speaker in this baby, though, so you access voice features through a hands-free kit (a speakerphone module costs extra). The less-pricey v100 lacks the glitzy color display and OS with application-adding capabilities, but still delivers text messaging and a WAP browser among other good on-the-road features.

These multipurpose products are pagers and PDAs first—phones second. If you crave crystal-clear voice quality, go with a cell phone. But these devices might have lower monthly charges and longer battery life than many phones or wireless Internet PDAs—again, figure out what matters most to you.

HOT TRENDS IN MOBILE DEVICES

The hottest mobile devices premiere every year at Germany's grand tech trade show CeBIT. The goods paraded down the aisles at CeBIT usually aren't ready for general consumption because they're still in development or first-production stages. These exciting toys from the 2001 CeBIT show should hit your local gadget store's shelves any day now (check the TechTV Web sites for ongoing news and manufacturer links):

- Microsoft's "Stinger" mobile operating system runs Sendo's new Z100 Multimedia Smartphone. The tri-band phone/PDA was scheduled for a late 2001 release.
- Digital signature was a noticeable trend. You'll soon be able to use your phone or PDA to sign your name thanks to secure information stored on your SIM (Subscriber Identity Module) card.
- Both Siemens and Nokia showed off MP3 players that double as hands-free accessories. Sony introduced the CMD-MZ25, an MP3 phone that stores music on a 64MB memory stick.
- The world's thinnest cell phone, Sanyo's SCP-6000, measured a mere 9.9 millimeters thick.
- The Siemens watch phone lets you talk Dick Tracy-style or use a hands-free accessory.

The biggest news at CeBIT 2001 was the impending 3G (third-generation) network standard, which promises faster Internet connectivity and the eventual arrival of quality video streaming on mobile phones. With the possibility of mobile streaming video comes the design of sharper screens. Ultra-sharp Organic EL (electro-luminescent) displays will offer more detail and better image quality on smaller screens.

Multimedia Phones Are Just the Tip

Morphing several mobile devices into one is a trend fueled by the telecom industry. Expect rapid-fire developments in mobile technology. Always-on, high-speed Net connections blur the lines between mobile phones and pocket computers, opening up brave new worlds of commercial markets for mobile devices. The industry will work hard to convince you that your cell phone is an essential companion in your mobile life. Multimedia phones are just the beginning; look for other device fold-ins, including music recorders, game machines, and digital cameras. And all of this stuff is going to have to come together in a small, functional, and easy-to-use package if consumers are going to bite. Look for trampling injuries in the mobile device industry as manufacturers race to deliver "firsts" in this wide-open field.

SYNCH YOUR DEVICES

No matter how much you "hybridize" your mobile devices, chances are good (for a while, at least) that you'll still use more than one on a regular basis. You can keep all of these road warriors marching to the same drum by synchronizing your devices on a regular basis. "Hot-synching" describes the process of copying data back and forth between your PDA and desktop or laptop PC.

Synchronizing can take a number of forms. You can synch through cables, through an infrared connection, over the Internet, or through e-mail. Whatever method you use, synching keeps your data safe and current—two important commodities in a mobile world.

It's on TechTV

TechTV's Fresh Gear tracks developments in mobile technology so our viewers can stay on top of developments in mobile communication tools. Watch the latest in these and other device developments at `www.techtv.com/freshgear`.

Synchronize Your Data with Web Apps

One of the TechTV reviewers' favorite super-synchers is a Web application called FusionOne (`www.fusionone.com`). You can use FusionOne to sync your home and work PCs, cell phone, and PDA. This application lets you retrieve your work e-mail on any of your systems, and it also gives you access to your calendar, bookmarks, and MP3s.

Using FusionOne is easy:

1. Log in to FusionOne.
2. Register each device (PDA, laptop, desktop PC, and so on).
3. FusionOne installs itself on each device and walks you through the installation process.
4. Select what you want to synchronize (FusionOne defaults to synching the My Documents folder).

FusionOne syncs applications and data automatically during installation. You also have 25MB of storage available on the FusionOne Web site, so this Web app is a synch *and* store solution—another two-fer! Security is an ongoing concern, but FusionOne seems to have set up a decent "digital vault" for its customers' data. According to FusionOne, your password is encrypted locally, and the data is also encrypted on its servers using Counterpane (`http://www.counterpane.com/`) Lab's Twofish cipher.

FusionOne has its limits; though it says it can sync with Outlook Express, but TechTV's reviewers could only get the full version of Outlook to sync. And FusionOne won't sync with some Web apps, such as Yahoo! Calendar or some Web-based e-mail accounts. And the 25MB of online storage isn't enough to handle a busy online life; you can get more storage space, though, for a monthly fee (the lowest current monthly service cost is $9.95).

Recently, Palm entered the online synching biz with MyPalm Portal (`www.palm.net`). This online storage and synching portal is free, which is good. But it doesn't sync all your information, which isn't good. MyPalm doesn't synchronize e-mail, expenses, and memo pad, and it doesn't support address book categories, either. If you've organized all your stuff into groups, those groups won't transfer to the Web. And if you use a Mac, forget it. MyPalm doesn't support Mac at this time.

Check Out Your PC Connection Options

When you choose a mobile device that you know you'll want to connect to your computer, make sure you check out its connection type. Most PDAs connect to PCs with a serial or USB cradle. Plug the cradle into the PC, settle the PDA in the cradle, and the devices synch by copying information between the two device memories (backing up your datebook, address book, to-do lists, and so on). You also use the synching process to load software. Synching with a USB cradle is easier than a serial cradle, so consider USB a plus in any system you're comparing. Although some Palm models don't come with a standard USB cradle, you can buy one for an additional $40. USB cradles are standard on most Visor PDAs.

Practice Safe Synching

Synching your PDA to your desktop or laptop computer is a pretty basic process, but that doesn't mean there aren't right and wrong ways to go about it. Your PDA came with step-by-steps for hot-synching. In general, the process involves hooking your PDA's cradle to your PC's serial or USB port, putting your PDA in the cradle, and pushing the cradle's Synch (or On) button. Sounds easy enough, and it is. But to keep the synching process swimming along, follow these tips:

- Be sure your cradle has batteries if it requires them.
- Don't synch when your battery charge is low. If the synch fails partway through, you're likely to lose data.
- Download software updates from your PDA manufacturer's Web site.
- Synch frequently. If you lose your PDA, or if your PC's hard drive crashes, you'll lose less data if your synchronization is current.
- Don't cancel a synchronization after it starts. You'll either lose or duplicate data, and the clean-up from either problem can be frustrating (not to mention annoying).

Could You Love a Web Companion?

If you think you might be interested in a Web companion—a wired or wireless non-PC device that gives you Internet access—ask yourself why. Don't feel like installing and configuring a PC? Most Internet appliances are easier to set up than a full PC, but some of them, such as AOL TV, aren't easy at all. And remember, that easy installation and flat learning curve result from the Web companion's lack of features. You can't download software and use applications such as word processors and spreadsheets with most of these things. Cost a factor? You won't save much over the cost of a cheap computer if you buy a $400 to $600 Web doodle, and then spend another $250 or so on the yearly usage charges (and some of these devices require that you sign up for a one- to three-year stint). Remember, you can buy some cheap PCs for around $500. So which is the bigger bargain? Depending on your needs and situation, a Web companion might be just right for you. But test-drive the device and factor in all the costs before you decide to hitch yourself to a Web companion.

LIGHTNING ROUND Q&A WRAP-UP

How can I synch my Palm Pilot with my Hotmail account that is being routed to Outlook Express?

Unfortunately, you're talking mission impossible. You can't sync a Hotmail e-mail account onto a PDA running the Palm OS, because the Palm will only synch to a default inbox. Palm PDAs are experts at synchronizing with the Microsoft Outlook and Microsoft Outlook Express e-mail clients. You drop them in the cradle with the proper setup, and the contents of your inbox instantly transfer onto your Palm. The problem is that you can't get the Hotmail contents to go into the default inbox.

You can configure Outlook to download your Hotmail, but it will go into an alternate Hotmail inbox. Try making a filter that orders all incoming mail with the word "Hotmail" in the "To" field to be sent to the primary inbox, and you'll be rewarded with a grayed-out button representing the said inbox. How about creating a new folder to filter the Hotmail and forward mail from the new folder to the primary inbox? Again, no luck. Unless you manually transfer individual messages into your inbox, then synchronize, this solution's another exercise in futility.

Bottom line: Hotmail, owned by Microsoft, is designed to function with Outlook and is not accessible through any other client.

I've heard that it's pretty easy to tap cell-phone conversations. How do I know if someone's listening in on my calls?

TechTV went to the pros for the answer to this question. Robert Weaver, assistant to the special agent at the U.S. Secret Service in New York City, and Eric Friedberg, senior litigation counsel for the U.S. Attorney's office of the Eastern District of New York, offers these tips on protecting yourself from cell-phone snoops:

- Don't divulge sensitive information, such as business secrets, credit card numbers, or private information about family or friends while on a cell phone.
- Contact your wireless phone provider to ask about cellular phones that use encryption. Phones that use encryption are more secure than those that don't.
- In general, digital phones are more secure than analog ones. It's easier to eavesdrop on and clone analog communications. But remember, most cell phones are dual band (meaning they switch between digital and analog depending on coverage). And just because a stream is digital doesn't mean it can't be illegally intercepted.
- Check your cell phone bill carefully for unfamiliar numbers. Some scams distribute over many numbers. Contact your cell phone provider to contest any charges you know aren't yours.

CHAPTER 16

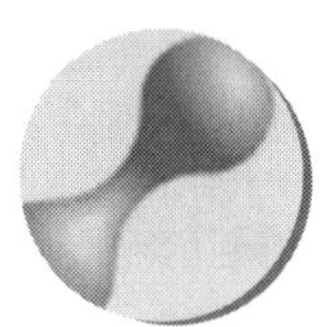

TAKE CONTROL OF YOUR PC GAMING

- Build your own gaming machine
- Upgrade an older PC for games
- Design your own games
- Jump into online gaming

Serious gamers often wonder whether to buy or build a gaming machine. You can buy some mighty powerful systems with graphics, sound, and speed that will get your heart thumping and set your hair on end. On the other hand, if you're interested in configuring your own custom game-ride, you can build your own system from the ground up.

This chapter shows you how to put together a no-holds-barred ultimate gaming machine, from case to keyboard. For those mortals among you, TechTV's favorite recipe for a smoking game box will set you back less than $1,000. And after you've built your own machine, why stop there? See how easy it is to design and create your own games in any genre.

BUILD A GAMER'S DREAM MACHINE

Gaming is good only when you can enjoy fast action, great sound, and killer video. Every serious gamer dreams of building the ultimate gaming PC, and in this section, we pull together *our* version of said mean machine. We know, we know, the specs of an "ultimate" machine change on a regular basis. But in this section, we show you how to build a screaming machine that, with periodic updates (and modifications to suit your own preferences) can stand the tests of time in any gamer's world.

It's on TechTV

Every year, TechTV builds a new "ultimate gaming machine." To catch the updates or learn more about any of the components mentioned in this chapter, visit `www.TechTV.com/products`.

Choose Your Core Components

What makes a killer gaming machine? A fast CPU is at the top of the list. Start your quest for the ultimate PC by choosing a processor that's both fast *and* reliable. Whether you go with an AMD or Intel platform, get the latest processor. AMD's 1.2GHz Thunderbird is fast, reliable, and reasonably priced, so that's the chip of choice for this machine. To complement that new T-bird, choose the A7V133 motherboard from Asus.

With the chip and motherboard in place, you need to add that RAM. The experts' best advice when deciding on memory is *get as much as you can afford*. 128MB is the baseline (for Windows 2000, consider 192MB the minimum), but you don't want to mess with minimums in a dream machine, do you? For TechTV's version of gaming heaven, add two sticks of Corsair 256MB PC2100 DDR memory, pushing the machine's RAM to 512MB. That oughta do.

Be Careful with That Microprocessor!

When you install the microprocessor, handle it with care. One wrong move and you can chip the chip. When that happens, your processor is toast (literally). You also need to keep processor-protection in mind when you install the cooling device. Again, if you get the device in the wrong position or try to force *anything* into place, you stand a good chance of damaging the processor (see Figure 16.1). Even if money is no object when it comes to your ultimate gaming machine, you could spend that $300 processor replacement cost on better speakers, right?

Pack in the Storage

Games hog disk space. On even a less-than-ultimate machine you need at least a 16GB hard drive that spins at 10,000 rpm. For *this* baby, though, go with two 45GB, 7200 RPM drives, to give the machine a total of 90GB of IDE hard drive space. While you're at it, go on and add four 73GB 10,000 RPM SCSI drives, for a total hard drive space of 383.6GB.

Removable storage options include DVD-ROM, DVD-R, CD-ROM, or CD-RW. Don't go with less than a 16x CD or 5x DVD, and TechTV recommends a 32x CD-RW (the Plextor Plexwriter is a great choice) and an 8x DVD-R.

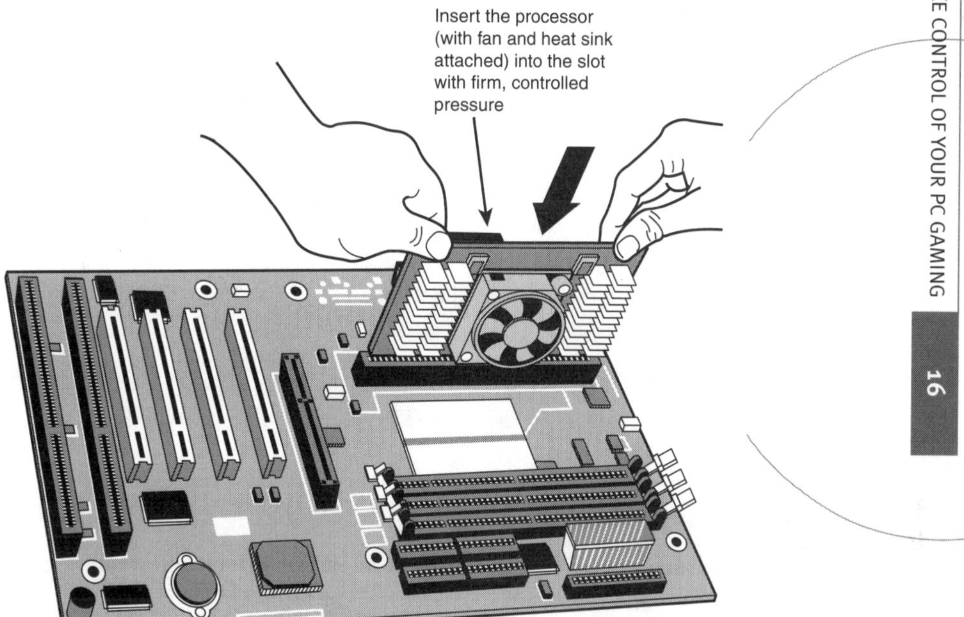

Figure.16.1

Take it easy when you install the processor and cooling devices. You can destroy the CPU if you try to force the module in place.

Get the Sound and (Graphics) Fury

After the CPU, sound and graphics components are the most important parts of a gaming machine setup. A hard-core gamer's graphics card should support the AGP bus and have no less than 32MB of memory. The TechTV ultimate gaming machine goes well beyond these minimums with its Gladiac Ultra GeForce2 Ultra Card. With 64MB of DDR memory and the nVidia GeForce Ultra GPU on board, this card screams.

To best use that card, put a 32-inch Arcadia AR3.2T monitor on your gaming machine. Not only does the sheer size of this monitor put you squarely in the gaming action, the AR3.2T is also an HDTV-compliant XGA monitor. That means you can get double-duty from the gaming machine by using it to watch HDTV or DVDs. If you have to keep your playing PC on a desktop, this big screen might be overkill—in that case, step down to a 19-inch or 21-inch display.

Surrounding yourself in fantasy means getting the best sound you can buy. At minimum, look for a 32-bit sound card with MP3 ripping software. The TechTV machine uses the Live! Platinum 5.1 card. This card's Live Drive 2 and Dolby 5.1 processing give full-theater sound to games *and* DVDs.

To put the bark in your system's sound bite you need a good speaker set. A five-speaker system with a good subwoofer will give you the surround sound you want with that high-quality sound card. The Klipsch THX-certified satellite speakers are favorites at TechTV, but speakers really are a "personal preference" component. Go out and listen to a variety of speaker systems to find the ones that sound best to you.

Box It Up and Cool It Down

That beefy 1.2-GHz chip we installed in our gaming machine puts off a lot of heat. When you construct your gaming PC, pay special attention to the system's power and cooling setup. You need a sturdy, well-ventilated case that can accommodate your cooling system. PC Power and Cooling's Steel Tower case is a good choice, with plenty of room and a 400-watt ATX power supply. A 300-watt power supply is a baseline, but if possible, go with 400 watts.

TechTV's favorite cooler is the Thermaltake SuperOrb. You should also use a few case fans and—if you think your gaming could get really hot—you could add a big-dog solution, such as the Turbo-Cool2X.

Get Your Hands on the Controls

Controllers are another "strictly your choice" PC component. Cool-hunting and trends aside, choose your game controller for function, not form. Go to the store and test-drive a variety of controllers, then buy the ones that feel and work best for you. Although the mouse and keyboard might be your controllers of choice, you'll also want to be able to game without wires. To meet that challenge, equip your ultimate gaming machine with a Microsoft Optical Intellimouse and the Intel Wireless keyboard.

Why PC When You Can Console?

Console games are ragingly popular. They're portable, easy to plug in and play, and the games ship in great, ready-to-use format—no "oops, we'll fix it later with a patch," as you sometimes see with PC games. But PC games are likely to be the favorite of serious gamers for some time, and with good reason. Games look better on PCs, thanks to VGA monitors and beefy PC processing power. And PC games are constantly evolving; you can add a new component to your system and get a better, bigger, faster gaming experience. A console is what it is. If you want to improve on it, you have to buy a new one. Finally, PCs can do many other tricks besides gaming, so a PC is simply more versatile than a game console. Next-generation consoles are in the works, and some folks predict that they'll kill PCs. But for now, many gamers will testify that for a really rich gaming experience, you gotta go with a PC.

To let you keep both hands in the game, this machine includes a Microsoft Sidewinder Strategic Commander—a multifunction USB control device designed for the left hand. To top off the set, we added a Microsoft Sidewinder Precision 2 joystick and a Sidewinder Game Voice, which is great for communicating with other online gamers and issuing voice commands.

BACK IN THE REAL WORLD WITH A SUB-$1,000 GAMING PC

So, are you saying, "Thanks, TechTV, but I don't want to take out a second mortgage to play Quake III"? Well, it's true that putting together a box like this gaming dream machine could set you back several thousand big ones. But TechTV does have a practical side, too.

Here's a short and simple recipe for a fast and mighty gaming machine that delivers blazing-fast 3D processing and smooth performance—for less than $1,000. Check out Table 16.1 for the components list and final tally.

You Can Beat This Deal

The prices listed in TechTV's "under $1K" gaming machine come straight from the shelves of the local electronics store. If you have the time and interest, you can do even better by shopping online bargain sites such as Price Watch (`www.pricewatch.com`). And there's a little nudge-room in the specs, too. Pack in a little less memory, or cut back to a GeForce2 Mx card, and you could save even more money and still get decent game-play.

TABLE 16.1 The TechTV Under-$1K (Before Tax) Screaming Machine Parts List

Part	Description	Price
CPU	AMD T-Bird 800 MHz	$129
Motherboard	ASUS A7V Socket A	$159.95
Memory	256MB PC133 SDRAM	$115
Graphics	Asus V-7700 Pure	$205
Sound	Creative SBLive! Value	$59
CD-ROM	Creative CD-ROM Blaster 52x (CompUSA)	$49.99
Hard Drive	IBM Deskstar 20GB 7200 RPM, UATA/100	$125.95
NIC	Smartlink 10BaseT/100 BaseTX Ethernet	$12
Fans	CPU/2 Aux case fans	$36
Floppy	Teac	$16.50
Case	ATX Mid-Tower w/300W Power Supply	$52
Keyboard	Generic	$15
Mouse	Kensington Mouse-in-a-Box	$15
Total Cost		**$960.39**

The earlier recipe for the ultimate gaming machine, presented the ground rules for choosing your weapons, and then proceeded to shoot well above the baseline in nearly every component category. This more down-to-earth gamer's playpen foregoes a lot of the frills without losing any of the power and speed good gaming requires. Here are a few points about the choices for this good gamer:

- This machine doesn't skimp on the chipset. The 800 MHz Thunderbird gives maximum performance per dollar in this machine. You can upgrade this component later, so 800 MHz is a fine starting point.
- 128MB of RAM is rock-bottom, but RAM is cheap. Using 256MB doesn't break the bank, and adding plenty now helps avoid the hassle of trying to match RAM with later upgrades.
- The Asus GeForce2 video cards offer strong performance. The GeForce2 GTS is the best video card out there for the money. If you want to drop another hundred bucks, go for the GTS Pro 64MB DDR card.
- The TechTV gamers chose the Creative Sound Lab's SBLive card and matched it up with a 52x CD-ROM. If you can find a less expensive CD-ROM drive that offers *at least* 32x speed, go for it.
- You won't find speakers listed here, because you probably have a pair of used speakers hanging around that will work for this machine. If you want to splash out on a pair of good speakers for this machine (and good speakers make for good gaming), you probably can pick up a pair of Klipsch pro Medias for less than $200.
- The hard drive listed here was an on-sale buy, but if you shop around online and keep your eyes open for sales, you should be able to match the quality and price.
- No need to cut corners on the case and cooling fans. This ATX Mid-Tower with its 300-watt power supply isn't expensive—and it's well worth every penny it costs.

The machine described here is strictly a gamer's friend. No DVD, no CDR/W, scanner, printer, or netcam. But this gaming machine is guaranteed to deliver every one of its $1,000 in pure gaming enjoyment.

THINKING OF UPGRADING AN OLD PC?

If you have an old PC beater stashed around the house, you might want to pump up its power and use it exclusively as a gaming machine. That can work, but you need a plan to make *sure* you follow the best path to gaming glory.

Upgrading your computer is serious business. When you start talking about things like upgrading your processor or motherboard, you're talking about major improvements (not to mention lots of money). Do your homework and don't go into the project blindly. These steps will save you time, money, and sanity during the upgrade process:

1. **Prioritize:** Have a good idea of what you want your post-upgrade computer to do. What do you want most, and what are you willing to settle for? What's more important, having great video or great sound? Is it more important to get a cool,

force-feedback joystick or to speed up the frame rate? By prioritizing what you want your computer to do, you'll be more likely to get what you want.

2. **Know the games you play:** Do you want to enter Quake III online frag fests? Or do you want to spend all your free time building theme parks in RollerCoaster Tycoon? Or maybe you just want to play e-mail Scrabble with your grandma in Tallahassee. Each of these requires different setups. Some games work best with a specific graphic card, and some games won't work at all with some cards. Research online and ask around to be sure you buy the card that best suits your gaming. The TechTV Web site (`www.techtv.com`) is a great place to find reviews of a number of graphic cards and links to the manufacturers' Web sites.
3. **The bigger, the better:** In gaming, size matters. The higher your machine's spec numbers, the better it will function as a gaming PC. Boosting RAM, for example, is a fast and cheap ticket to better frame rates and less lag time. And go with high-quality Grade A RAM. Anything less could result in system crashes. But don't forget to match your RAM to your chipset (keep reading to learn more about that choice).
4. **Know your chipset:** A computer's chipset determines how much and what type of RAM you should use in your system. Check the manufacturer's specs to find out what RAM is best for your motherboard and processor.
5. **Read, read, read:** Pick up some gaming magazines, read online reviews and visit good online gaming spots like Gamespot.com (see Figure 16.2). Then, talk to other gamers to be sure you know what you want your computer to do, and the best way to do it. You can't over-work this stage of your upgrade, so dig into all the info you can find.

Figure 16.2

You can learn a lot about what's happening in the gaming world at `Gamespot.com`. This site lists the latest in games and gaming hardware, and it's a great way to keep up with the latest in gaming news.

Can Windows Get Game?

Windows 98 proved to be a strong OS for a wide variety of games, but many folks who upgraded to Windows 2000 discovered that it doesn't play nice with many games. Microsoft didn't leave its Windows 2000 users gameless, though. If you use Win2K, download a patch that fixes game compatibility issues at `www.microsoft.com/windows2000/downloads/deployment/appcompat/default.asp`. Now, how about Windows XP? The jury is still out, but you can follow developments by watching TechTV and visiting `www.techtv.com`.

CREATE YOUR OWN VIDEO GAMES

Have you ever dreamed of creating your own video game? Chances are that you can. But if you aren't comfortable with dabbling around in programming languages, don't expect to author the next Quake or Doom. Programming a full-fledged video game that really works the latest technology requires a lot of skill—and a fair investment of time and patience to boot. You don't *have* to do all the programming to create a video game. Go all the way or dabble in game creation—the choice is yours.

Feel Up to Programming?

If you're ready and able to tackle programming, you can write powerful games using the C or BASIC programming languages. Before you quit your day job though, get comfortable with programming terms such as vector graphics, parallax scrolling, polygon rendering, and pixel plotting.

If you work in C, pick up a copy of *The Black Art of 3D Game Programming* by Andre LaMothe. This book delivers detailed C++ source code for every facet of game programming, including writing your own high-end 3D engine. Although the bundled CD and the source code are designed for Windows PCs, the techniques and concepts apply to all computers.

If BASIC is your language of choice, grab a copy of a programming tool called DarkBASIC (`www.darkbasic.com`). DarkBASIC lets you create your own 3D games and demos using the BASIC programming language. The tool's in-depth tutorials should get you started, even if you're a first-time coder.

Get Gaming Advice From the Pros

Whatever gaming info you're hunting, you'll find it at Gamespot's PC Games Workshop (`www.gamespot.com`). Gamespot lists a wide variety of gamers' news, product reviews, and links to the newest game downloads and demos. The site's beta center and release calendar keep you on top of new and upcoming releases, and Gamespot's hints and strategies can improve your game in any genre, including Action, Role-Playing, Sports, Sims, and Strategy. Gamespot also walks you through the specs of *its* version of the ultimate gaming machine, with links to component vendors.

Take the Less Complicated Path

You can still exercise your inner game-maker, even if you never master a programming language. MODs—or game modifications—have given lots of nonprogrammers the opportunity to dabble in game development. MODs let you customize a game by adjusting some of the game's parameters, including model skins, level maps, game physics, and sound.

MODs are easy to use and even easier to conceptualize. Using MODS is like customizing a car or redecorating your house. The framework stays the same, but the game's "feel" and function change just enough to give you your own, custom-made rush.

For expert guidance through a "no-experience-necessary" process of creating games and sims, try Stagecast Creator (`www.stagecast.com`). Stagecast Creator has a built-in tutorial called Learn Creator. Using the tutorial, you can make your first game in one or two hours. Stagecast supplies the expertise—you supply the ideas.

Step Through the Design Basics

Designing a game or sim can seem like an overwhelming process—and, as we've mentioned, detailed programming takes some skill and expertise. But whether you plan to program your way to 3D action or work through your design with the help of a program like Stagecast Creator, your game design involves the same basic steps:

- **Design your characters and decide how they'll appear**: You have to determine what pieces or characters appear in the game. Most characters can appear several different ways, by facing right or left, looking angry or surprised, and so on. Your design determines how and when the characters move. You decide whether they do something—move, make noise, change appearance, interact with another character—while the user is just watching, or react only to user-input.
- **Make the rules**: You determine the rules of your game, including how users play the game and how the game responds to controller commands (arrows, mouse clicks, and so on).
- **Create levels and stages:** Most games have levels that get more complicated as the players move through the game. Determine how many levels your game has and how hard each level should be. Each level should go on a different "stage" or back-

Check Out These Game-Building Resources

If you're serious about creating your own game, you need to take advantage of the best resources you can find. Ambrosine.com (`www.ambrosine.com/resource`) maintains an exhaustive list of game development news and resources, engines, and authorware for nonprogrammers. You'll find graphics, music, and other tools for putting together heart-thumping games—and you don't have to be a programmer to use many of them.

ground, and each instruction screen, help screen, and scoring screen is also a stage. How many stages will your game have? What will the user have to do to get from one level to the next? You have to design the look of each stage by determining the color and size of the stages and the size of the grid that the characters move across.

When you've created your characters, rules, levels, and stage backgrounds, you're ready to put them all together into the game you've designed. Whether you program code or follow a game-design tutorial, creating a working video game takes time and skill. But what a cool accomplishment—you'll have created your own gaming masterpiece!

GETTING INTO ONLINE GAMING

Online gaming is a great way to pit your wits against thousands of fellow gamers. You can play games such as chess, backgammon, and euchre against real, live opponents from around the world. Some game rooms only allow serious competition, while others are more social. If you're not the competitive type, you can play crossword puzzles, word searches, and trivia games. Visit `www.boxerjam.com` and the MSN Gaming Zone (`www.zone.msn.com`) for some of these great online challenges.

Check out these gaming hangouts:

- **First Person Shooter:** Quake III or Unreal Tournament both make it easy to jump into an online match (and Unreal Tournament has a great tutorial). If you want to take it up a notch, try Counterstrike. This game emphasizes teamwork and currently is the most popular online first-person shooter. Tribes 2, another teamwork-based game, is the new kid on the block. You can find all these games at your local software store; playing online is free.
- **Strategy games:** These usually take place in real time, meaning that all players begin the game at the same time. One of the easiest games to get into is Blizzard Entertainment's StarCraft (`www.blizzard.com/starcraft`). You can access the game's free matching service, Battle.net, from within the game to find thousands of willing opponents. Warning: real-time strategy games take a few hours to play, so be sure you have time to finish the game before you start.
- **Role-Playing:** These games often involve thousands of players, all playing at the same time. The virtual worlds (and play) go on, even when you log out. Although role-playing games aren't much more than glorified chat rooms, playing with others who share your style can be a lot of fun. One of the most popular games in this category, Everquest, requires that you buy the software and pay a monthly subscription fee (about $10) for access to the online world. Other titles offer the first month free. Or, try a total freebie, Subspace (`www.subspacehq.com`); this game's like a multiplayer version of an old computer game called Space War.

You're playing with real people here, in real time. Among the thousands of players you'll encounter, some will be as creepy as the visual effects in games they play. Play nice, play clean, and keep telling yourself that it's only a game.

LIGHTNING ROUND Q&A WRAP-UP

Since I installed my firewall, I've had problems hooking into online games. Do I have to choose between the firewall and Everquest?

Most multiplayer online games work just fine through a firewall, but sometimes you have to open specific ports to allow certain traffic to reach the game firewall (each firewall has its own process). If you host an online game, you can count on having to open specific ports to allow others to connect to you. If you're in doubt as to which ports to use, check with the manufacturer of the game. Here's a list of a few games and the ports they use (with an address, where a Web site is available):

- **Age of Empires** (`www.ensemblestudios.com`)—Initial TCP 47624 Outbound 47624 Inbound Connection

  Subsequent TCP 2300-2400 2300-2400 Inbound

  Subsequent TCP 2300-2400 2300-2400 Outbound

  Subsequent UDP 2300-2400 2300-2400 Inbound

  Subsequent UDP 2300-2400 2300-2400 Outbound
- **Battlezone 2** (`www.activision.com`)—UDP—17770 and 17771
- **Descent Freespace** (`www.descent-freespace.com`)—Freespace itself, 4000 (UDP) and 3999 (TCP)

  Descent Freespace PXO chat server, 7000 (TCP)

  Descent Freespace PXO user tracker, 3493 (UDP)

  Descent Freespace PXO game tracker, 3440 (UDP)
- **Diablo 2** (`www.blizzard.com`)—Battle.net, 6112-6119, 4000 TCP and UDP

  Diablo 2 non-Battle.net, 4000 TCP
- **EA Games** (`www.ea.com`)—Typically TCP 1791
- **Everquest** (`www.everquest.station.sony.com`)—This game is complicated to set up. See the instructions at the Web site.
- **Klingon Honor Guard**—7777
- **Half-Life**—(`www.sierrastudios.com`)—27015
- **Heretic 2**—(`www.robertgraham.com`)—28910
- **Hexen 2**—26900
- **HexenWorld**—26950
- **Quake**—26000
- **Quake 2**—27910
- **Quake 3** (`www.activision.com`)—Port numbers vary depending on server, but they're typically 27960-27963
- **Red Alert 2** (`www.westwood.ea.com`)—1234, 1235, 1236, 1237

- **Sin**—22450
- **Starsiege TRIBES**—28000-28008
- **TRIBES 2** (`www.planettribes.com`)—28000-28009, 6667-6669, and upper UDP ports 1024+
- **Unreal**—7777
- **Unreal Tournament**—7778

My friends and I want to network our computers to play games and send and receive files. We live about a mile from each other, so a normal network will not do. Is there any software out there that can network at least three computers over the Internet?

Yes, and you have a few options for setting up a network to share files and play games with your friends over the Internet. Start by doing a PC-spec inventory. Find out which of the computers in the group is the fastest and has the most available space, and designate that machine as the "server."

Next, you need a safe and secure way to share files over the Net without creating a WAN (wide area network). For this job, you can use Hotline (`www.bigredh.com`), a program developed originally for the Mac. Besides letting you safely share files over the Internet, Hotline features real-time chat, conferencing, messaging, data warehousing, and file transfer and viewing. Install the server edition on the computer you've designated as the server. Everyone else on the gaming network installs the client version on their machines. The Hotline tutorial walks you through the process of configuring the server and explains how to grant access rights.

Most popular multiplayer games ship with TCP/IP support and let you connect with whomever you like. Configure the server to allow connections, so you can connect players from different locations. You should be able to do that configuration from within the game software. Then, just be sure everyone in the gaming group knows the server's IP address. After they configure their machines to point to the server (also within the game software), your gaming network is good to go.

My son likes to play Quake and other games online. I've had some strange things happen to my computer since he started playing these games. Are there ways for anyone to do something bad to my computer while he is gaming online?

It sounds like you might have received a Trojan horse while your son was gaming online. Trojan horses appear to be harmless files and can lie dormant for long periods of time. The best thing you can do to avoid getting one is to buy and install Norton Antivirus (`http://www.symantec.com/nav/nav_9xnt/`) and regularly watch for updates. The updates feature all the latest antiviral medicine your computer needs to repair itself if you receive a virus not registered with Norton.

You also might want to ask your son to curb any risky game habits. One popular lure with playing Quake online is the ability to play in levels or maps that someone else has created. If your son downloaded and installed a custom level, he could have brought the Trojan Horse into your machine with that level. A simple solution to this is to only let your son play in levels that are created by the game's manufacturer. But that won't offer you 100 percent protection. Chat rooms with the capability to share files also present risky scenarios. If your son trades files in chat rooms, he's setting your PC up for an eventual Trojan Horse invasion. Tell him not to trade anything in a chat room but chat.

CHAPTER 17

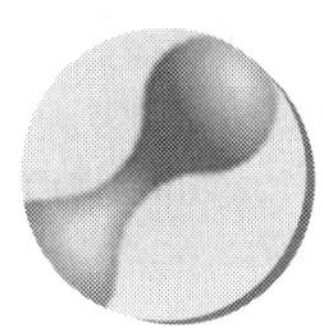

HAVE IT ALL: THE JUKEBOX/MUSIC STUDIO/RADIO/MOVIE THEATER PC

- Get inside MP3
- Find, play, and play *with* MP3s
- Track down a good MP3 player
- Use your PC as a music studio
- Tune into Internet radio
- Dig into DVD

Your computer is a lot more than a "work station." In fact, it can be the ultimate entertainment machine. In this chapter, you learn how to extract maximum entertainment value from your time at the box. If you haven't jumped into the world of MP3 swapping, it's never too late to start. Here, you learn where the MP3 action is and how to get there. You also find out about cool software and hardware setups that can turn your PC into a good-as-the-pros music production studio, an all-the-hits-all-the-time radio that broadcasts just the stations you want to hear (from anywhere on the globe), and a director's-cut dream machine for watching DVD movies.

DEMYSTIFYING MP3S

If the whole MP3 thing has passed you by, don't just stand there with that puzzled expression on your face. There's nothing complicated, difficult, or (in most cases) illegal about downloading and listening to MP3s. This fast, easy-to-read section explains the whole process to you in a few pages.

Sample MP3 Technology

First, a moment of definition. MP3s are audio files that have been compressed so that they transfer easily from an online site to your hard drive, a CD-RW, or other storage medium. MP3 uses the third audio layer of the MPEG (moving picture experts group) compression standard, and that's where it gets its name.

By removing superfluous sounds—which the ear doesn't register, anyway—from audio tracks, the MP3 format shrinks the original recorded sound by a factor of 12. That makes the files smaller without sacrificing much quality. Smaller files equal zippier transfers and more efficient storage, making those once-bulky audio files more usable.

A Closer Look at MP3 Sound Sampling

Your computer can't represent the sound of a recorded music track exactly as it is in the real world—that takes too much data. Instead, the computer *samples* the music. It listens to a sound a certain number of times per second, and each time it listens it assigns a number to the sound-bit, based on the sound's sine wave. In CD-quality sound, the computer listens to a sound about 14,100 times per second. That means that each second of music you hear on a CD recording is made up of approximately 14,000 sound numbers, glued together to represent the smooth curve of the actual sound. Even on an MP3 recording, which reduces the sound bits on a CD recording by a factor of 12, the human ear can't easily tell the difference between the "sampled" sound and the original recorded sound.

Is This Stuff Legal?

This technology doesn't sound like anything revolutionary, does it? But MP3s have changed the way people acquire and listen to music, and that's what sparks the interest of the music industry (and its attorneys). Because people can download, listen to, and share copies of copyrighted material, many in the music industry see this technology as a "pirate enabler" that cuts into revenues of musicians and the record companies who produce and distribute their music.

On the other hand, MP3 technology makes it possible for musicians to record and distribute their own music directly to their fans, bypassing the record companies completely. The fans can get cheaper music, and more of the profits go directly into the pockets of the musicians. Are you beginning to see who's screaming the loudest over the MP3 revolution?

So, is it legal to download MP3s? The answer is, "maybe." Creating and playing an MP3 on your home system is legal. Downloading an MP3 from a Web site is legal *if* the song's copyright holder has granted permission to download and play the song. However, it's *illegal* to encode MP3s from CDs and trade them without permission from the copyright holder. Think of MP3s as having the same legality as Cuban cigars: It's OK to have them, it's OK to smoke (or play) them, but it's not OK to buy them or send them to someone.

Why MP3 Matters to Most of Us

You might be wondering why, if you're not a musician or a record company executive, you should care about MP3. If you're a music lover, you should care a lot. This technology lets you download and store music right on your computer, turning your PC into your dream jukebox. You can create a huge music library, filled with hard-to-find favorites that would take years (and lots and lots of moola) to acquire through

Follow the Action in the Napster Wars

On the front lines of the MP3 battle, the pioneering MP3 distribution site Napster has been suffering the slings and arrows of litigation almost since it hit the Net. In March 2001, a federal appeals court ruled that Napster had to block the trading of copyrighted files on its system in response to a lawsuit by the world's five biggest record companies: Vivendi Universal's Universal Music, Sony Music, AOL Time Warner's Warner Music, EMI Group, and Bertelsmann's BMG. Napster instituted the screening mechanism and began constantly tweaking the filters to detect intentional misspellings. The number of files per user fell dramatically after the filter was put in place—from 220 to 34 within the first month. Congressionally mandated licensing might be Napster's best hope for survival, but executives from the Recording Industry Association of America (RIAA) and the Motion Picture Association of America (MPAA) balked at compulsory licensing. Looking forward to the day when movies are widely distributed online, the MPAA hasn't exactly come out in favor of compulsory licensing. And many observers have accused RIAA of hypocrisy, noting that record labels have a history of shortchanging artists on royalties to maximize profits. Critics see the RIAA's current quest to neuter Napster as a reflection of the group's desire to extend its control of music distribution into cyberspace. The battle rages on, but here's the bottom line: Music equals money, and the highest bidder just might walk away with the prize in these rock-star wars.

traditional music retail outlets. MP3 lets you manipulate the music like you never have before. Burn your own music on MP3 format, edit the tracks, and—with a CD-RW—rip CDs from MP3s or create MP3s from CDs.

ALL THE HOW-TOS OF MP3

The beauty of the MP3 process is that it's so sweet and simple. To download and listen to MP3s you just need a computer, an Internet connection, and MP3 player software. Then, you're ready to start grabbing those MP3s and listening to your own private play lists. We like these players:

- **Winamp** is the standard Windows MP3 player. You can download it free at `www.winamp.com`.
- Although the CD-writing features only work with the CD-R in the Power Mac G4/466, G4/533, and G4/667, **iTunes** is still useful for any Mac user. It can organize your play lists and convert your files to MP3. What's more, it's free (for now, anyway)! Download your copy at `www.apple.com`.
- **MusicMatch Jukebox** (`www.musicmatch.com`) is probably the best jukebox program around. Use it to play and convert MP3, WMA, and WAV files, manage your music, and burn CDs. It offers changeable skins and visualizations, so your music experience never gets boring. You can go for the free version, but we suggest that you pony up $20 for the Plus flavor, which offers faster encoding and burning, along with other functions not found on the freebie.

Find MP3s

When you have your player, you need the MP3 files. Peer-to-peer file sharing, real-time chat trading, FTP, and newsgroups are among the many ways to find and download MP3s. The most popular peer-to-peer applications include

- **Gnutella** (`www.gnutella.wego.com`): Developed by the same team that brought the world Winamp, Gnutella is similar to Napster, but it doesn't use a centralized server to facilitate transfers.
- **Audiogalaxy** (`www.audiogalaxy.com`): Use its Web site to select which songs to download from other members, and then watch the client software facilitate the file transfer. It works best with Internet Explorer.
- **KaZaA** (`www.kazaa.com`): This peer-to-peer file-sharing program is similar to Gnutella, but KaZaA finds the fastest download.
- **BearShare** (`www.bearshare.com`): BearShare, one of the most user-friendly applications for grabbing MP3s, lets you search for, download, and share files with everyone on Gnutella's global peer-to-peer network.

Attention Napster Users: R U Experienced?

If you're an experienced Napster user, you can use OpenNap, the open source Napster service. OpenNap is *not* a Napster client; it's an open source server for connecting Napster clients. You can use an application such as Napigator (www.napigator.com) to navigate to the connected Napster servers and find information about each server's current state, including its real-time server statistics, ping times, what files it has available, and the number of its users online. If you learn to access and search OpenNap servers, you can find the fastest download times, and you can track down really obscure titles that you'd have trouble locating in mainstream sources. Best of all, if Napster suffers the worst possible fate, you won't be cut off from the directories of those MP3s you love. You can learn more about the OpenNap project at www.sourceforge.net. Visit the ZeroPaid OpenNap Server Listing at www.zeropaid.com/napster/opennap/servers.php3.

If you're interested in real-time chat trading, you can trade MP3 files using the file transfer feature of popular chat clients such as ICQ (web.icq.com), mIRC (www.mirc.com), or Aimster (www.aimster.com). FTP (file transfer protocol) sites are an excellent source for MP3s. You also can collect MP3s through newsgroups, but it's more work-intensive than most of the other methods we mention here. If you want to give newsgroup MP3s a whirl, you can find out how by reading the FAQ at www.mp3-faq.org.

You can listen to and download MP3s from a number of Web sites. Try www.mp3.com and www.mp3board.com. Web-based MP3 search engines, such as Audiovalley (www.audiovalley.com) or Audiophilez (www.audiophilez.com), are a sure-fire way to track down more MP3s.

Remember Downloading Safety

Any downloading experience can lead to disaster if you don't use the proper virus protection and safe downloading practices. If you need a refresher, see "Downloading Files" in Chapter 4, "The Good Life Online."

Download and Play MP3s

The next part of the process—downloading the MP3—is a breeze. Your player and the MP3 download site will offer good step-by-step instructions, but (in general) here's an easy way to download an MP3 from the Internet:

1. Right-click on the link that points to the file and select Save Target As or Save File As (depending on which browser you use).
2. Select the directory that you want to save the song to and (if you'd like) rename the song.
3. Click the Save button.

The download process begins at this point. Don't lose patience—depending on your connection and the source of the MP3, the download can take a while. The average download takes about 15 minutes, so don't expect instant gratification from this experience.

Playing MP3s is even simpler than downloading them. Open up the files in your MP3 player, and then click the Play button.

Don't Lose Track of Your Tracks

Different players have different processes for storing downloaded MP3s. Get to know your player's setup so you can keep track of your tracks. If you left-click (instead of right-click) the Download link, the song should save itself automatically either to a temporary directory, a personal folder, or directory on your hard drive. Or you might get a pop-up prompting you to "Open the file" or "Save to Disk." If you get this pop-up, choose Save to Disk. When your computer asks where to save the file, choose a destination you can remember so you can find the MP3 later. Most players have a settings area where you can specify how you'd like to download songs. Try playing around with these settings to see which process you like best. If you continue to have problems, check your browser settings to be sure they aren't shunting downloads to some obscure location.

Create MP3s from CDs

Want to add your favorite CDs to your growing MP3 library? It's easy enough to do. If you're using our ripper/player/burner of choice, MusicMatch Jukebox, you already have the software you need to *rip* (or convert) audio CD tracks into MP3s. Armed with that software, you need to make three up-front decisions:

- **What track-naming convention will you use?** The program lets you select seven fields to include with every CD you encode. Selecting only Artist, Album, Track Number, and Track Title should give you enough information to get your collection going. If you have the time later, you can add additional tags such as Tempo, Lyrics, Mood, and Cover Art to individual tracks or entire albums. To modify the order of these fields, choose Options, Settings, and then select the Music Library tab.
- **What bit rate will you encode in?** The higher the bit rate, the more hard drive space each song fills. You can get near-CD quality at 96Kbps, but for true CD quality, encode at 128 or 160 Kbps. To change the bit rate settings, single-click Options, mouse-over Recorder, and then select Settings. Choose the bit rate that's appropriate for you. If you have the hard drive space, leave it at 128Kbps.
- **Where will you store the ripped tracks?** By default, MusicMatch stores ripped MP3s in the MyDocuments\MyMusic\ directory. Remember this, so you don't lose your tracks. To change the storage location, single-click Options, mouse-over Recorder, and then select Settings. Select the Songs Directory button, and point it to the folder where you want to store the tracks.

Is Your Drive Designed for Ripping CDs?

Your drive might or might not be set up to handle digital-audio extraction—that's the fastest way to rip songs. You can check your CD-ROM drive specs to find out whether it has digital-audio extraction capabilities. MusicMatch checks this for you. If you bought the drive within the last year or so, it probably can handle digital-audio extraction. Even if it can't, you can still rip songs with the drive, but the process takes the same amount of time as playing the songs.

Now, you're ready to rip. Connect to the Internet, then follow these steps:

1. Open MusicMatch and insert a CD into your CD-ROM. The program automatically recognizes that an audio CD is inserted and initiates the Recorder to begin searching the online CD database.
2. If it finds a match for your CD, MusicMatch fills in all the album information for you automatically. If it doesn't find your CD's info online (a service provided by the Gracenote compact disc data base), you can type in this info.
3. When you input artist/album name and all the track titles, click the REC button on the recorder. Depending on the speed of your PC, you should have the CD fully ripped in less than 10 minutes.

Don't Be a Pirate!

When you convert commercial CDs to MP3 format, don't forget that the music is covered by copyright laws. You should only do this with music that you already own, for your own personal listening, and so on and so forth. You aren't a pirate, aahhhrrrrrrr you?

Burn MP3s to CDs

Burning CDs has become a 21st century tradition, but unless you have one of those new MP3-CD hybrids, listening to your precious MP3s on the road can be a pain (see the following section, "Take it With You: Portable MP3 Players"). Thanks to versatile jukebox programs, you can convert your MP3s to the CD-audio compatible WAV format, then burn them to a CD-R. The benefits of burning your MP3s to CD go beyond portability, because you can create your own personalized mixes.

To do this trick, you need a CD burner, some CD-Rs, and a jukebox program like MusicMatch Jukebox. Here's how to burn a CD that will work in any CD player:

1. Open MusicMatch. Create your play list by dragging and dropping MP3s from your music library into the play-list windows (in the upper-right corner of the MusicMatch screen). Remember that most CD-Rs can hold about 74 minutes of music.
2. Click the CD-R button. A new window appears with many options. Select Audio.

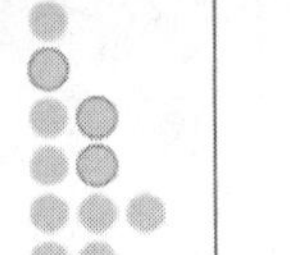

3. Notice the status bar at the bottom of the window. It indicates how much room you have left on the CD. Fill that baby up. It's easy to add or delete tracks from this window.
4. Select Test And Write CDs if you want to check the quality of your recording before you commit. If you're in a rush, just click Write. If you're creating a mixed CD, leave the two-second gap box unchecked.
5. Drop a blank CD-R in your drive and click Create CD.

MusicMatch converts your MP3s to the WAV format, and then burns your tracks onto the CD-R. This process can take a while, but don't use your computer for any other applications while it's going down. You get the fastest conversions if you buy the full version of MusicMatch for $30, instead of using the free downloadable.

TAKE IT WITH YOU: PORTABLE MP3 PLAYERS

The portable MP3 player market has emerged for those music mavens who want to carry their ripped or downloaded tunes with them. The most popular form of portable MP3 player is a compact, handheld device that looks like a radio Walkman. These devices either have onboard flash memory or use removable media like SmartMedia, Compact Flash, or MultiMediaCards. Because the players have no moving parts, they play music skip-free—unlike some portable CD players. They sound good, too, boasting near CD quality if it was encoded at 128Kbps (see Figure 17.1).

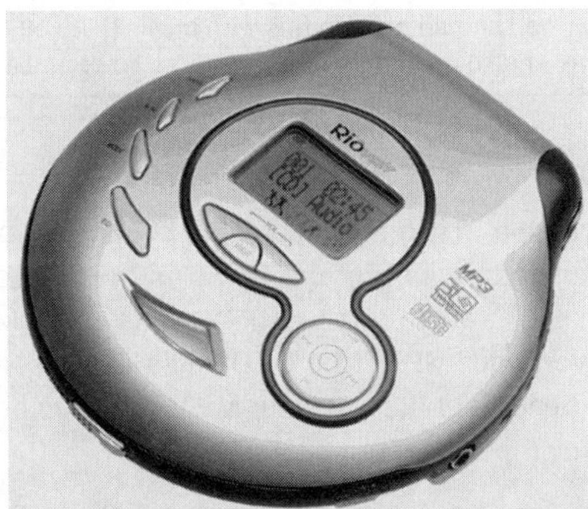

Figure 17.1

Use a portable MP3 player to take your music with you.

Now, for some Tales From the Downside. Portable MP3 players tend to be expensive, at about $200 to $300. The players have short memories, too; most come with 32MB or 64MB of memory (though many have a memory expansion slot). Sixty-four megs of memory will hold about an hour of music encoded at 128Kbps.

The following are some of the models and features available:

- Creative's Nomad series has a wide range of models, features, and prices. The Nomad II MG, for example, has a built-in FM stereo, a voice memo recorder, a nice pair of headphones, 64MB of memory built in, and a slot for memory expansion. Find out more about this series at `www.nomadworld.com`.
- Sonicblue's players are classics. Sonicblue's Rio was the first portable MP3 player to make it big, and it still delivers good, dependable quality at a (relatively) reasonable price. Find out about these players at `www.sonicblue.com`.
- Intel's Pocket Concert is worth a look, too. It's compatible with both the MP3 and WMA formats, is firmware-upgradable, and includes an FM receiver. The Pocket Concert has good sound quality and is well designed. Find out more at `www.intel.com` (see Figure 17.2).

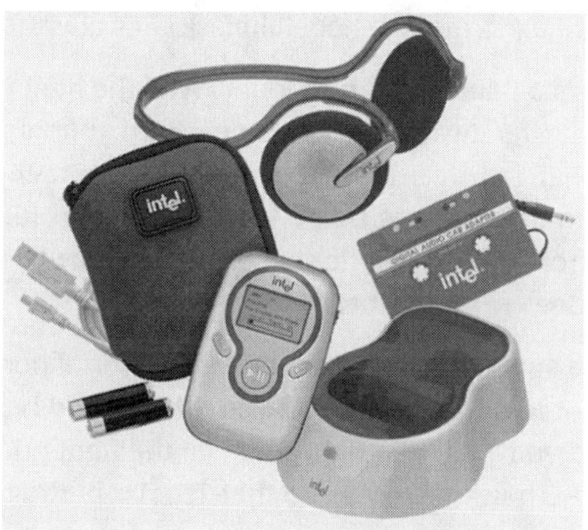

Figure 17.2

Intel's Pocket Concert—shown here with accessory kit, including docking station, car cassette adapter, RCA cable, and rechargeable batteries—is available for about $320.

To get the most portable music for your buck, consider an MP3/CD hybrid player. You can burn more than 10 hours of MP3s to a CD, and then take the tunes with you in one of these CD-sized portable players. Improved RAM buffers eliminate the skipping problems of earlier portable CD players, and at $100 to $200, a portable hybrid offers you a lot of listening time per dollar.

To learn more about hybrids, check out TDK's Mojo (`www.tdk.com`), with its wonderful interface that breaks down a CD's content by artist, album, track, and playlist information. Other hybrid players include Sonicblue's Rio Volt and RCA's RP2410 (`www.rca.com`).

Find the MP3 Player You'll Love

If you go shopping for an MP3 player, follow these tips for tracking down a good one:

- Memory equals music storage. Look for a unit with at least 64MB of storage and a slot to add removable flash memory cards.
- Be sure the software is compatible with your computer.
- Simple, easy-to-operate controls are a must.
- An ample LCD screen makes for easier song navigation.

TURN YOUR PC INTO A MUSIC STUDIO

In days gone by, if you wanted to get a music contract for your almost-famous garage band, the first thing you had to do (besides learning to pick out *Smells Like Teen Spirit* on your guitar) was to get a studio to give you a budget to cut a demo. The expense of booking studio time put a halt to many a hopeful musician's quest for stardom.

That stumbling block's a thing of the past today. With the right music production software and production-friendly hardware tweaks, you can turn your humble home computer into a recording studio that can rival those expensive by-the-hour behemoths any day. You need to know how to use a mixing board and other music studio tools, of course, to get the best recordings from your PC music studio. (And, even with the best synth software, a little musical ability doesn't hurt, either.)

With just a little time and energy, you can build a powerful home music studio into your desktop computer for less than $1,000. Cruise through the hundreds of music resource pages out there, and you'll find the right setup (at the right price). This section gives you an inside look at a PC music studio setup that TechTV put together for under $1,000 in early 2001.

Use this collection as a starting point. Before you buy any products, check the specs to be sure they're compatible with your system. The prices we list here were current when the system was built, but you can expect those prices to have changed by the time you read this list. And, as always, visit `www.techtv.com` for more product reviews and the latest information on these components. Without further ado (shameless self-promotion and boring disclaimers), here's the TechTV PC Music Studio setup:

- **Sound card:** The TechTV music studio is equipped with the Sound Blaster Live! Platinum 5.1 (`www.americas.creative.com`) card because it sounds better and has more options than most cards costing double its list price ($200 in 01/01). It has EMU wavetable synthesis with 64-note polyphony and effects processing. The rear interface supports four speakers, so you can take advantage of Creative's EAX surround sound. The card's front panel interface mounts into one of your computer's drive bays. It has MIDI in and out; a separate 1/4-inch headphone jack with its own volume; SPDIF and optical ins and outs; and an adjustable 1/4-inch microphone input (if your mic uses an XLR connector, you can pick up an XLR-to-1/4-inch adapter for about $10). You also get a killer bundle of software with this card, including Cubasis VST, Wavelab, and Recycle.

- **Microphone**: You'll need a good basic mic for sampling, rapping, and singing. The TechTV music machine boasts the Shure SM48 Microphone. It's known worldwide for its versatility and durability, and it's great for sampling and live performance. This SM48 listed for $137, but most online stores carried it in early 2001 for under $70.

Don't Put Your Mic Where It Doesn't Belong

Never try to plug a professional mic in a 1/8-inch jack, even with an adapter. That hookup is bad for the input; without an adjustable input, the audio will be distorted and unusable. If your sound card doesn't have an XLR or 1/4-inch mic input, you'll need to use a small mixer or mic preamp.

- **Headphones or speaker system:** You'll want to hear everything that your soundcard has to offer. Most professional mixers use headphones, but you may prefer the wide-open spaces of speaker sound. If you want to go with speakers, a good inexpensive choice is Boston Acoustics Digital BA790 Speakers (ours were $99.95; check current prices at `www.bostonacoustics.com`). For the headphone set, Sony's MDR-V600 Headphones ($130 list, $80 to $90 street; check `www.sel.sony.com`) will do the trick.
- **Synthesis program:** ReBirth 2.0 (`www.propellerheads.se/products`) has a lot to offer the beginning or advanced musician who wants to make rap or dance music. This dance-driven digital synthesis program contains two virtual TB-303 bass machines and two virtual drum machines—a TR-808 and a TR-909. It also offers sequencing and effects. The real versions of these machines, which were created by Roland in the 1980s, cost about $1,000 each. Rebirth 2.0 lists at under $200.
- **Recording and sampling:** If you want to save some money, stick with the Cubasis VST program that comes with the Sound Blaster Live! Platinum 5.1 Sound card. Cubasis has 32-track recording capability, synthesis, and sampling. We ponied up $400 for Cool Edit Pro's 64-track mixing, recording and editing package (`www.syntrillium.com`). It features sound generation, sampling at up to 192 KHz, a huge 32-bit effects palette, and it works in 25 different audio formats.

That's it. Street prices on these products brought the TechTV music studio PC in at about $919 before tax and shipping. With smart shopping, you might do even better—on pricing and performance. Good luck, and happy hunting.

BRING RADIO TO A PC NEAR YOU

In many parts of this fine country, radio broadcasting is limited to a dismal mix of just-alike-top-40s and less-than-golden-oldies programs, and idiotic DJs laughing insanely at their own lame jokes. Fortunately, Internet radio gives us another listening option by bringing radio broadcasts from around the globe to our computers.

Because you're not limited to what you can pick up with your antenna, Internet radio lets you listen in on your favorite college sports team, talk radio from a city across the country, or international news from the BBC in London. Even if your radio can't pick up your favorite station at home, you can listen in via your laptop.

Yahoo! Broadcast (`www.broadcast.com`) is the largest provider of radio-station Web casts, and a good place to start listening to Internet radio. Yahoo! Broadcast features a variety of formats from around the world, including music, business, sports, news, education, and even spiritual programming.

If you want to hear a specific station, the most comprehensive list is The MIT List of Radio Stations on the Internet (`www.radio-locator.com`). The MIT list links to more than 9,000 stations worldwide. Use its searchable database to find stations by call letters, format, or country. Other Web sites with listings of radio on the Internet include

- Internet Radio Online Directory (`www.radiotower.com`) lists more than 1,100 stations worldwide.
- Live Radio on the Internet (`www.liveradio.net`) includes great cross-platform how-to instructions on finding and listening to radio stations from all over the world.

Pac Man Goes Hip Hop

If you're into producing your own tracks, and you have warm, fuzzy memories of all those Commodore games from the 1980s, you have to lay your hands on the Elektron SidStation synthesizer. Techno and hip hop producers are always on the lookout for cool retro sounds, and the SidStation delivers the goods with its Commodore 64 sound chip. The SidStation gives you access to 90 preset sounds from some of those all-time Commodore favorites such as Pac Man, Tempest, and Centipede. You also can edit or build a sound from the ground up using four intuitive real-time controllers, then use the same controllers to tweak the sounds in real time. The sounds are MIDI controllable, either by a keyboard or an external sequencer (like a PC). This synthesizer module is well-designed and beautifully engineered (at well over $500, it should be). Find out more about the SidStation at `www.sidstation.com`.

Internet Radio in Your Hand

When it comes to Internet radio, you *can* take it with you. If you're near an Internet connection, you can tune into your favorite Internet radio station with a boombox like the Kerbango (`www.kerbango.com`). Portable Internet Radio boomboxes operate from any Internet connection, offer good quality (boombox-style) speakers, and let you take your favorite programs with you on the road. The first streaming MP3 player for the PocketPC platform, Live365.com, gives you wireless access to thousands of online streams, in a simple browser and player interface. Wireless access is still expensive, and the first beta of Live365.com was a bit buggy. But look for this technology to improve dramatically by mid-2002.

GET THE SCOOP ON DVD, DVD-ROM, AND MORE

DVD (digital versatile disc) is one of the hottest storage technologies to hit the streets since the CD. In just a few years, the number of games and movies issued on DVD has skyrocketed—and so has the number of home DVD players. DVD drives are an increasingly common component of new computer systems. Some analysts predict they'll soon replace audio CD, videotape, laserdisc, CD-ROM, and even videogame cartridges.

So what's so hot about this technology? Capacity is DVD's ace in the hole. At its core, DVD is really a bigger, faster CD that holds both audio and video on a single disk. Although it's the same physical size as a CD, a DVD disc can hold about eight hours of VHS-quality video or 160 hours of audio on a single layer.

DVD falls into two main categories. A DVD player hooks up to your TV to play videos and movies. A DVD-ROM drive is a computer component that reads both data and video disks. The difference between the two is similar to the difference between standard music CDs and the CD-ROMS you use to install data into your hard drive.

How to Be Sure Internet Radio Keeps Streaming To You

Internet radio takes advantage of media streaming technologies, and those technologies have four basic components: the player that Web surfers use to play the media file, the server component that transfers the media from the Web site, the encoding tools that create the compressed media files, and the compression technologies used to create the files. You can listen to Internet radio using any media player, including RealAudio's RealPlayer, Microsoft's Media Player, or Apple's QuickTime. The quality of the broadcast (reception, not program content) is determined by the oomph of the server and how well it can implement the scalability scheme of your player. Some sites support all the major players, but many others *don't*. The chances are good that you'll run across a site that doesn't support the player of your choice, so you might have to install all of the "big three" on your machine.

Untangling Recordable DVD

The DVD-ROM and DVD-Video formats are well established and completely standardized. Unfortunately, the other side is more confusing, with four recordable versions of DVD-ROM: DVD-R, DVD-RAM, DVD-RW, and DVD+RW.

DVD-R can record data once, whereas you can rewrite DVD-RAM, DVD-RW, and DVD+RW a thousand times or more. Each format comes as a computer drive for recording data, and currently every format can hold 4.7 billion bytes (4.7GB) per side.

- **DVD-R** is primarily designed for DVD production. The drives are expensive ($1,000) and the discs cost about $30 each. The advantage of DVD-R is that the media works with many existing DVD-ROM drives and DVD-Video players because it uses organic dye polymer technology, like CD-R.
- **DVD-RAM** drives cost $500 and up, with blank discs priced at about $30. DVD-RAM isn't currently compatible with most DVD-ROM drives and DVD-Video players. Think of it as a removable hard disk that can also read DVD-ROM discs. DVD-RAM is supported by Panasonic, Toshiba, Hitachi, and others.
- **DVD-RW** works with many existing DVD-ROM drives and DVD-Video players. Right now, DVD-RW is primarily supported by Pioneer, who released the DVR-A03 drive in April 2001. The DVR-A03 can read and write to DVD-R, CD-R, and CD-RW formats.
- **DVD+RW** is scheduled to become available in the summer or fall of 2001. It will be compatible with most existing DVD-ROM drives and DVD-Video players. DVD+RW is supported by Sony, Philips, Hewlett-Packard, Mitsubishi/Verbatim, Ricoh, and Yamaha.

If the industry doesn't lock on a standard soon, consumers will look elsewhere for a dependable, portable high-capacity optical storage solution. A standard could evolve any

D-VHS: The Next "Best Thing"

With DVD bogged down in legal problems surrounding DeCSS (software that defeats DVD-scrambling technology) and copy protection, and the failure of the industry to come to an agreement on a single standard for recording, JVC is hoping lightning will strike twice with its VHS format through a new Digital VHS, or D-VHS.

D-VHS can record and play back four hours of video in high-definition mode—as many as 1,080 lines per inch, or more than double the resolution of DVD, according to Allan Holland, national product specialist in the consumer video division at JVC. It can also record at the standard VHS resolution of 240 lines per inch.

day, so keep your eye on TechTV's News Headlines for the latest developments. Until you're sure your DVD recordable technology won't go the way of Beta Max, your best bet is to follow the industry and wait for a standard.

Play DVDs on Your PC

To get good quality DVD playback on your PC, the machine needs to be fast. Unless your system includes a dedicated DVD decoder board (which you learn more about in just a minute), all the real work of MPEG-2 decoding happens in software run on your computer's main processor.

DVD movies squeeze onto a DVD disc via MPEG-2 compression, which takes lots of power to decode. If you decompress DVD in software only, you can do it with a 350-MHz Pentium II system (or AMD equivalent). You should also be sure your system has a graphics board that offers Motion Compensation (MC). If your system couples that graphics board with iDCT (one of the most processor-intensive stages of MPEG-2 decoding), you draw even less on your CPU and get a better viewing experience.

If you want the best possible playback on a slower processor, buy a dedicated DVD decoder card, such as Sigma Design's REALmagic Hollywood Plus. According to Sigma Designs, the board can deliver decent DVD playback on a machine equipped with nothing more than a 133-MHz Pentium, or AMD or Cyrix equivalent, with 16MB of RAM. That's probably pushing it, but a decoder card will definitely make a difference in the quality of your viewing.

And why bother with the surround sound and special effects boost of DVD if you don't have a good sound card and speaker system? Without a good sound setup, you won't get the full DVD viewing experience.

With twice the resolution of DVD and a high-definition recording option, D-VHS could give DVD a major run for its money since the recordable standard for DVD still isn't set, and now DVD discs are vulnerable to piracy.

But don't declare your DVD player obsolete just yet. Video on D-VHS tapes is uncompressed, so it's enormous. A 75GB hard disk can hold around 30 minutes of the video, according to company officials, making the trading of HD content over the Internet impossible.

The JVC D-VHS deck hit the market in May 2001 at about $2,000, and blank media costs between $10 and $15. JVC's only TV to support HDCP is the D'Ahlia system, which sells for a whopping $10,000.

Play DVDs on Your Powerbook

We don't suggest that you buy a PowerBook just to watch DVDs. But if you already have a PowerBook, why not pop in a feature film? Here are our suggestions for better DVD viewing on an external monitor or television (possible with a PowerBook's S-Video output port):

- For viewing on an external monitor, turn Video Mirroring off. The DVD software doesn't work right with Video Mirroring turned on.
- Move the menu bar to the monitor where you want to watch the movie. Open the Monitors control panel (or Monitors and Sound if you use an OS previous to OS 9). In the Arrange window, drag the tiny representation of the menu bar from the PowerBook's screen to the external monitor's screen.
- The Mac's video is anything but crystal clear on a TV. Choose a resolution of 640×480 (NTSC) in the Resolution control strip module to make those fuzzy icons and menus large enough to see.

And don't forget these keyboard shortcuts for fast-action playback control:

- Command+W closes the Monitors control panel.
- Command+Option+P presents video in the viewer.
- Spacebar starts and pauses the movie.
- F3 and F4 increase and decrease the movie's volume.
- Command+Q quits the DVD Movie Player application when you finish the movie.

LIGHTNING ROUND Q&A WRAP-UP

I want to become a laptop DJ and mix my own music or MP3s and WAVs I've downloaded. I've heard of programs such as Virtual Turntables, but I can't seem to find them. What can you tell me about these DJ programs?

Several programs allow you to mix your own music files. Most of them attempt to simulate real turntables and mixers by adding key DJ-ing elements like pitch control, cue points, and even scratching. You can get a copy of the shareware product you mention, Virtual Turntables, at `www.carrotinnovations.com`. Virtual Turntables is one of the easiest ways to get started as a laptop DJ. It allows for real-time mixing, volume and pitch control, playlists with AutoDJ functionality, and a number of user-definable special effects such as scratching and backspins. Right now, this program is free to try, $42 to keep.

If you want MP3 mixing software with features designed for professionals, check out Vsiosonic's PCDJ Red (`www.pcdj.com`). PCDJ Red offers exact cueing to a fraction of a millisecond, instant start, back cueing, 20 independent cue memories per track, ripping, recording, looping, turn table brake, automatic pitch matching, and auto-BPM detection. The interface completes a DJ's fantasy, featuring a host of tweakable controls and a convenient "record bag." This software carries a professional price tag at $199.00. A free, less feature-rich version, called PCDJ Silver, is available at the same site.

My Power Mac G4 launches the DVD Player before the Multiple Users login screen comes up. I'm tired of restarting. What's the deal, here?

Mac models released in the summer of 2000—specifically the Power Mac G4, iMacs, and G4 Cube—launch the Apple DVD Player before the Multiple Users login screen appears if you have a DVD-ROM in the drive. The workaround is simple: Don't leave a DVD-ROM in the player when you shut down or restart your Mac if you turn on Multiple Users.

How can you condense a whole movie onto the 650MB of a CD?

Can you stuff an entire DVD video movie onto a CD-R? Sure, if you compress the heck out of it using a variation of MPEG4, a.k.a. the DivX;-) codec. You will lose some of the DVD quality, getting motion artifacts and blockiness on the screen. On the flipside, you get a huge reduction in file size, so a 4GB DVD video might require less than 650MB, the magic number for a CD-R disc.

Now for a word of legal warning: Don't crack DVD movies and post them up on the Web. It's illegal, it's sleazy, and it can get you deep in litigation stew. On the other hand, you're perfectly legal if you use this process for distributing your original content, such as a movie you created or family videos, out over the Web.

SmartRipper 2.0 is a great tool for pulling the video off the DVD; try using Flask to compress it down into single .AVI file. To use DivX;-), which is essential to get the tight compression, download and install it, too.

You need a DVD drive and at least 5GB open hard drive space to do this. And don't hold your breath waiting on the thing to finish. At the fastest compression setting (that delivers the worst quality), it takes more than three hours to compress a 104-minute movie on an 800-MHz Intel Pentium III with 128MB of RAM. Higher quality on a slower processor can easily push the encoding time for an average video to eight to 10 hours.

Here's the how-to for fitting a DVD on a CD:

1. Download all the software.
2. Insert the DVD into your DVD drive.
3. Launch SmartRipper and pull the DVD Video off the disk and onto your hard drive.
4. Launch Flask, select your quality and output settings, then click Run/Start Conversion.
5. Go to bed for the night, or work on another computer for the next few hours.

CHAPTER 18

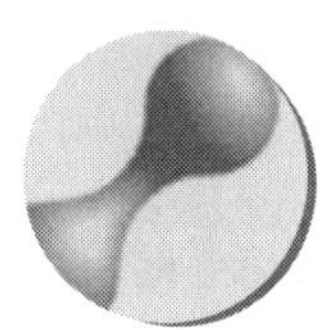

DIGITAL IMAGING EQUIPMENT IN FOCUS

- Understand digital imaging basics
- Find the digital camera that's right for you (and use it right)
- Buy a digital video camera and edit your masterpieces
- Choose and install a netcam

People love digital cameras; manufacturers shipped more than 4 million units in 2000 alone. Digital cameras are easy to use, and with prices falling, you can bet sales will keep on climbing. The rest of the digital imaging product line gets tastier all the time, too. Video cameras, printers, scanners, netcams, and other peripherals are improving in quality even as their prices go down, down, down.

If your digital imaging know-how could use a tune-up, you've come to the right place. In this chapter, you learn some of the best ways to choose and use digital imaging equipment—from still cameras, to scanners, to netcams. Getting the most from your digital imaging investment of time and money is simply a matter of keeping your equipment in harmony with your needs, your interest—and your wallet. So make the most of TechTV's best shopping tips, and then take a look at this chapter's important how-to info for shooting good digi-cam photos, editing digital video, and going live with a netcam.

DIGITAL IMAGING FAST FACTS

Digital imaging has made processing and storing visual images on a computer possible by making the stored files small and easy to transfer over the Internet. How does it do that? A digital image captures enough data of its subject to present a good picture, but it leaves out enough data to keep the file size manageable. Think of a digital image as being like your view through a window screen. The screen wires edit out part of the image, but your eyes see enough of what's out there to record a clear view of the great outdoors (is it time to mow again, already?).

With that peaceful view in mind, look over these fast facts about the digital imaging process:

- Digital imaging captures and stores images electronically for processing on a computer. The lens registers an image as a series of data bits. Some of the "connecting" bits drop out, and the remaining bits join up to create a clear—but condensed—picture of the subject.
- Digital images are stored as bitmapped graphics made up of pixels. The more pixels, the better the image resolution will be. One-million pixel (one-megapixel) images have low-end resolution, while six-megapixels make up a professional, high resolution image.
- Bit-depth—the number of data bits in each pixel—affects image quality. The more bits of data that each pixel contains, the richer the image color will be.
- You can adjust resolution and bit-depth when you record an image and when you reproduce it—whether that's on a computer monitor, through a printer, or in a scanner.
- You can use image-editing software (like Adobe Photoshop or MGI PhotoSuite) to sample up or scale down the number of pixels or image size in your digital images.

That's a bare-bones look at the technology, but it's enough to show how flexible and useful digital imaging can be. You can use it to record photos and see them in an instant, send home movies as e-mail attachments, and store your entire family photo album on a single disc. Not bad for one technology, huh?

HOW TO CHOOSE AND USE A DIGITAL CAMERA

Digital cameras have gone mainstream. Taking photos with a digital camera is a fun, easy, and convenient way to capture the moment. You can see your photo on a color LCD panel just seconds after snapping the shot. If the picture's lousy, you can erase it and try again without wasting an exposure (unlike film, you can reuse memory cards more than 1,000 times). Sony and Canon produce some popular digital cameras, including

- The Sony DSC-S85 digital camera, which delivers 4.1 megapixels of resolution for around $800.00. It can be found at `www.sony.com`.
- The Canon Powershot A20 (2.1 megapixels) and A10 (1.3 megapixels), both of which come with built-in flash and 3X optical zoom. They are available at `www.canon.com`.

You save time and money by not having to get the photos developed at a processing lab. (One-hour wait? No, thanks.) To get physical prints with a digital camera, attach the unit to your PC, send the files to the hard drive, and print them out on an ink-jet printer. Or don't print your pics at all. Instead, post them on a Web page, place them in an electronic photo album, look at them on a TV screen, or display them in a digital photo frame.

What to Look for When Buying a Digital Camera

As digital cameras drop in price, bargains get easier and easier to come by. Low prices also mean that you don't have to sacrifice quality to get a good, affordable camera.

- **Resolution:** Resolution is the clarity and detail of a recorded image, measured in megapixels. A digital camera's lens sends the image to the camera's CCD (charged-coupled device), which captures the image in pixels. One-megapixel and two-megapixel cameras represent the low-end norm; three-megapixel cameras are great, and six-megapixel models are the current top o' the line. Most cameras offer variable resolution settings, from "best" to "good," so you can adjust the resolution to suit the purpose of the image.
- **Removable media:** The cheapest digital cameras don't offer removable media, and you don't want to get stuck with *that* limitation. When you fill up a fixed-media camera's storage, you have to stop shooting until you offload the images to a PC. Removable storage lets you change cards—like you change film in a traditional camera. Most digital cameras use removable SmartMedia (maximum capacity of 64MB) or CompactFlash (maximum capacity of 192MB) cards. The type of camera you buy will determine which you use, and the average camera comes with an 8MB card.
- **A USB connection:** Some inexpensive digital cameras attach to your PC via a serial port. Try to get a camera with a USB interface, which transfers images to your computer 10 times faster than a serial connection can. Besides, USB cameras are much easier to attach to your PC.

Don't Forget the Video Port!

When you shop for a digital camera, get one with a video port. A video port lets you attach the camera to a television set so that all the people in your living room can look at your pictures at the same time. You can even videotape your picture show and send it to relatives who don't have a computer. Video ports aren't expensive "extras," so this is a great feature you shouldn't pass up.

- **A good LCD display:** Even low-end digital cameras should offer a good color LCD display window, so you can preview your pictures before you save and store them. But don't get a camera that uses an LCD display as its viewfinder. LCD displays sap a tremendous amount of battery life. With any decent camera, you ought to use the optical viewfinder rather than the LCD when snapping a picture.

- **A good zoom:** Some low-end cameras come with 2x digital zoom, and that's OK for so-so snaps. But an optical zoom will give you much better image quality. If you can spend a little more, look for a digital with 3x optical zoom. You'll get higher-quality images.

Shop for Digital Camera Bargains

It used to be that buying a digital camera meant shelling out at least $300. But today's low-end cameras are affordable, and offer decent imaging in an easy-to-use form. If you're looking for a low-cost entry into digital imaging, here are three cameras you might look into:

- **Kodak DC3200** (`www.kodak.com`): This one-megapixel digital takes crisp, clear pictures and makes a good start for someone entering the digital photo world. This rugged and sturdy little camera has all the basic features, weighs less than 8 ounces, and has 2MB of memory to hold 5 JPEGs at "best" resolution and 22 at "good" resolution. The Kodak is easy to use, but not as speedy as higher-priced models, and it won't transfer to Macs. The price is right at $200.
- **Hewlett-Packard PhotoSmart 215** (`www.hp.com`): This 1.3-megapixel digital is simple to use and takes good-quality photos. It weighs about 10 ounces and includes a 4MB CompactFlash card that holds 36 JPEGs at its lowest resolution. The PhotoSmart also comes with a built-in 2x digital zoom lens (remember to expect less-than-professional close-ups) and ArcSoft's PhotoImpression 2000 and PhotoMontage 2000 Photo-editing software packages. At $199, it's a bargain.
- **Intel Pocket PC** (`www.intel.com`): The USB-based Intel Pocket PC camera successfully walks the line between an expensive digital camera and a single-function netcam. Like most netcams, it captures a clean, bright video signal while attached to

What's the Difference Between an Optical and Digital Zoom?

Digital cameras support two types of zooms, optical and digital. Optical zooms use real lenses to magnify the subject, while digital zooms magnify your subject electronically. Although optical zooms can't magnify a subject as much as digital zooms, they give you much better image quality. Those digital zooms are just blowing up pixels to increase the image size, and that's not the same thing as actually magnifying the size of the camera's "capture" of your subject's image.

your PC. But when unplugged, it can take quick low-resolution snapshots, and 10-second video as well. Of course, this device won't compete with the average digital still or digital video camera. But then again, at $149, it's not claiming to.

Don't forget that 1-megapixel cameras are low-end entries into digital imaging. As mentioned previously, you can't expect high-quality images, a wide range of features, and broad format capability in these cameras.

Fast Tips for Great Photos

Few folks take the time to get to know their digital cameras before they start snapping photos, and that can lead to missed shots and frustrated photographers. Follow these quick tips to keep your next picture-perfect moment from becoming a missed opportunity:

- Before taking a picture, push the shutter button halfway down to allow the camera to auto-focus and set auto-exposure levels.
- Set your image resolution to low for online use and high for pics you will later print.
- Carry extra batteries. Digital cameras eat up power, especially when you use the flash and LCD screen.

BUY A DIGITAL VIDEO CAMERA

If you're interested in editing your videos without losing any of the original quality, DV is the way to go. When the DV urge strikes, decide what type of camera you need *before* you shop to buy.

- **What is your budget?** Consumer digital video cameras cost between $300 and $2,000. That's a wide spread. Set a realistic price range to narrow down your choices.

Move Beyond Point-and-Shoot

If you're a serious photographer, you might want more than a simple point-and-shoot camera, but that doesn't mean you can't go digital. Digital SLR (single lens reflex) cameras—the Canon EOSD30, the Fuji FinePix SI Pro, and the Nikon D1—offer professional photographers a manually controllable digital camera option. When TechTV tested these digital SLRs in early 2001, their quality still lagged behind the fine-grained results you can get with 35mm film, but we expect the digital SLRs to keep getting better. The pros like these cameras for their large and high quality CCDs, precise optics, and the modern conveniences of digital "film." Digital SLRs are professionally priced, most costing just under $6,000 for the body alone (although that sounds expensive, keep in mind that professional studio cameras cost $10,000 and up).

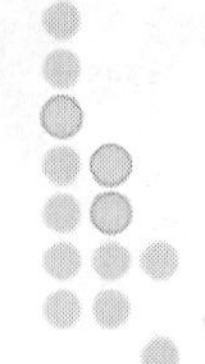

- **What do you need?** Read up on DV and think about how you'll use your camera. Check out TechTV's reviews and other online product comparisons (at `www.techtv.com`), and read through electronics magazines at the newsstand. Ask friends who own these cameras what they like, don't like, and wish they had on their cameras.

Don't Get Trapped by Feature Creep

When developers create software, they often end up ruining perfectly good applications by overloading them with a bunch of bells and whistles no one will ever use (remember Clippy?). Too many features can make any program—or product—expensive, difficult to use and maintain, prone to break-downs, and nearly impossible to repair. When you shop for a digital video camera, avoid falling into a feature-creep danger zone by shopping—and paying for—*benefits*, not features. For example, look for benefits like the camera's optic quality, ease of use (size, weight, controls), battery life, image stabilization, and good zoom control. If you don't use a DV camera for still shots, don't pay more for that feature. And if you don't need professional-level results, don't pay extra (substantially extra, by the way) for separate green, red, and blue CCDs. When you see a long list of features on a DV camera, look hard at what they do and how likely you are to use them. Then you'll have a better idea whether the camera's "nice" is worth its price.

Weigh Your Options

Choosing a good DV camera is tricky only because you have so many options to choose from. But beyond "nice to have" extras, you need to be certain that the camera will provide the basic quality that you want in your videos.

- **Optic quality**: Pay close attention to the camera's lens quality and CCD (charged coupled device). This electronic piece inside the camera is laden with thousands of individual, light-sensitive pixels. The CCD captures the image, converts it into a digital signal, and sends that signal to tape. The more pixels contained in the CCD, the higher your picture quality will be.
- **Zoom:** A 10x optical zoom suffices for most general DV filming. Some zooms are 100x or more, but don't let the high number drag you in if you don't intend to use the camera for shooting close-ups of things that are exceptionally far away.

Give It a Zoom

Test-drive a DV camera before you buy it to be sure you like the way it feels and works. Check how the camera's weight and size feel in your hand, see how easy or difficult it is to focus manually or how well the auto-focus features work. Try the zoom to be sure the control is ergonomically placed, and has a speed control to give you accurate and smooth zooming action. And check the image stabilization to see whether your hand-held camera work looks steady and stable (or seems to be registering about .5 on the Richter scale).

- **Image stabilization:** Most of your camera work will be handheld, so image stabilization is important to reduce jiggling. Image stabilizers come in two types: optical and digital. Optical systems use little gyroscopes within the lens to steady the image and produce a smoother look; they cost more. Digital stabilizers use an electronic circuit and software to stabilize the image. These stabilizers cost less, but they can introduce weird artifacts in your image. If you opt for a digital stabilizer, be sure it has a switch so you can turn it off for better image quality.
- **Battery life:** Obviously an important issue, unless you plan to stay plugged into the AC all the time. Check how long the battery will run while recording—some last 4 or 8 hours.
- **Viewfinder versus LCD panel:** Larger LCD viewfinders (3-inch or 3.5-inch) are great, but can be very expensive and gobble up batteries fast. Be sure the optical viewfinder is easy to see into and has a flexible rubber boot to block the sun.
- **Manual controls:** Point and shoot means all you have to do is know how to start the tape rolling, operate the zoom, compose a shot, and hold the camera fairly steady. If you want the ease of point and shoot, but think you also might want to use special settings, be sure the auto-features have a manual override option.
- **Special effects:** Some cameras have special effects built right into the camera. These include strobe, old-fashioned movie, monochrome, sepiatone, and special presets for specific lighting.

Not to make things sound more complicated than they are, but consider what formats you want to shoot in. The format determines both the type of storage medium you'll use and the quality of the final video. Factor the tape costs into your total "cost of ownership" equation.

- **VHS-C** plays back in any VHS deck by using an adapter. Unfortunately, tapes hold only 20 minutes. We wouldn't consider VHS-C because the cameras are big and the tapes are too short. VHS-C 30 cost about $4.
- **8 mm** format gives almost the same picture quality as VHS, but the tape length goes up to 120 minutes. This format isn't great for shooting documentaries or footage for TV broadcast, but it works fine for home movies. Tapes in 8 mm cost about $3 for 120 minutes.
- **Hi 8** gives better picture quality than 8 mm (more lines of resolution) but costs more, too. Some Hi 8 cameras also record digitally, producing excellent results, and can even digitize your existing 8 mm and Hi 8 tapes into DV format for computer editing. Hi 8 tapes typically run about $6 for 120 minutes.
- **MiniDV** format typically produces the best image quality in the smallest form. MiniDV stores images in a compressed, digitized format on a small, 60-minute (maximum) tape. MiniDV tapes cost about $12 each. If you hope to make a movie, documentary, or broadcast your material, you'll need a MiniDV.

Go Pro with MiniDV

The whole point of having a DV camera is to perform digital editing without loss of quality. If you intend to do non-linear video editing with MiniDV, get a camera with a FireWire port. Almost all DV cameras have FireWire (IEEE 1394) ports these days. Be sure you have software and driver compatibility, too. You can control any camera with a 1394 port if you have access to the right drivers.

TIPS FOR EDITING DIGITAL VIDEO

Chasing fresh video footage with your digital camcorder is only half the story. To make your video worth watching, you still need to edit it. Editing lets you trim out bad or unnecessary footage so you can make your video viewable and compelling.

Video editing used to require a ton of expensive and specialized hardware. Today, you can do it all on your desktop PC. Best of all, editing video on your PC is "non-linear," which means you can quickly grab random scenes from any part of your footage and attach them together.

You'll find several good digital video editing programs on the market. These software applications run the gamut from sub-$100 beginner's programs to semiprofessional programs for creating works like documentaries and short films. Names to keep in mind are Adobe Premiere (`www.adobe.com`), Digital Sonic Foundry's Vegas Video (`www.sonicfoundry.com`), MGI VideoWave (`www.mgisoft.com`), and Ulead VideoStudio (`www.ulead.com`).

You'll learn the most about video editing by playing around with the software. Most programs come with a tutorial, and you usually can find help on the manufacturer's site as well. Here's a basic, general guide to the video editing process:

1. Launch the software.
2. Import clips. Click on the Clip icon and browse your drive to select the video clips and sound files you want to work with (they appear as blocks to be placed on the time line).

Edit Analog Video on Your PC

Although lots of people don't know it, you can edit analog video on your PC. Most people began shooting in analog, so this is a popular process. To do this type of editing, you need to get a good video card for your PC; we recommend the ATI Radeon All-In-Wonder (`www.ati.com`). It costs about $200 and it does everything. Then, pick up a program called Pinnacle Studio DC10 Plus (`www.pinnaclesys.com`). The program costs $100 or so. It lets you capture full-screen, full-motion video from your camcorder, edit it, and then copy your edited tape back to video or in digital form, for easy storage or e-mailing.

3. Drag the clips to a player. Watch each clip and decide how you want to edit it.
4. Pick in and out cues. Play the clip and edit it to your liking with the in and out cues.
5. Drag the clips to the time line. This adds each clip to the work in progress.
6. Add stills, using the same process you use to import video clips.
7. Select transitions by clicking on the transition bar in the time line and choosing from the various transitions offered.
    - **Cuts** are the editing all-star. Most often, the best way to transition between scenes is simply to cut from one to the next.
    - **Fades** are the basic "curtain up, curtain down" switch between scenes, and they can have some surprising twists. One of our favorites is to let the visual fade down and back up. The audio you play during the fade pulls the viewer into the next scene.
    - **Dissolves** set the mood. If you want to make people cry, it's hard to beat a series of dissolves, slow motion, and sad music. Dissolves are easy to do, but don't let that encourage you to overuse them. If your video isn't changing scene and mood, a dissolve can seem mushy. And too many dissolves will put the audience to sleep.
8. Create text and paths for titles. Usually, the Effects menu lets you add titles at the desired time and location. (Remember that you have 15 frames per second of footage, so you don't want to title something for just one frame—you won't see it!) Next, move the text across the screen in any path you like.

Do You Have A Right to That Sound?

iMovie and many other video editing software packages let you import CD music, but if you have any intention of Net-distributing your movie, be careful about using recorded music. Posting already-published music without paying ASCAP or BMI fees violates copyright laws.

Time for Linear Editing

Some video and sound editors are *linear*, which means they show their data as a time line with time code at the top, increasing from left to right. For example, if your video clip is two minutes long, a block will appear on the time line from 0:00 to 2:00. When you're editing more than one clip, the clips occupy more than one horizontal block (usually with one shown above the other), and you can set transitions between them.

Creating with Sound

When you work with your video's audio, play around with the sound. Try to find cool and unexpected ways to use dialogue, music, and special-effects sounds to make your video's message loud and clear. Some of your audio is supplied by the spoken words of the people on tape. You can pick up natural sounds, like the wind or the ocean, from one clip and put them on another. You also can import audio from another source, such as a CD, and you can add narration with the DV's built-in microphone. Special effects sounds can be a lot of fun, and you can fake your own, just like they do in Hollywood. Silence can be a powerful attention-grabber, too. Use your imagination and really get into making your video, so your viewers can really get into watching it.

9. Preview. Always, always, always preview. Why waste disk space rendering if the video has a mistake you could have spotted in the preview? (Some software will not play the audio in preview mode.)
10. Check the codec (the compression/decompression technology). Choosing the right codec is important if you're working with vmails or any other highly compressed video. You'll need to select a codec that the software understands (to learn more, visit `www.icanstream.tv/CodecCentral/GenInfo`).
11. Build. To render your video edit to disk, just click Build (or whatever command your editing software uses to create the final version of the edited video).
12. Save. Give it a long descriptive name (so you'll remember it) with the project extension .prj.
13. Play your video to see how the final product looks.

GET ONSCREEN WITH A NETCAM

There's no doubt that TechTV *is* the Netcam Network. We aren't alone in our fascination with these devices that capture and send live images over the Internet. With a growing number of broadband subscribers, not to mention PC users in general, netcams are finding their way into a lot of homes, cubicles, and classrooms.

People use point-to-point video communication for all sorts of reasons: Business types have face-to-face meetings with associates around the globe, grandparents see and talk to growing grandchildren, and befuddled computer users call us at TechTV for tech support. Many folks use their netcams to record video e-mail attachments, known as vmail.

Choose a Netcam

You might have a netcam that you never intended to own. Some computer companies bundle them with PCs, and ISPs (such as Earthlink) give them away for free. But if you have shopped for a netcam, you know that consumers have many to choose from. They come in all shapes, sizes, and colors, and although the majority of them stack up to one another spec-wise, performance results can vary widely.

- **Price:** Price isn't necessarily linked to netcam performance. You can get some good values for less than $100, if you shop wisely.
- **Resolution:** Many netcams offer 640×480 VGA resolution and a frame speed of 30 fps (frames per second). These specs work fine for most purposes. Your camera's processor speed can also affect the quality of the netcam's broadcast image, especially in terms of its fps.
- **Connector type:** Netcams use either a parallel port or USB connector. USB is by far the most popular type of connection because it's so much easier to install.
- **Bundled software:** With the proper software, you can send video mail, capture stills and edit them, communicate via video-conferencing software such as Microsoft's NetMeeting, and even set up motion-sensing monitors that will alert you via pager or e-mail. Compare software bundles when comparing netcams.

Like all products, opinions on netcam image quality can be subjective. Inspect a netcam's quality and decide for yourself whether it meets your standards.

It's on TechTV

TechTV is the home of the Netcam Network (find it at `www.techtv.com/callforhelp/netcamnetwork`). There, you'll find more useful information about netcamming than anywhere else on the Net, and you can use the chat rooms to get information and meet other netcammers.

Install a USB Netcam on a PC or Mac

When you pick up your netcam, you'll get a full set of installation instructions, along with these basic components:

- A video camera to capture images
- A power adapter (usually PS/2 or AT reversible)
- Video software

Follow the instructions carefully, and you should be starring in your own netcam broadcasts in a matter of no time. Most installations are a snap, and involve some variation on these basic steps:

1. Before you plug your netcam into the USB port, insert the install disk into your CD-ROM drive. The installation program should automatically start and load the drivers you need.
2. When the drivers install, your computer prompts you to plug your netcam into the USB port. Be sure you keep the install disk in your CD-ROM drive.

3. Your computer should then recognize the camera. The install disk will walk you through the software installation.
4. Finally, plug your microphone into your sound card. Some netcams have built-in microphones, or you can use an external microphone.

Tips for Better Netcamming

These tips help you land in high-quality netcamming land:

- Use your friends to help tweak your system, even if they don't have a netcam yet. As long as they have NetMeeting installed, they can see (and hopefully hear) you.
- Bandwidth and processor power is the key to a better picture. Shut down any unnecessary programs and your browser while netcamming.
- Adjust your settings in NetMeeting to ensure quality. Choose a small picture and set the slide bar for "faster video" while receiving—especially if you don't have a powerful system. Trying to use the large picture setting will probably result in a broken up picture, and could lock up your computer.

LIGHTNING ROUND Q&A WRAP-UP

Where can I get a free download to paste together pictures to make a 360° panoramic picture?

We like Cool 360, created by Ulead (`www.ulead.com`). The program is free to try for 15 days or $39.95 if you decide to keep it. After downloading and installing the program, you can use Ulead's online tutorial to learn how to use it.

To get the best results with Cool 360, use a tripod with degree markers. Snap a picture, and then turn the tripod every few degrees. Doing this will ensure you get a full panoramic view without missing any parts. Take as many pictures as needed to achieve a 30- to 50-percent overlap.

The program automatically outputs panoramic pictures in a variety of formats like JPEG, QuickTime (MOV), and UVR. You'll need browser plug-ins to view both MOV and UVR.

I want to use my netcam to monitor the front of my house. How long can my parallel cord be? Do you know of any program that will capture and upload streaming video?

Parallel cords are limited to six feet lengths. Unless your computer is close to your front door, connecting your netcam to your computer probably isn't the best option. You do have three alternatives, which vary in price and capabilities (use the Web site addresses to check current prices, updates, and so on):

- Purchase an Earthcam (`www.webcamstore.com`). This industrial camera comes in eight groovy colors, but that's not what makes it special. The Earthcam has a choice of connections—Ethernet, serial, or traditional video-out. The camera features a built-in computer that simply outputs video. You won't have to connect it to your home computer to run the system. The Earthcam costs about $800.
- Inetcam VTS 8500 (`www.inetcam.com`) comes complete with everything you need to transmit live video feeds from your home computer. It comes with two cameras, software, a switcher, cabling, and even a power supply. This complete system costs around $430.
- Eyes&Ears (`www.zdnet.com/downloads`) shareware integrates your netcam into a surveillance system. Eyes&Ears is sound and motion-sensitive, and it automatically captures changes. This shareware is free to try, $21.95 to keep.

I was wondering if it is possible to use a camcorder as a netcam. If so, what video card would be the best?

Not only is it possible to use a video camera in lieu of a netcam, but the video camera will produce a better picture. Netcams are inexpensive for a reason. They have a fixed focal length, no special features, and they serve one purpose: to get your image across the Internet. Camcorders cost hundreds of dollars, have lots of features, and provide a better-quality picture.

A number of video-capture cards on the market allow you to hook the video camera directly into your computer. The video-capture card turns the analog data from your video camera into bits that the computer can process. Our favorite video-capture card for this setup is the Winov Videum AV (`www.winnov.com`). After you install the card and drivers, connect the video camera via RCA jack to RCA to get your software to recognize the video camera.

CHAPTER 19

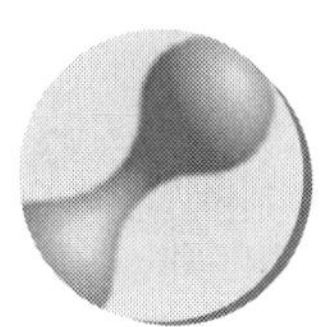

MAINTENANCE MATTERS AND MINOR FIX-UPS

- Benefit from basic backups
- Clear the junk out of your hard drive
- Add storage with a second hard drive
- Protect your system from crash disasters
- Restore lost files

You might not consider yourself a computer technician, but you use a computer, and you should expect some minor fix-up chores to fall your way now and then. In this chapter, you get TechTV's best advice on the most basic tasks for keeping your computer ship-shape. Of course, you learn about the all-important backup routine that every user should know and follow. But the chapter also offers good tips for keeping your hard drive slick, clean, and solid.

The more messy program build-up you let accumulate on your hard drive, the more crashes and error messages you'll suffer. Follow TechTV's advice for hard drive maintenance, and you'll avoid the majority of those sorry blue-screen mess-ups. You also learn you how to beef up your machine's storage by installing a second hard drive, and in the process you learn how to partition the drive for even better performance. Finally, find out how to get back those precious files you accidentally banished from your life. None of these jobs is particularly difficult, and they can make your computing faster, easier, and a heck of a lot less frustrating.

BACK UP! BACK UP! BACK UP!

Stop right there!! Back up your system before proceeding with any of the other suggestions in this chapter. Design a backup plan that's as simple or complicated as it needs to be to protect your data, but then *do it*. Your system will crash—that's a given. So if you don't want to lose big pieces of your data (that just might represent big pieces of your life), use the following suggestions to pull together a backup system that works for you.

Back Up All the Right Stuff

Businesses make backing up simple. They buy big tape drives and back up absolutely everything all the time. For businesses, where every minute of downtime means dollars lost, that makes sense. But most individuals aren't willing to pay the money or take the time to constantly back up every bit of data on their machines.

For the rest of us, the essential rule of backing up is "Make a copy of anything you can't otherwise replace." That means you copy your personal data. If you have the original master disks for your OS and your apps, don't copy those programs. Rebuilding your hard drive from the original program disks isn't the end of the world. What you *do* want copies of, however, are your precious data files. On-time backups will be easier if you follow these guidelines:

Special Backup Advice for Quicken Users

Most recent Windows programs store their data inside a My Documents folder, but one critical exception is Intuit's Quicken. Quicken stores data in its own program directory, unless you save it elsewhere. If you use Quicken, right now, before you forget, open Quicken and save a copy of your data to the My Documents folder. Once you do that, Quicken will continue to keep it there, and you'll have quick and easy access to it for backups.

- **Back up as needed:** Back up some files every time you change them. For example, you back up your accounting package data every time you balance your checkbook. Though you may choose to back up some files at regular intervals, we suggest you back up all of your personal data at least weekly, and save a copy of the backup offsite.
- **Store docs in a central location for easy backup access:** Store all your documents in one folder. Recent versions of the Mac system software automatically create a folder called Documents, so Mac users should get in the habit of storing all their work inside that folder. Windows automatically creates a My Documents folder. Windows users can simplify backing up if you direct all programs to store documents in the My Documents folder.

Now, you're creating regular backups of all of your personal document files. Your system has other files squirreled away that you need to back up as well. Here are a few candidates for regular backup and hints on how to find them:

- **Saved games:** If you want to back up saved games, find them inside the game program's directory. Look for files with the .sav extension.
- **E-mail:** If you use your e-mail for anything other than sending and receiving bad jokes and chainmail hoaxes, you need to back it up. Every program stores these files in a different directory. Eudora stores its e-mail and address book in .mbx files in the main Eudora folder. Outlook Express lets you specify the location of its mail file, so it could be anywhere. Netscape Messenger defaults to C:\Program Files\Netscape\Users\your name\Mail. Outlook stores everything in a .pst file in the C:\Windows\Application Data\Microsoft\Office8.5\Outlook folder.
- **Templates:** You might have put a lot of time into these, so you don't want to lose them. Most programs, such as Microsoft Office applications, store these in a separate Templates directory.
- **Internet Bookmarks and Favorites:** Your browser determines where to store your Web site "speed dial" list. Netscape defaults to C:\Program Files\Netscape\Users\your name\bookmark.htm. Internet Explorer stores Favorites as individual files in the C:\Windows\Favorites directory.
- **Preference and settings:** Your preferences and settings are scattered all over your hard drive, usually in files with the .ini extension. You probably don't need to back up Windows .ini files, but you might want to back up preferences from other programs. And don't forget to jot down your Dial-Up Networking and TCP/IP settings while you're at it. Mac users can bring this information on-screen, then press Cmd+Shift+3 to save the screen image, then double-click the file and print it.

You might have other important data hidden away on your hard disk. Look around to see what else is in there. To see every file that your system has stored recently, search your disk by file creation date. Most of the newest files will be those you created, or backups your system automatically creates and stores for you. This hard-drive tour will give you a good idea of exactly what's being kept on your drive—and where.

Back Up Your Data on Removable Media

If you can't haul it away from your computer, it's not a backup. So you want to use some form of removable media for your backup, but choosing the right *kind* of removable media can be difficult.

You can back up to floppy disks if you have no other choice, but floppies aren't reliable for long-term archival storage. Filling dozens of floppies takes so much time that the very idea of it might encourage you to put off backing up until it's too late. Many people back up to tape drives. Tapes are cheap, and their huge capacities make it easy to back up an entire hard drive. Tape is better than nothing, but you can't really be sure that your data is really there on the tape.

You might prefer to work with removable storage, such as Iomega's Zip (`www.iomega.com`) or Imation's SuperDisk (`www.superdisk.com`). These disks hold 100MB or 120MB respectively—plenty of space to back up the average user's irreplaceable data. Zip drives are fast and reliable. Best of all, you can access the data stored on the disk, so it's easy to verify that the copy actually took. If your computer isn't equipped with either a Zip or a SuperDisk drive, you can buy one for $150 or less. Disks cost $10 or so.

Some TechTV staff use a simple shareware program called Second Copy (`www.centered.com`) to automatically back up data every few hours to a Zip disk. If you use this backup solution, have three disks handy and rotate them on a daily basis. Take the most recent to work with you, so you have three copies of your data, one of which is offsite in case of a major disaster.

A Backup Solution Even Slackers Can Love

Answer these three questions:

- Do you only want to back up a few megabytes worth of data?
- Do you have horrible self-management skills?
- Do you feel your data is secure on a remote computer?

If you answered yes to all of these questions, you might want to give online backup a go. With an online backup service, instead of backing up your data on tapes, CD-Rs, or Zip disks, you send your data to another computer, which acts as your backup. If ever you lose a file, you contact that remote computer to retrieve the lost file. Services such as BackupNet (`www.backupnet.com`) offer a number of backup providers, many available on a free trial basis. As the questions indicate, if you have to back up lots of data and you want absolute control over the storage location, online backup may not be for you. Otherwise, it's a good way to keep your data safe without putting undo wear and tear on your attention span.

Looking for Long-Term Storage?

For long-term archival data storage, consider using a CD-R or CD-RW drive. CD recorders cost as little as $100, with blank CDs costing just a buck each. Because each CD stores 650MB, monthly backup of all data onto CD is an affordable option. CD storage is compact, compatible with nearly every PC on the market, and likely to last for several decades. Recordable CDs are as close as you can get to backup nirvana.

CLEAN UP YOUR HARD DRIVE

When your hard drive gets full, your system slows to a crawl and using any productivity app becomes a painful process. No matter what you've heard, it's fairly easy to create more space on your hard drive. In this section, you learn a few simple tips that can get your drive cleanup project off the ground. We have no way of knowing exactly what files you should or shouldn't delete from your system, so read the following sections carefully to choose the suggestions that seem appropriate for your system setup.

Get a Smaller Recycle bin

The Recycle Bin's maximum capacity is ridiculously large, with a default size of one-tenth of your hard disk. If you have a 6GB hard drive, you could have a whopping 600MB worth of unwanted stuff cluttering and slowing down your hard disk before Windows reminds you to dump the trash. To lower the percentage at which Windows nags you about the bin, do this:

1. Right-click on the Recycle Bin.
2. Select Properties.
3. On the Global tab, drag the Maximum Size of Recycle Bin (Percent of Each Drive) meter to about five percent.
4. Click Apply.

Of course, your best bet is to empty the Recycle Bin often, whether Windows reminds you or not (right-click it and choose Empty Recycle Bin). But if you forget, an early reminder can stop you from piling up your own data landfill.

Delete Leftovers

If you don't use an uninstaller to get rid of unused programs, you might have a lot of useless leftovers on your system. The best way to flush out this program residue is to buy or download uninstaller software. The reviewers at TechTV like Norton CleanSweep (`www.symantec.com`). For the complete scoop on uninstallers, see "Using Installers and Uninstallers," in Chapter 12, "Hard Facts About Software."

Clean Out the Junk Drawers and Empty the Trash

Your hard drive probably harbors the equivalent of a busy family's junk drawer, with folders that have been storing copies of files you no longer need, misplaced downloads, and files set aside for destruction, then forgotten. Welcome to the most-overlooked areas of a hard drive: its Temp folder(s), Recycle Bin, and Internet Temp folder (sometimes referred to as your browser's cache).

Cleaning out these data junk drawers is easy if you use the Disk Cleanup Utility.

1. Go to your desktop and double-click My Computer.
2. Right-click the drive where Windows is installed (usually C:), and then choose Properties.

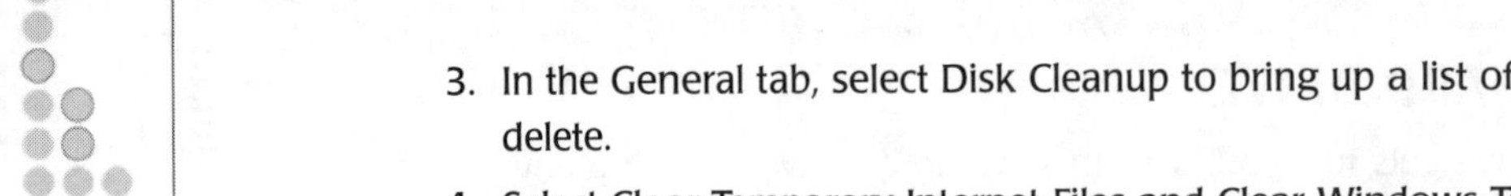

3. In the General tab, select Disk Cleanup to bring up a list of folder contents to delete.
4. Select Clear Temporary Internet Files and Clear Windows Temporary Files.
5. You also can choose Clear Downloads Folder and Empty Recycling Bin, but only if you know these contents are OK to delete. If you're unsure, select the Recycle Bin and choose View Files. You can do the same to each of the items on the list.
6. When you're sure of what you want to delete, choose OK.

To automatically empty Mac trash on startup or shutdown, use this good housekeeping AppleScript:

```
tell application "Finder"
empty trash
end tell
```

To run this script automatically on startup, use Script Editor to save it as a run-only application, and drag the resulting file into the Startup Items folder inside the System Folder. If you'd rather have the script run when you shut down, put the file in the Shutdown Items folder, also inside the System Folder.

Search and Destroy: Oversized Personal Files

You could be storing large files that you simply don't need any more. Do a search to produce a list of all files larger than 2MB (if that size isn't practical for the types of files you store, set the size to another of your choice). Then, go through the list and delete those that you no longer need. To set up the search, use a wild card like *.* (instead of a file name), and then set your size limitation in the Advanced tab. When you delete files, a good rule of thumb is: If you're unsure, leave it alone. Here are some recommendations for files you should—and shouldn't—delete:

- Delete oversized and unnecessary pictures (.bmp, .gif, .jpg), audio/video (.mp3, .mpg, .mov, .rma, .ra, .wmv, .wav, .avi), and documents (.txt, .doc) from the list.
- File extensions you *don't* want to delete are .ini, .swp (swap file), .cab, .dll, .bat, .sys, .exe, and .reg.

SOLVE STORAGE PROBLEMS BY ADDING A SECOND HARD DRIVE

If your current hard drive runs out of space due to all those Gnutella downloads, or if you'd like a quick and painless way of doing weekly data backups, install a second hard drive. This isn't as scary as it sounds. In fact, you can be up and running with a shiny new hard drive in less than an hour.

Although hard drives are relatively cheap these days (you should be able to pick up a 20GB drive for less than $100), you don't have to buy a new one. If you can't afford a new drive, ask your friends if they can spare an old hard drive. As long as it works, well…it works.

If you're comfortable opening up your computer and performing basic installations and adjustments, you should have no problem adding a drive (remember that Windows 95 tops out at 32GB; you'll need Windows 98 or above to add 40GB or larger drive. Adding a second hard drive involves opening your computer's case, setting jumpers to designate the master and slave drives, mounting the new drive, running a partition program, and then formatting the new drive to complete the process. Did you get all of that? Just kidding. Keep reading for details.

Take Care Before You Open 'er Up

Before you open the case on your computer, unplug your computer from the wall. Then—and only then—should you open the case. Consult your manual if you need help with the specifics of opening your computer's case. And before you start poking around inside, be sure you're properly grounded. Static electricity can short out the delicate circuitry inside your motherboard. Wear a grounding wrist strap and, for maximum protection, set your computer on a grounding mat.

Prepare for the Installation

You start the installation by opening the case and getting a feel for the new drive's neighborhood. Double-check that you have an extra slot for the new hard drive, an extra spot on the IDE ribbon that connects to the other hard drive on your system, and an additional four-prong female power supply adapter.

- Most computers have ample room for additional hardware. Look directly under or below your current drive. You should find an empty spot for the new drive there.
- The IDE ribbon is always gray (sometimes with a red or blue stripe) and about two inches wide. The primary IDE ribbon is the one connected to your current hard drive. That ribbon should have a second connector identical to the one occupied by your current hard drive (see Figure 19.1). You will attach your new drive to this second connector.

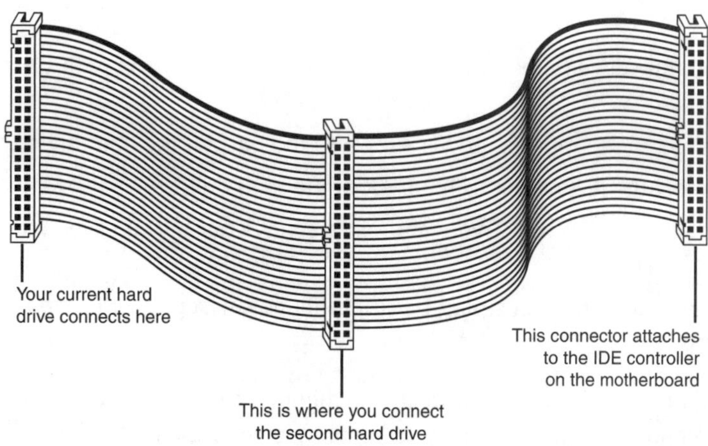

Figure 19.1

Most IDE ribbons come with an extra connector for adding a new drive. As a rule, you should designate the second hard drive as the slave and leave the original drive as the master.

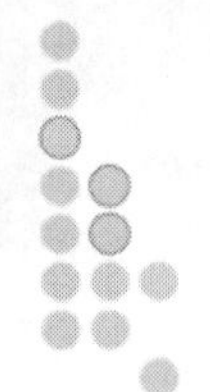

- To find the extra power adapter, follow all the cords coming from your power supply. Most computers have one or two extra adapters to support additional drives. Look for an extra four-prong female adapter to supply power to your new hard drive.

Before you can install a second hard drive on your computer, you have to designate one drive the master and the other the slave. Usually, the master drive holds the OS and is your computer's boot drive. The slave is simply any second hard drive you connect to your system. The IDE's jumper controls determine master and slave settings. Check your drives' documentation to determine how your jumpers should be configured for each drive's make and model.

Your current drive probably is set as a master, because most hard drives come that way. The top of each drive should be marked with a diagram for setting the jumper (the diagrams show sets of pins with a black box around two of them). On your new drive, find the diagram for the slave jumper setting. Then, grab a pair of tweezers and reposition the pins to match the slave jumper settings shown on the new hard drive.

Get a Positive ID on Your Master Drive

While you have your machine open for the new drive installation, verify that your current hard drive is set as the master. Chances are that it is—almost all drives come that way. But you might as well double-check now, so you can avoid any chance of having to get back in the case and fiddle with the settings after you complete the installation.

Install the Drive

Okay, with your jumpers configured and your connections all lined up, you're ready to proceed with the installation.

1. With the power supply still unplugged, place the new drive into the open drive slot.
2. Mount the drive to the computer by screwing two screws on both sides of the chassis.
3. Connect the four-prong power supply to the back of the hard drive.
4. Connect the IDE ribbon to the back of the hard drive.
5. Get all of your screwdrivers and extra screws out of the case, and then close it up.
6. Insert your computer's plug back into its power supply, and then turn the computer on.

When you turn your computer on, it should automatically detect the new drive. As it boots up, the computer will list a primary IDE master drive and another drive labeled primary IDE slave. Each drive listing will include a manufacturer's serial number.

If your system doesn't recognize the new drive, then you'll need to go into the BIOS to designate the new drive as a primary IDE slave. Check your system manual for guidelines on that operation.

Partition a PC Drive

Windows comes with a built-in utility for drive partitioning known as FDISK. That program requires that you format the drive, so it works just fine for this new drive installation. A number of commercial programs, such as PowerQuest's PartitionMagic, can partition drives without destroying the drives' data. Here, TechTV shows you how to use FDISK to partition your new hard drive into two virtual drives.

Here are the three most important facts you should know before you begin:

- Only primary partitions are bootable. They're always the C: drive when active. Normally you can only have one.
- If you want more than one partition, you must use an Extended partition. You can only have one Extended partition.
- You can create more partitions by adding Logical Drives in the Extended partition. Since you can only have one Primary and one Extended partition, Logical drives are the only way to extend your partitions beyond this two-count limit.

Here's how to use FDISK to partition your new hard drive:

1. Click the Start menu and select Run.
2. Type **fdisk** at the command line, then press Enter. FDISK opens and asks if you'd like to enable large disk support. Y should be selected by default.
3. Press Enter again. A menu appears with a list of options. Choose number 5, Change Current Fixed Drive, and press Enter.

Why Do You Want to Partition Your Drive?

Partitioning divides a single hard drive into logical partitions. To the OS, these partitions look like multiple hard drives. Why would you want to fool your operating system? First, partitioning simplifies file organization. If you want to run multiple operating systems, for example, you create a partition for each OS. But maybe the best reason for partitioning is that it can improve the performance of large hard drives. Even Windows' 32-bit file-allocation tables can use storage space inefficiently. By dividing your hard drive into multiple partitions, you give the OS smaller clusters in which to store data, and that results in more efficient, less fragmented storage. Less wasted storage space equals better drive performance. And that's the only reason for partitioning you really need—isn't it?

4. On the list of drives and numbers, find the number next to your new drive, which should be listed as the Current Fixed Hard Drive. If it is, the number next to it will be any number other than 1. If you have just added a second hard drive, the number probably is 2. Double-check that the Current Fixed Hard Drive is the new hard drive you just installed. When you have identified the number of the Current Fixed Drive (your new drive), type that number beside Enter Fixed Disk Drive Number, and press Enter. This will take you back to the beginning screen.

Don't Mistake the Current Drive!

When you're telling FDISK which drive you want to partition, it's vital that you don't accidentally choose your original drive instead of the new hard drive you just installed. If you do, FDISK will seriously mess up and destroy data on your original drive in the process of partitioning it. By default, FDISK thinks it's partitioning your original drive, so it lists drive 1 in the Enter Fixed Disk Drive Number line. Be sure you change that number to the number of your new drive—which is probably 2, but definitely *any number other than 1*.

5. Select 1 to choose Create DOS Partition or Logical DOS Drive, then press Enter.
6. Select 1 again to choose Create Primary DOS Partition, then press Enter. For the next few minutes, your computer verifies the new drive's integrity. When it finishes, a screen message asks "Do you wish to use the maximum available size for a Primary DOS partition?"

   Here's where the directions take a great divide: To create just one partition, proceed with step 7. To create multiple partitions, leap to the next set of steps.

Choose Your Partitions

Many people just create one additional partition on their second hard drives, but you don't have to limit yourself to one. For example, one TechTV host partitioned his second hard drive at home this way:

- Windows/Programs/Data
- Temporary Files
- Optional:
  Games
  Kids
  Office

You can set up as many partitions as you like, and allocate a specific amount of space to each one. Use your partitions to help keep your drive's data organized, accessible, and easy-to-find.

7. Press Y if you only want to create one partition. The computer creates the partition, then transfers you back to the beginning screen, where you can press 4 to inspect the new drive's partition. Essentially, you're finished with the whole partitioning thing. Press ESC twice to exit FDISK.

To create multiple partitions on your new drive, follow these steps:

1. At the "Do you wish to use the maximum available size for a Primary DOS partition?" screen, press N, then Enter.
2. A screen message asks you to "Enter partition size in Mbytes or percent of disk space to create a Primary DOS Partition." We suggest you enter a percentage here, rather than trying to calculate the specific number of megabytes for each partition. When you finish entering the size of the new partition, press Enter to create it.
3. Press Esc to return to the new drive's main menu.
4. Select 1 to "Create DOS Partition or Logical DOS Drive."
5. Now it's time to create the Extended partition. To do this, select 2 from the menu and press Enter.
6. A screen that says "Enter partition size in Mbytes or percent of disk space to create an Extended DOS Partition" appears. You should notice that the computer did the math for you and filled in the remaining hard drive space to be partitioned. If this number is OK, press Enter to complete the process. If it's not, and you plan on creating additional partitions, lower the number accordingly and then press Enter.
7. After FDISK creates the partition, press Esc to return to the new hard drive's main menu.
8. Before the new Extended partition will work, it needs to have a Logical DOS Drive. To create the drive, select 1 on the list to "Create DOS Partition or Logical DOS Drive."
9. Select 3 from the list to "Create Logical DOS Drive(s) in the Extended DOS Partition" and press Enter. Your computer verifies the drive integrity and automatically delivers the size of the extended drive. You should see a number next to "Enter logical drive size in Mbytes or percentage of drive." This number should equal the size of the extended drive you created earlier.
10. Press Enter to "Create Logical DOS Drive(s) in the Extended DOS Partition." FDISK assigns a new letter to the new partition you just created.
11. Press Esc to exit this screen and return to main menu.
12. Choose option 5 to "Change current fixed disk drive," then press Enter. You should see a list of all the drives on your computer, including the two you just created.
13. Press Esc twice to exit FDISK.

Check Your Drive's Space

You can monitor the state of any drive on your computer any time by checking its properties. Open My Computer, then right-click on the drive you want to check. Choose Properties. A pie chart appears showing the used and unused space on your drive, along with the exact amount of each in MB.

You've partitioned your new disk! You have to restart your computer so it can recognize the new partitions. Then, all that's left to do is format the partitions so they'll be ready to use.

Partitioning a Mac Drive

In most cases, you have to reinitialize your Mac hard drive before you repartition it. So, the first step in this process is to back up all your data, because it will be lost in the reinitialization phase of partitioning.

You can use Drive Setup—an application that comes with your OS and is stored in the Utilities folder—to partition the hard drive on your Mac. When you open Drive Setup, it automatically scans your bus and lists your drives. Just click and highlight the drive you want to partition, and then click on Initialize. Finally, follow the application's step-by-step instructions and make your personal selections as you go.

Format Your New Drive

Disable your anti-virus programs, and then follow these steps to format your new drive:

1. Double-click My Computer.
2. You should see an additional drive with letter D: and a possible third with the letter E: (if you created multiple partitions).
3. Right-click your new D: drive and select Format from the list.
4. Change the Format Type to Full.
5. Press the Start button to begin formatting the drive.

Anti-Virus Equals Anti-Format

Before you start formatting, you have to disable your anti-virus programs (you *do* have anti-virus programs on your computer, right?). Those programs won't allow anything to modify the master boot record, so they'll block the formatting. But when you're finished with the format process, don't forget to turn your virus protection back on!

Repeat those steps to format any remaining partitions you created on your new hard drive. Your new drive is ready for action, and your storage problems are over (for a while, anyway).

MAKE YOUR PC (ALMOST) CRASH-PROOF

Time for some brutal honesty: The info in this section will not protect your PC from every future crash. That's because there *is* no way to absolutely crash-proof your PC. But TechTV is your best source for warding off most crashes, and that's what you learn how to do in this section of the book. With this information under your belt, you can compute with some peace of mind (depending upon what's happening in the cubicle next door).

Face Your Crash-Enablers

The first step in fighting any problem is to admit that you have it. When the problem is PC crashes, you probably have several problems to combat. Why, oh why, do bad crashes happen to good people?

- **A DOS-based, GUI OS:** Okay, yes, this means Windows, but TechTV doesn't get its kicks from picking on Microsoft. See, the first Windows system was designed to just glide along on top of MS-DOS. But by the time Win95 hit the streets, the OS had become this huge behemoth that was still trying to skate on top of good old DOS lake. The MS-DOS ice just isn't thick enough to support the 32-bit Windows weight, and so the crashes began. Windows 2000 and XP have resolved many of these issues, and are infinitely less "crash-prone" than their predecessors.
- **Bloated software:** Windows isn't the only heavyweight on the block. Most of today's software is overloaded with features. Users love those features, and each new one requires the addition of lines and lines of code. And every time you add a line of code to software, you introduce more opportunities for bug infestations. More bugs equals more crashes.
- **Cheap computers:** Not to shock you, but the ultra-cheap PCs available today aren't made of the best materials (that's how you get the "cheap" part of the product). None of the run-of-the-mill PCs on the shelves today are built to be beefy. Manufacturers want to sell as many PCs as they can, and they sell a lot more PCs when they keep their prices low. So most users aren't out there buying super machines that were designed with stability in mind. They'd rather save a few thousand dollars and settle for a PC that crashes now and again (until it does, of course).
- **DLL Hell:** DLL incompatibility is one of the major causes of computer crashes. DLLs (dynamic link libraries) are small programs that larger programs rely on in order to accomplish tasks. Several applications can share a DLL. Microsoft Word and Excel, for example, use the same DLL to send documents to the printer. When you install new software, it might overwrite a DLL with an older version bearing the same name. Then, another application looks for the good old DLL it's always used, finds the newcomer's version, and—in a fit of application anger and confusion—crashes.

So, do you see why you can't really crash-proof your PC? Instead, your goal is to cut down on the number of crashes your system suffers. And you can do that.

Keep It Clean and Lean

The best way to make a Windows PC crash infrequently is to keep it lean. When you have some free time, perform a clean install of Windows, and only install the applications that you actually use. If you don't play the games or use the freeware, don't install them. You'll not only cut down on software conflicts, you'll cut down on drive-space consumption and speed up your system.

Don't add stuff to your system that you don't need or plan to use. Every time you load new software into your system you threaten the peaceful, less-crash-happy kingdom you've created. Remember: Every piece of new software brings with it the opportunity for new conflict-related crashes. When you do add new software, back up your system first, so you can revert back to the old, stable configuration if conflicts erupt.

Avoid Betas

In your quest for a less crash-prone existence, steer clear of beta software. The joy of being one of the first people to use a new product soon falls prey to the frustration of never-before-diagnosed bugs and conflict disorders. Wait until the software reaches general release, then give it a whirl. Major new software releases are as prone to problems as new or radically redesigned cars. Service pack releases usually follow the major release, full of fixes for those new-version bugs. Even with the relatively short lifespan of most software releases, it pays to get a version with at least some post-release polish.

Don't over-indulge in open programs. Running too many programs at once saps your system's resources and sets you up for crashes. Close programs you're not using, and save yourself some hassles.

Maybe You Need More RAM

If you frequently want or need to work with several applications open at once, add more RAM to your system. One of the reasons computers crash when you have a bunch of applications open at once is that they run out of memory. For Windows computers, the RAM sweet spot is between 64MB and 128MB—and most new computers ship equipped with that much RAM. If your system isn't, upgrading the RAM is a cheap and easy process that can make your system less crash-prone.

Consider Switching Your OS

If you suffer lots of crashes and you can't take it any more, consider switching to an alternative operating system like Linux or BeOS. Both are nearly crash-proof, but they're also difficult to use and offer far fewer software options than you'll find for Windows or Macintosh platforms.

If you do move to an alternative operating system, set up a multi-boot system, so that—for a while, at least—you can run the new OS and your old one at different times. That way, you won't be singing the blues if you decide you never should have left your old system in the first place. To set up a multi-boot system, buy a hard drive partitioning utility such as PowerQuest's Partition Magic (`www.powerquest.com`) or V-Communications Partition Commander (`www.v-com.com`).

Many Mac users swear that their computers crash less than PCs, but many PC users claim just the opposite. Switching from a PC to a Mac means replacing all your software and some of your hardware. You'll invest a lot of time and money in the shift, and you'll probably find that Mac users have fewer software products available. All that hassle won't guarantee that you'll suffer fewer crashes, either.

If your life revolves around Windows, you can probably cut down on your crashes by switching to Windows 2000 or XP. These later versions of Windows were built from the ground up—no skinny DOS legs, here. These Windows versions are preemptive, multitasking operating systems, meaning the OS itself, not your applications, controls the allocation of the CPU's power. No one application can hang your entire system, and every app gets its own space. A nicer, less crashy arrangement.

Reformat Your Hard Drive

If your machine has a serious case of the crashes, the best—but most drastic—thing you can do is to rebuild your hard drive from scratch and eliminate all the software flotsam and jetsam. Reformatting your hard drive can dramatically improve your machine's performance; to be safe, you should reformat your hard drive once a year.

Reformatting is a big deal. **It completely destroys the info you have on your hard drive**. So your first step is to do a major backup, as described earlier in this chapter.

Second, pull together a complete inventory of all the hardware on your system. Open the system Control Panel, click the Device Manager tab, and then click the Print button. You'll get a printed summary of the full system, including all your system configuration information.

While You're At It, Update Those Drivers

If you're reformatting your hard drive, now is a good time to update your device drivers to the latest versions. Updated drivers give you better performance and more stability. Because those are two of the biggest reasons to reformat your drive, you might as well do all you can to hit your goals. Go to each manufacturers' Web site, download the latest drivers for your hardware devices, and put them on a backup medium (a Zip disk works great). Windows 98, 2000, and XP all come with a nice set of drivers, but if you use Windows 95, you'll definitely need to update your drivers if you haven't done so recently.

No Silver Bullets

Many software companies sell products that sound as though they'd make your PC crash-free. The thing is, none of these programs really make your PC completely crashless. In fact, some people claim that they actually cause crashes. They do monitor your system and warn of impending crashes, and (in some cases) they'll automatically save your data when a crash occurs. Bottom line: You can't rely on any anti-crash program as a preemptive strike. To date, TechTV reviewers haven't run across any anti-crash program that actually prevents crashes. And with some users reporting that they've had more crashes *after* installing these programs, you should just steer clear of the lot of them.

As a final step in your prep, absolutely be sure you have a boot disk and the boot disk can see the CD drive! Without a boot disk, you CANNOT reinstall Windows. Windows 95 users take special note, because the Win95 rescue disk won't let you reinstall Windows after you delete the OS from your system. Learn how to create a boot disk in the "Lightning Round Q&A Wrap-Up" section of Chapter 2, "Set Up Your Home Computer." Try out your boot disk before you proceed with the installation. Reboot from your floppy drive, put the Windows CD in your D drive, and then type **D:**. The screen should show you the D: drive and read the contents of the Windows CD.

With a boot disk handy, formatting your hard drive is a cinch. Insert the boot disk and reboot your PC to the command line. Enter your format command, which involves typing the command so that it affects just the drive or partition you want to reformat. In most cases, type **format C:** to format the entire hard drive.

Be sure that you are formatting the intended drive. If you wish to format a drive other than the one on which you are currently working, you must type the letter of that drive before the slash (/). For example, if you are working on the C: drive and want to format the A: drive to make a boot disk, you would type **format a:/s**. If you are working on the C: drive and want to format the C: drive, simply type the commands as they appear above.

After you type your command and press Enter, the computer gives you one last chance to back out before it starts deleting the data on your drive. If you tell it to go ahead, it begins reformatting your drive and displays a tracking marker so you can follow its progress.

When your drive is reformatted, re-install Windows and your other backed-up files. Now, you have a fresh, clean start on your computing life—one that should be relatively free of crashes and other blue-screen frustrations.

Variations on a Format Theme

The format command gives you plenty of muscle for transforming the contents and condition of your hard drive.

- **format /q:** Quick reformat of a previously formatted disk. This format deletes the disk's file allocation table (FAT) and root directory, but it doesn't scan the disk for bad areas.
- **format /s:** Copies system files to the formatted disk (to make a boot disk).
- **format /b:** Allocates space on the formatted disk for system files.
- **format /c:** Causes format to retest bad clusters (otherwise, the format marks the clusters as bad, but it doesn't retest them).

RECOVER LOST FILES

During all of this feverish PC cleanup campaign, you might trash something you didn't want to lose. If you accidentally erase important data, you have a few options. You can restore your entire hard drive from the backup file you created or you can start a selective search for the missing gold.

You already know to check the Recycle Bin first, right? This is the quickest and easiest way to recover a deleted file. If the deleted file appears in the archive list, you're in luck. Just highlight the file, then choose File, Restore to save a new version to your hard drive.

If your file doesn't turn up in the list of previously erased files, you have a small challenge ahead of you. When a file has been emptied from the Recycle Bin, your computer erases a directory entry of where that file is placed on your hard drive. The file might still exist on your computer if the hard drive hasn't allocated its space to a new file yet. If you act quickly after deleting a file from the Recycle Bin, you might be able to get it back using an undelete utility.

Using Windows 9x? You Might Be Undeletable

If you use Windows 95, 98, or Me you have an UNDELETE program that you might be unaware of. Microsoft stashes undelete.exe on the Windows CD-ROM, in the \Other\Oldmsdos folder. Copy that program into your \Windows\Command directory, then follow these steps:

1. Choose Start, Shutdown, then choose the Restart the Computer in MS-DOS Mode option.
2. At the DOS prompt, type **lock** and press Enter. Then type **undelete** and press Enter. This command runs the UNDELETE utility.
3. When the utility finishes running, type **unlock** and press Enter. Then type **exit** and press Enter to restart Windows.

The utility should have recovered most, if not all, of your lost files. Windows 2000 doesn't support this command. And be very careful when working in DOS; if you aren't completely comfortable with your DOS skills, don't tackle this process.

Some programs can restore life to files you've accidentally banished into never-never land. The best example: the Norton Utilities 2001 package (`www.symantec.com`). The UnErase Wizard in this suite will restore deleted files with little muss or fuss, and the package runs a system check to diagnose system problems that might have resulted from accidental deletions. You can download a demo free, or pay $45 for a retail version.

LIGHTNING ROUND Q&A WRAP-UP

My computer runs great when I'm just using my apps, but the machine's Web performance is crummy. How can I track down the cause?

If you use Internet Explorer 4.x or higher, you can take advantage of an easy way to test your PC's Web performance. Visit PC Pitstop (`www.pcpitstop.com`). After you register (which is free), you download and install a small ActiveX applet that runs the tests on your machine.

After running through the tests, PC Pitstop presents a clear and concise overview of its findings, and offers ways you can improve your PC's condition. It also returns a detailed inventory of your machine's hardware, in case you purchased your machine without a full knowledge of what was "under the hood." Most results link to even more information.

If this isn't enough, PCPitstop also helps you run a Web-based virus scan, test your Internet connection, test the health of your hard drive, or visit the forums to get advice and tips from other users. Unfortunately, because Netscape's system doesn't support ActiveX, you can't run PCPitstop from the Netscape browser. PC Pitstop is considering releasing a Netscape version in the future.

How can Safe Mode help me troubleshoot my computer? It sounds like a problem preventer, not a problem finder.

If your computer runs on Windows 95/98/2000, chances are you've seen safe mode. The name can be misleading, because Safe Mode is useful only when there's something wrong. You can't use it to fortify your desktop against viruses, or prevent damage when your laptop falls off the kitchen table. It's a special operating mode used for troubleshooting.

When you enable it, Safe Mode starts your computer with only the mouse, keyboard, and standard VGA device drivers loaded. This minimization allows you the opportunity to locate problematic operations, like a faulty software installation, local printing malfunction, or blurred video display. If you've installed a driver that doesn't work, you cannot enter Windows and fix the problem without Safe Mode.

To start Windows in Safe Mode, Press F5 at startup, right before the Windows graphic comes up. An easy way to get this timing right is to repeatedly tap F5 from the first moment of startup.

Once launched, safe mode begins to diagnose your computer using a file known as bootlog.txt, a system file hidden in the root directory. It goes through a step-by-step assessment of your PC's startup devices. Bootlog will produce a list of the devices (more than likely, the last on the list is the driver that's crashing). However, the contents of the bootlog may be cryptic. For bootlog assistance, you can download Boot Log Analyser (`www.zdnet.com/downloads`). The program's fast and easy to use, and it'll help you understand what bootlog tries to tell you.

My Mac has never had crash problems before, but now it's become one crash-happy machine. How can I troubleshoot the source of the problem?

Whenever a previously trouble-free Mac starts crashing, you almost always can suspect a new installation of hardware or software has caused an extension conflict. Before you call tech support, try to reboot by holding down the Shift key to turn the extensions off.

If your Mac stops acting up, that means you do, in fact, have an extension conflict. Open the Extension Manager control panel under the Apple menu to turn off any new extension. If that doesn't work, you may have to manually turn extensions on and off until you find the culprit. To make this process faster, do yourself a favor and turn off a quarter of your extensions at a time, not one by one.

PART V

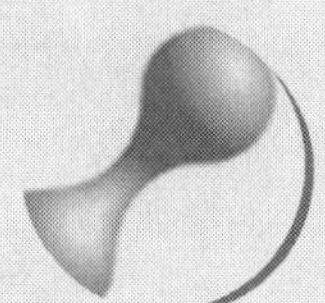

APPENDIXES

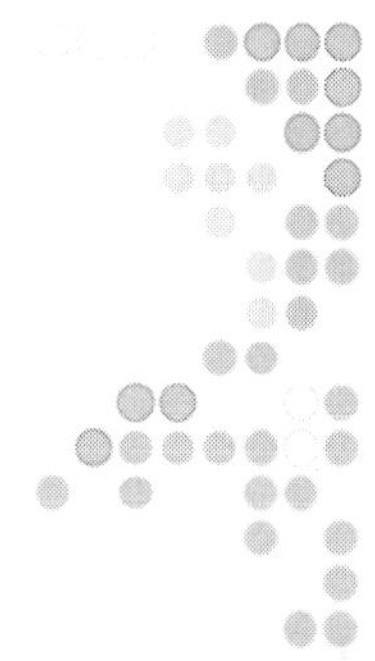

GLOSSARY

bandwidth The amount of data a system can transmit over a given bandwidth during a fixed amount of time. In other words, the amount of information that can flow through "the pipes" into and out of your computer. Bandwidth of digital devices usually is given in bits per second (bps) or bytes per second. Analog devices list bandwidth in Hertz (Hz).

bloatware Software that eats up large quantities of space on your computer system. Bloatware is famous for offering tons of features that offer little or no value to the user.

Bluetooth A wireless technology that may (or may not) end up defining the wireless age of computing during the next year or so. Using the unlicensed 2.4-GHz band, Bluetooth changes its signal 1600 times a second. Because Bluetooth uses a frequency hopping spread spectrum (FHSS) technique, its multidirectional radio waves can transmit data through walls and other non-metal services at speeds of 720 Kbps within a range of 30 to 300 feet (with a power boost). Problems of interference from other devices can eat into those transmission speeds, though, so this technology may need a few more rounds of development before the tech community declares it ready for prime time.

broadband A transmission technology capable of transmitting several channels at once over a single medium. The technology is used to deliver high-speed, two-way access to the Internet via satellite, cable modems, or high-speed telephone connections. The content delivered through these media is also referred to as broadband.

cable modem An Internet access technology used to send to and from the Internet using cable television lines.

cache An area of computer memory that stores frequently accessed data for faster repeated access. Browsers also use their own cache to provide quick re-access to previously visited Web pages.

CCD A *Charged Coupled Device* or CCD sensor is an electronic chip used by digital imaging devices to capture and transmit images to a computer processor or storage medium. The chip's light-sensing capacitors (called pixels) are "charged" by light that reflects through the camera lens. When the exposure finishes, the CCD transmits the image for display or storage.

CDDB *CD Database*, now known as Gracenote Disk Recognition Service, is an online database of information about music CDs, their tracks, titles, artists, Web links, and other information. Users of CDDB-enabled players can load a CD and click on a track to access and retrieve information about the song, artist, contributing musicians, and so on.

CD-ROM *Compact Disk Read-Only Memory*, a device that plays compact discs or runs computer programs stored on a compact disc.

CD-R *Compact Disk Recordable*, a recordable compact disc.

CD-RW *Compact Disk Read-Write*, a device that can both play and write (or burn) compact discs.

client A network-connected device that runs applications but depends on a server to manage Internet, file, and shared drive access.

cluster The smallest amount of disk space to which data can be allocated.

codec *Compressor/decompressor* is a technology used in both hardware and software to compress and decompress data. Telecommunications uses the term to refer to a device used to convert binary signals into analog signals.

cookie small pieces of data sent and retrieved by Web sites to record information about your visits. Web sites can read only their own cookies, and there are limitations on the quantity and kinds of information sites can store.

CPU Central Processing Unit. See *processor*.

DHCP Dynamic host configuration protocol; a protocol used to assign IP addresses on a network.

DIMM *Dual Inline Memory Module*; a circuit board that holds memory chips and has a 64-bit path.

distribution An operating system that has been developed by adding commands to a kernel. Several distributions can be created from a single kernel, and each distribution can be unique, depending upon what installation, running, and interface commands it contains.

DLL *Dynamic Link Libraries* are small programs that larger programs rely on to perform specific tasks, such as sending documents to a printer.

downloading The act of physically transferring and storing a media file to your computer. See also *uploading*.

DRAM (pronounced dee-ram) *Dynamic Random Access Memory* is a type of memory used in most personal computers.

DSL *Digital Subscriber Lines* are a type of Internet connection that support the transfer of data at high speeds.

DVD Stands for *Digital Video* (or *Versatile*) *Disk*, a removable storage medium that can store even more data than a CD and that plays high-quality video images.

DVD-ROM A read-only compact disk that can hold up to 4.7GB of data—a full-length movie's worth of data and then some. There are four recordable versions of DVD-ROM: DVD-R, DVD-RAM, DVD-RW, and DVD+RW.

EIDE *Enhanced Intelligent* (or *Integrated*) *Drive Electronics*, a mass storage device that supports data rates between 4 and 16.6 Mbps.

Ethernet A local area network (LAN) protocol that supports data transfer rates of about 10 Mbps (megabits per second). The newer 100Base-T, or Fast Ethernet, supports data transfer rates of 100 Mbps, and Gigabit Ethernet supports transfer at up to 1000 megabits, or 1 gigabit, per second.

FAT32 A version of the file allocation table (FAT) available in Windows 95 OSR 2 and later.

firewall A system used to protect hardware and software from unauthorized access.

FireWire See *IEEE 1394*

FTP *File Transfer Protocol* is an Internet standard for the exchange of files.

GNU *GNU's Not Linux*, a UNIX-compatible software system.

GPL *General Public License* is a licensing certificate that accompanies open-source software. A GPL gives everyone the right to use and modify the material as long as it is available to everyone else with the same licensing stipulation.

hard drive The place where a computer stores and retrieves data. When you buy a new computer, any preloaded programs come installed on the hard drive.

IEEE 1394 This external bus supports rapid transfer of massive amounts of data—as fast as 400 million bits per second. You can use one of these ports to connect 63 external devices. This technology is important for anyone who uses computers for advanced photography or video production. Apple has trademarked the term FireWire to refer to its version of this technology.

IRC *Internet Relay Chat* is a real-time, Internet-based chat service.

IrDA *Infrared Data Association*, a consortium of device manufacturers that developed a standard for transmitting data using infrared light waves. Some laptops, printers, and PDAs come equipped with IrDA ports that let devices transfer files and data without needing extra cables.

IRQ *Interrupt Request line* refers to hardware lines over which devices can send interrupt signals to the microprocessor.

kernel The essential core of an operating system that contains all of the boot information and a few running commands. Vendors build an OS by adding installation, support, and interface commands to a kernel.

LAN *Local area network* is network of computers linked within a limited area by high-performance cables. LAN users can share information, peripherals, programs, and data.

modem A device that allows a computer to transmit data over telephone lines, cable lines, and DSL lines. Modems are used to connect to the Internet and to send/receive faxes.

motherboard A large circuit board that contains the computer's central processing unit, expansion slots, microprocessor support chips, and random-access memory.

MP3 A file extension used for MPEG audio level 3 files. MP3s are audio files that have been compressed for easy transfer over the Internet to a hard drive, CD-RW or other storage medium.

MPEG Although the acronym stands for *Moving Picture Experts Group*, the term usually is used to refer to an audio file format for compressed digitized stereo audio. The MPEG group developed the format's standards.

NIC A *Network Interface Card* is an adapter that lets you connect your computer to a network cable.

open source A certification standard that indicates the source code of a program is available free of charge to the public. Programmers can read, modify, and redistribute open-source code. This process helps to create programs with fewer bugs and increased usability. UNIX, Linux, and FreeBSD are examples of open source codes. The Open Source Initiative issues open source (OSI) certification.

PCI *Peripheral Component Interconnect* is a local bus standard developed by Intel.

PDA A *Personal Digital Assistant* is a handheld computer, usually used to provide schedule, calendar, address book, e-mail, and other tools for day-to-day personal organization.

Peer-to-Peer (P2P) Peer-to-peer networking is an Internet file exchange technology that allows you to share files from your desktop with others who use the same software. Napster, with its music-trading revolution, was a prime source of content trading via P2P.

PPP *Point-to-Point Protocol* is the mechanism you use to run IP (Internet Protocol) and other network protocols over a serial link. You can use PPP to connect to a PPP server and gain access to the resources stored on the network that the server's connected to. If you set up your PC as a PPP server, other computers can dial into your computer and access its resources (or those of your local network).

processor The processor is the brains of a computer; it's capacity for processing information is measured in MHz (megahertz). For example, a 75-MHz processor is slower than a 100-MHz processor.

proxy server A device that connects a client application to a full server. The proxy server intercepts requests from the client to the full server, fulfills the requests it can fulfill, and forwards all other requests to the full server.

RAID *Redundant Array of Independent (or Inexpensive) Disks* is a category of disk drives that use two or more drives in combination to offer better fault tolerance and performance. RAID drives appear more commonly in servers than in personal computers.

RAM *Random Access Memory* is the place where computer programs store data for quick access. The more RAM your computer has, the more efficiently your computer operates. RAM is the most important area to invest in when you buy a new computer.

RDRAM *Rambus DRAM* is a type of memory developed by Rambus, Inc. RDRAM transfers data at speeds as high as 600 MHz.

scanner A device that converts paper documents or photos into an electronic format.

SDRAM *Synchronous DRAM* is a type of memory that can deliver data at a maximum speed of about 100 MHz.

server A device used to manage file, drive, printer, Internet, and other types of network access. In a client/server network architecture, client devices run applications and depend on server devices for access to shared network resources.

SIMM *Single Inline Memory Module* is a type of circuit board that holds memory chips and has a 32-bit path.

sims Computer games that simulate some aspect of real life, such as driving a race car, flying a DC-10, or raising a family. Good sims are open-ended and allow players to have a high degree of control over the game's content, characters, and action.

software Computer programs that have a specific use, such as word processors, spreadsheets, or games.

streaming The process of watching or listening to media files that are stored on a computer other than your own. You request a media file from the remote location and it travels to you in data packets.

USB A *Universal Serial Bus* is a type of connection that lets you easily install an additional device (such as a scanner or CD-RW) on your computer without having to open up the case and tear into guts of the machine. One end of the USB cable plugs into the device, and the other plugs into the computer.

vaporware Software that's been announced, but never actually hits the marketplace. Sometimes a company will announce that it's going to release a new software product simply to gauge consumer interest in such a product or to undermine the success of a competitor who's preparing to release a (real) similar product.

VPN A *Virtual Private Network* is a protected, private network constructed by using public wires to connect nodes. VPNs are only accessible to authorized users; encryption and other security measures prevent VNP data from being intercepted.

WAP *Wireless Access Protocol* is both an environment and a set of communication protocols that allow wireless devices to access Internet and telephony information and services.

Wi-Fi A term used to name the 802.11B wireless networking technology. Wi-Fi began as a business networking standard, but then moved into hotels and airports, and has recently become a popular home networking method.

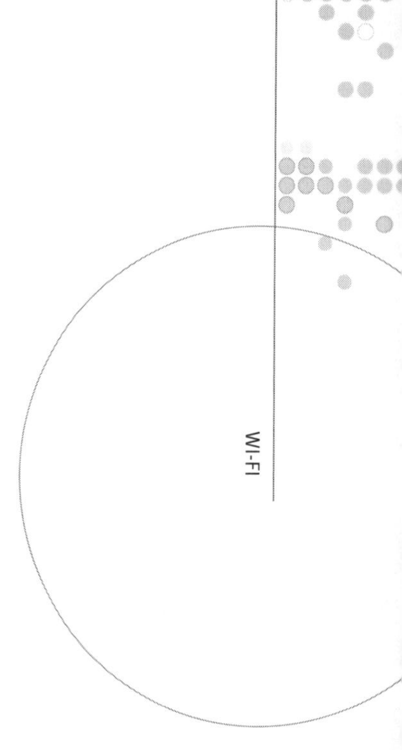

APPENDIX B

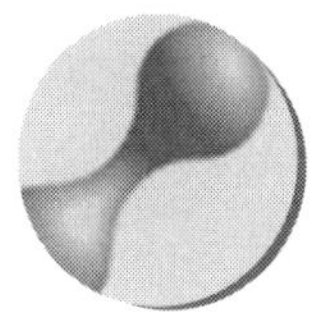

Q&A COLLECTION

SYSTEM AND SETUP BASICS

What is MOBO?

MOBO stands for motherboard. That's the big circuit board in your computer that holds the processors, memory, slots for cards, and so on. It's sometimes called the main board, but we like motherboard because it is, indeed, the mother of all circuit boards!

How do I find out the maximum RAM my motherboard can handle?

The best way is to check the documentation for the system either in the manual or online.

How do I synch Outlook?

If you use Outlook 2000 and want to synchronize your calendar between your desktop and laptop, use a Web-based calendar as an intermediary. TechTV reviewers like FusionOne (`www.fusionone.com`). It's free and it will synchronize your datebook, address book, notes, tasks, bookmarks, files, and even browser cookies.

What's with disk free space discrepancies?

When you right-click on a folder and select Properties to check the folder size, Windows reports two numbers: size and size on disk. To understand the two numbers you have to know how a computer uses a hard drive to store information. For efficiency, the drive is divided into clusters. On PCs each cluster usually holds 8,096 bytes, or 8KB (kilobytes). That's the smallest amount of space a file can take.

If you save a 2KB file it will take up 8KB on disk. The remaining 6KB remains as unused, or slack, space. A 36KB file will use five clusters, or 40KB, wasting 4KB of space. If you have enough files on your hard drive you can waste 20 or 30 percent of your space.

Using a smaller cluster size will help, but only to a point. Slack space is just the price we pay for using Windows.

What in the heck is that wheel on the front of my CD-ROM?

On most CD-ROM drives you can plug a pair of headphones into the front of the drive, so you can use them to listen to audio CDs without bothering anyone nearby. The wheel controls the volume to that headphone jack. It doesn't affect the audio volume coming through your computer speakers.

Is moving a cable modem connection to a new computer a hassle?

If the new computer has its own network interface card, just swap the cable, update the network settings on the new computer to match those of the old, and go. You might have to unplug your cable modem for a few minutes to get it to update its hardware info. If it doesn't work, contact your cable company. In some cases they have to reset their hardware.

If you don't have a network card in the new computer, you'll have to move the card from your old box. That's a little trickier, but if you've ever installed a card in your PC you should be able to handle it.

How do I disable apps before defrag?

Restart your computer in safe mode. Safe mode only loads the core software and drivers you need on your computer. Defrag works much better in safe mode.

What's the difference between a recovery disk and a boot disk?

You use a boot disk, or start-up disk, to start your computer. As we've mentioned before, everybody needs a boot disk. Re-create your boot disk whenever you make system changes, such as installing a new OS or adding new drivers.

An emergency recovery utility, or ERU, is a different beast altogether. The ERU is a program located on Windows installation disks. ERU saves critical information onto the hard drive, and you can use it to save must-have system files to a disk or other removable storage medium, in case of damage to your system. The ERU is a "hidden" feature that doesn't install automatically with Windows. Microsoft hides it because it considers this feature to be for tech-support people only. If you plan a hard drive reformat or other major change to your system, the ERU is an added safety measure. If you want to install it, here's how:

1. Go to the Windows CD directory named Other/Misc.
2. Drag and copy the folder named ERU to your Drive C:/ (or other hard drive of choice).
3. Double-click the new ERU folder on your hard drive.
4. In the ERU directory, locate the file ERU.inf.
5. Right-click on the ERU.inf file.
6. Click Install on the menu that pops up.

OS SOLUTIONS

How do I fix my slow Mac bootup?

A viewer told us his Macs began booting slowly after he upgraded to Mac OS 9. If that happens to you, check the Servers folder inside your System folder. Delete any aliases inside. The Mac will attempt to mount these servers even if they don't exist, and that can take a lot of time.

What's the best way to escape from a crashed program on a Mac?

Try pressing the Option, Command, and Escape keys at the same time. Exit the program in question when the prompt comes up. Continue by saving any open files and then stop working. Count yourself lucky and reboot. During the reboot you will have to wait for a disk check.

How can I enlarge the Windows taskbar?

Hover the mouse over the edge of the taskbar until the cursor turns to a double-headed arrow. Then click and drag the edge up to enlarge the task bar. Shrink it the same way.

SOFTWARE ANSWERS

How do I read my AOL e-mail when I'm not signed on to AOL?

Reading AOL e-mail offline used to be called Flash Sessions, but now AOL refers to this practice as Automatic AOL. Here's how to do it:

1. On the Mail Center menu, click Set up Automatic AOL (Flash sessions).
2. Select the tasks you want Automatic AOL to perform (retrieve unread mail, and so on).
3. Click Select Names.
4. Select the screen names for which you'd like the tasks performed.
5. Type the passwords for each screen name you select in the box provided.
6. Click OK.

To Run Automatic AOL, click Run Automatic AOL Now on the Mail Center menu, and then click Begin.

This file has no extension. How do I know if it's a JPEG?

JPEGs are a good way to send images with e-mail, but they don't always have the JPG or JPEG file extension. The best way to tell if a file is a JPEG is to open it with an image editor. If it's not a JPEG, save it as one to save space. You can find out any file's type by right-clicking and choosing Properties.

WEB WORK

How do I add a link to the browser bar?

Want to add a link to a website to your browser's toolbar? That's easy enough. Go to the site you want to save, and then drag the icon from the address bar to the toolbar.

In Netscape, you first bookmark the link. Then, click on Bookmarks, Edit Bookmarks, and drag the desired link into the personal toolbar folder.

How can I make a browser font larger?

In most browsers, you can click the Text Size item under View and enlarge the font. Sometimes Web designers keep you from increasing font size. Windows users can override that setting and get the text size item to work by following these steps:

1. Open Internet Options.
2. Click the Accessibility button.
3. Check the Ignore Font Sizes Specified By Webpages box.

How do I delete all the Web sites I've visited in the past from my hard drive?

Here's how to delete your Web history in Internet Explorer:

1. In Internet Explorer, go to the Tools menu and select Internet Options. Click the General tab.
2. In the Temporary Internet Files box, choose the Delete Files button. This gets rid of all cookies and Web sites you've visited.
3. To see what you're deleting, select Settings (found in the same pop-up window next to the Delete Files button).
4. At the bottom of the pop-up window, select the View Files button. Here you will see all your cookies and Web sites.
5. While you're in the Tools menu, clear the files in your history folder. This will erase all the URLs in the drop down bar of your address bar.

Here's how to erase your Web trail in Netscape:

1. In Netscape, go to the Edit menu and select Preferences.
2. Click the Clear Location Bar button.
3. To further clear your cache, in the Preferences window click the plus sign next to Advanced in the Category section, then select Cache.
4. Choose the Clear Memory Cache button and, while you're there, select the Clear Disk Cache button.

Download TweakUI (`www.zdnet.com/downloads`) to automate both of these tasks. Click on the Paranoia tab to see all the options for hiding your tracks.

MUSIC, VIDEO, AND MORE

Know of a good Napster replacement?

Napster is the program that helps you find MP3s on other users' hard drives. The classic Napster replacement is Gnutella (`www.gnutella.wego.com`). It's free. Many TechTV viewers also like CuteMX (`www.globalscape.com`), though some viewers have reported that they think CuteMX is a major resource hog. Both programs can search for more than just music.

Can I save video to a floppy?

One viewer wanted to save movies from the Net to floppy, but he was worried that it would be bad for the drives. The floppy grinds a lot—meaning it sounds like it's dying—but that's normal. Floppies are much noisier and slower than hard drives, but they won't break if you use them, so go ahead.

Can I improve MIDI playback quality by recording to a WAV file?

Unfortunately, the answer is no. MIDI files are essentially musical scores. They tell the computer what notes to play and which instruments to use. The quality of the playback depends on the quality of the sound card.

Here's a good solution from a TechTV viewer. QuickTime has an improved MIDI playback that uses its own high-quality instrument samples. Download a copy free for Windows or Mac at `www.apple.com`.

How do I clean my CDs?

First of all, how do you know when your CD needs cleaning? Any of the following could be a sign that your CD's gotten a little gamy:

- It just looks dirty.
- The CD skips both sounds and graphic images.
- It won't play at all.

You could buy a cleaning product made especially for CDs, but they're often costly and unnecessary. All you really need is some gentle soap, water, a soft cloth (you can buy inexpensive pads at most music stores), and most importantly, a soft touch.

Contrary to popular belief, CDs are not indestructible! Be especially careful when cleaning the data (clear) side of the disc. Avoid even getting fingerprints on it. To preserve the data, clean the disc from the center out, and not parallel to the data grooves. Do not even think of using harsh household cleaners, as they can destroy the disk's data. Just a very gentle dish soap should do.

Does a slow burn speed make a better CD?

You might have heard that burning at a lower speed improves the quality of the CD. But unless you're experiencing buffer underrun errors that cause skips or a blown disk, slowing down the burn speed won't affect the quality of the audio CD.

How fancy does my computer have to be to use MusicMatch Jukebox? Will it do the same thing as Napster?"

According to the MusicMatch Web site, you need a 200 MHz processor or better, Windows 95/98/Me/NT/2000, 32MB RAM, and 50MB hard drive space. It's not a huge resource hog, but it does need some processing power so your music doesn't skip as it plays.

As far as Napster qualities, Music Match is not Napster-esque, but it does have many cool music-related capabilities. MusicMatch Jukebox burns music files to CD. It does not, however, allow you to share files across the Internet the way Napster and other peer-to-peer file sharing programs do.

Can I put a music track behind my PowerPoint 97 presentation?

You can do that with PowerPoint 2000, but we're not sure about 97. You have to turn the PPT presentation into an AVI movie, and you do that by recording the screen.

Office 97 comes with Microsoft Camcorder, a program that can record the screen. Microsoft doesn't ship it with Office 2000 because Camcorder doesn't work so well with the latest software and operating systems. We also recommend a shareware program called HyperCam (`www.hyperionics.com`).

What is BURN-Proof?

BURN-Proof is a new technology that eliminates buffer underruns, making CD recording much more reliable. You can read all about it on the BURN-Proof site (`www.burn-proof.com`).

If you're buying a new CD recorder, be sure it includes BURN-Proof. It makes a big difference. Our two favorite drives, the Plextor Plexwriter and TDK's VeloCD, both come with BURN-Proof.

APPENDIX C

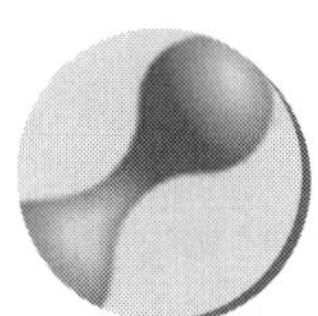

TECHTV QUICK FACTS

Boasting the cable market's most interactive audience, TechTV is the only cable television channel covering technology information, news, and entertainment from a consumer, industry, and market perspective 24 hours a day. Offering everything from industry news to product reviews, updates on tech stocks to tech support, TechTV's original programming keeps the wired world informed and entertained. TechTV is one of the fastest growing cable networks, available around the country and worldwide.

Offering more than a cable television channel, TechTV delivers a fully integrated, interactive Web site. Techtv.com is a community destination that encourages viewer interaction through e-mail, live chat, and video mail.

TechTV, formerly ZDTV, is owned by Vulcan, Inc.

AUDIENCE

TechTV appeals to anyone with an active interest in following and understanding technology trends and how they impact their lives in today's world—from the tech investor and industry insider, to the Internet surfer, cell phone owner, and Palm Pilot organizer.

WEB SITE

Techtv.com allows viewers to participate in programming, provide feedback, interact with hosts, send video e-mails, and further explore the latest tech content featured on the television cable network. In addition, `techtv.com` has one of the Web's most extensive technology-specific video-on-demand features (VOD), offering users immediate access to more than 5,000 videos as well as expanded tech content of more than 2,000 in-depth articles.

INTERNATIONAL

TechTV is the world's largest producer and distributor of television programming about technology. In Asia, TechTV delivers a 24-hour international version via satellite. TechTV Canada is a "must-carry" digital channel that will launch in September 2001. A Pan-European version of TechTV is planned for 2002.

TECH LIVE QUICK FACTS

Tech Live is TechTV's unique concept in live technology news programming. Tech Live provides extensive coverage, in-depth analysis, and original features on breaking technology developments as they relate to news, market trends, entertainment, and consumer products. Tech Live is presented from market, industry, and consumer perspectives.

Mission

Tech Live is the leading on-air resource and ultimate destination for consumers and industry insiders to find the most comprehensive coverage of technology and how it affects and relates to their lives, from market, industry, and consumer perspectives.

Format

Tech Live offers nine hours of live programming a day.

Tech Live is built around hourly blocks of news programming arranged into content zones: technology news, finance, product reviews, help, and consumer advice.

Tech Live news bureaus in New York City, Washington D.C., Silicon Valley, and Seattle are currently breaking technology-related news stories on the financial markets, the political arena, and major industry players.

The TechTV "Superticker" positioned along the side of the screen gives viewers up-to-the-minute status on the leading tech stocks, as well as additional data and interactive content.

Tech Live runs Monday through Friday, 9:00 a.m.–6:00 p.m. EST.

NETWORK PROGRAM GUIDE

The following is a list of the programs that currently air on TechTV. We are constantly striving to improve our on-air offerings, so please visit `www.techtv.com` for a constantly updated list, as well as specific air times.

AudioFile

In this weekly half-hour show, Liam Mayclem and Kris Kosach host the premiere music program of its kind that dares to explore music in the digital age. From interviews with artists and producers, to insight into the online tools to help create your own music, *AudioFile* discovers how the Internet is changing the music industry.

Big Thinkers

This weekly half-hour talk show takes viewers into the future of technological innovation through insightful and down-to-earth interviews with the industry's most influential thinkers and innovators of our time.

Call for Help

This daily, hour-long, fully interactive call-in show hosted by Becky Worley and Chris Pirillo takes the stress out of computing and the Internet for both beginners and pros. Each day, *Call for Help* tackles viewers' technical difficulties, offers tips and tricks, provides product advice, and offers viewers suggestions for getting the most out of their computers.

CyberCrime

This weekly half-hour news magazine provides a fast-paced inside look at the dangers facing technology users in the digital age. Hosts Alex Wellen and Jennifer London take a hard look at fraud, hacking, viruses, and invasions of privacy to keep Web surfers aware and secure on the Web.

Extended Play

In this weekly half-hour show, video game expert hosts Kate Botello and Adam Sessler provide comprehensive reviews of the hottest new games on the market, previews of games in development, and tips on how to score the biggest thrills and avoid the worst spills in gaming. This show is a must-see for game lovers, whether they're seasoned pros or gaming novices.

Fresh Gear

A gadget-lover's utopia, host Sumi Das supplies viewers with the scoop on the best and brightest technology available on the market. In this weekly half-hour show, detailed product reviews reveal what's new, what works, what's hot, and what's not and offers advice on which products to buy—and which to bypass.

Silicon Spin

Noted technology columnist John C. Dvorak anchors this live, daily, half-hour in-depth look at the stories behind today's tech headlines. CEOs, experts, and entrepreneurs cast a critical eye at industry hype and separate the facts from the spin.

The Screen Savers

Whether you are cracking code, are struggling with Windows, or just want to stay up to speed on what's happening in the world of computers, *The Screen Savers* is here to help. Leo Laporte and Patrick Norton unleash the power of technology with wit and flair in this live, daily, hour-long interactive show geared toward the tech enthusiast.

Titans of Tech

Titans of Tech is a weekly hour-long series of biographies profiling high tech's most important movers and shakers—the CEOs, entrepreneurs, and visionaries driving today's tech economy. Through insightful interviews and in-depth profiles, these specials offer viewers a rare look at where the new economy is headed.

INDEX

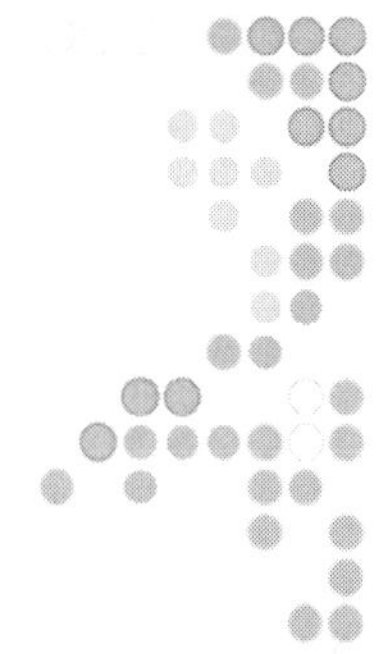

Symbols

A

B

Q-R

S

T

U

V

W

X-Y-Z